Teaching, Tutoring and Training in the Lifelong Learning Sector

Fourth edition

Teaching, Tutoring
and Training
in the Lifelong Learning Sector
Fourth edition

Susan Wallace

Los Angeles | London | New Delhi
Singapore | Washington DC

First published in 2001 as *Teaching and Supporting Learning in Further Education*
Reprinted in 2002
Reprinted in 2003 (twice)
Reprinted in 2004 (twice)
Second edition published in 2005
Reprinted in 2006
Third edition published in 2007
Reprinted in 2008 (twice)
Reprinted in 2009
Reprinted in 2010
Fourth edition published in 2011

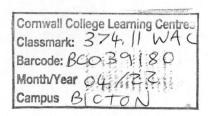

British Library Cataloguing in Publication Data
A CIP record for this book is available from the British Library.

ISBN: 978 0 85725 062 9

This book is also available in the following ebook formats:
Adobe ebook ISBN: 978 0 85725 069 8
EPUB ebook ISBN: 978 0 85725 068 1
Kindle ISBN: 978 0 85725 070 4

Cover design by Topics – The Creative Partnership
Project management by Deer Park Productions, Tavistock, Devon
Typeset by PDQ Typesetting Ltd, Newcastle-under-Lyme
Printed and bound in Great Britain by Ashford Colour Press Ltd, Gosport, Hampshire

Learning Matters
An imprint of SAGE Publications Ltd
1 Oliver's Yard
55 City Road
London EC1Y 1SP

SAGE Publications Inc.
2455 Teller Road
Thousand Oaks, California 91320

SAGE Publications India Pvt Ltd
B 1/I 1 Mohan Cooperative Industrial Area
Mathura Road
New Delhi 110 044

SAGE Publications Asia-Pacific Pte Ltd
3 Church Street
#10–04 Samsung Hub
Singapore 049483

Contents

Acknowledgements

The author and publisher would like to thank the following for permission to reproduce copyright material:

Ball, S., Maguire, M. and Macrae, S. *Choice, Pathways and Transitions Post-16*. Copyright © 2000 Routledge Falmer. Reproduced by kind permission of Taylor & Francis Books UK;

Hyland, T. *Competence, Education and NVQs*. Copyright © 1994 Cassell. Reproduced by kind permission of Continuum International Publishing Group;

Usher, R. and Edwards, R. *Postmodernism and Education*. Copyright © 1994 Routledge. Reproduced by kind permission of Taylor & Francis Books UK.

Carr, W. and Kemmis, S. *Becoming Critical*. Copyright © 1986 Falmer Press. Reproduced by kind permission of Taylor & Francis Books UK;

Every effort has been made to trace the copyright holders and to obtain their permission for the use of copyright material. The publisher and author will gladly receive any information enabling them to rectify any error or omission in subsequent editions.

Introduction

This book was written in response to the Standards for QTLS (Qualified Teacher Learning and Skills), which replaced the FENTO standards in 2007. It is designed to support all teachers, trainers and tutors in the sector, who are now required to regularly update their continuing professional development (CPD). It is intended to be particularly useful for student-teachers, both those on pre-service teacher training programmes who are entirely new to PCET, and those who are already employed in the sector, already have some experience – perhaps even lengthy experience – and who are undertaking their professional qualifications as part of their in-service professional development. It will hopefully also be a useful and accessible source of information and ideas for qualified teachers, and for teacher trainers and mentors. This edition contains a new chapter (Chapter 17) which provides practical guidance on achieving a teaching qualification in the Lifelong Learning sector, with an emphasis on how to succeed in your observed teaching sessions.

How to use this book

The chapter titles are designed to make explicit the link between their content and the domains and values which give structure to the QTLS Standards. These can be mapped as follows.

- **Access and Progression (Chapters 2 and 12).**
- **Professional Values and Practice (Chapters 1, 2, 3 and 16).**
- **Specialist Learning and Teaching (Chapters 5 and 6).**
- **Planning for Learning (Chapters 8, 9 and 17).**
- **Learning and Teaching (Chapters 10, 11, 15 and 17).**
- **Assessment for Learning (Chapters 12 and 13).**

Underlying the six domains, there are three more areas of knowledge and understanding which are essential to effective professional practice. These are:

- **an understanding of the context of FE and the Lifelong Learning sector (Chapter 4);**
- **an understanding of key theories of learning, and how they apply in practice (Chapter 7);**
- **an understanding of the issues surrounding learners' motivation and behaviour, and how these can be improved (Chapter 14).**

The values set out in Domain A – *Professional Values and Practice* – although covered explicitly in Chapters 1, 2, 3 and 16, also run like a thread through all other chapters, as indeed they must. Reflecting on your own practice, promoting equality and recognising diversity, treating others with respect, communicating appropriately, working cooperatively to the benefit of learners: all these are essential practices if we are to call ourselves professionals.

Each chapter follows the same structure, with the exception of the final two whose contents require a slightly different format. In all the others we begin with the chapter objectives, which are listed clearly as bullet points. Each of these objectives is cross-referenced clearly to the QTLS Standards, so that the reader can map the ground they have covered. There then follows an introductory paragraph which sets the context for what is to follow. As well as offering realistic examples and scenarios, each chapter includes **tasks, discussion,** and guided reflection in the form of **Close focus** questions. The tasks and Close focus questions are ones which can be addressed by the reader alone or, if the reader is engaged in professional development along with others, the questions can be explored as a group task which encourages the sharing of ideas and understanding. Towards the end of each chapter you will find a summary of the key points. These are followed by a set of three **branching options**, which will allow you to consolidate what you have learnt and to stretch your skills and understanding at a level that seems appropriate to your current professional development. Broadly speaking, these levels are designed to correspond to National Qualifications Framework (NQF) levels 5, 6 and 7. In terms of named qualifications, these might be seen as applicable, for example, to Cert Ed (NQF level 5), PGCE (NQF level 6), and M level (NQF level 7). This last level of option is intended to support those who wish to take advantage of the QTLS Standards' provision for the accumulation of credit at M (postgraduate) level where appropriate. Of course, some readers may find it interesting and challenging to choose to work through two or even all three levels, regardless of the end qualification for which they are aiming.

Finally, at the very end of each chapter you will find a list of references, suggested further reading and useful websites.

The sequencing of chapters and tasks

The sequencing of chapters does not follow any rigid system of progression. We cannot claim that we, as teachers, must be able to plan before we can assess, or assess before we can make an informed choice about what methods to use for teaching and learning. The skills teachers must develop are by their very nature integrated and interdependent; and the process of teacher education may in this respect be described as holistic. Chapters, therefore, do not imply a modular sequencing of course content and can be read in any order. And, just as with the areas of the Standards, you will find a degree of overlap between chapters. Again we cannot, for example, discuss planning without touching upon assessment, or supporting learners without looking at methods and techniques. Chapter 1, which focuses upon keeping a reflective journal, is, however, placed early in the book in order to establish the importance of reflective practice. The chapters that follow draw and build upon this central aspect of continuing professional development.

Chapter content

Chapter 1 focuses on reflective practice. This is one of the core values which underpin the Standards, and is therefore a good place to start. Using extracts from teachers' journals, it explores what constitutes reflective practice and why this is important to the teacher's professional development. In the process of analysing journal extracts, it shows how to structure reflective writing in such a way as to review existing practice and use what we have learnt to inform our planning of practice for the future.

Chapter 2 addresses Communication and Teamwork. Effective communication is not only an essential skill for teachers. It is also an area in which we have the opportunity to provide a model of good practice for our learners. One-to-one communication is particularly important in our role as tutors, and Chapter 2 makes a clear link between communication and tutoring skills. In this chapter we also look at several key aspects of communication, from communication theory to the literacy content of the minimum core; and from effective classroom management to body language. An exploration of the skills we need to work effectively as part of a team follows on quite naturally from our discussion about communication. The QTLS Standards place an emphasis on the teacher's role as a team player in the support of learning, and this chapter encourages the reader to evaluate their own skills and values in this respect, as well as to consider what makes a successful team and an effective team member.

Chapter 3 explicitly addresses one of the Standards' most important underpinning themes: that of recognising diversity and supporting equality. Like reflection, communication, and teamwork, issues of diversity and equality are themes that run throughout most of the chapters of this book. In Chapter 3, however, we take the opportunity to focus on what these values mean in practice, and to look at some of the most recent anti-discrimination legislation. And then, in Chapter 4, we turn our focus to the organisational, local and national context of Lifelong Learning, and summarise some of the philosophical, social, political and economic issues which have shaped the sector we know today. This chapter also encourages the reader to explore some of these issues further and to analyse the impact they have had on their own college or organisation.

These first four chapters, then, address important themes and issues which inform, or provide a context for, the development of our professional skills. They set the scene for Chapters 5 to 15 where the emphasis turns to the practice and theory of teaching and supporting learning. Chapters 5 and 6 invite the reader to focus on their role as a subject specialist and to consider issues of professionalism and scholarship, how to keep their subject knowledge and expertise updated, and the ways in which their subject will inform their planning and choice of learning activities. Chapter 7 looks at theories of learning and how these can be applied to practical teaching and learning situations in order to gain a clearer understanding of how and why our learners learn, and what we can do encourage them and make the learning as accessible to them as possible.

Chapters 8 and 9 examine how we plan and resource the teaching and learning experiences for groups and individuals, and how we evaluate them. Continuing the theme of reflective practice, these chapters use journal extracts and learning plans to illustrate some of the important features of good lesson planning. They take a problem-solving approach, inviting the reader to analyse and comment on examples of planning and evaluation, and to undertake some planning and evaluation of their own. In Chapters 10 and 11 we go on to look at methods and strategies for teaching and supporting learning. Chapter 10 focuses on selecting and using methods appropriately to meet learner needs, while Chapter 11 is aimed at encouraging the reader to extend their range of methods to include higher risk activities such as role-play and less familiar modes (to some at least), such as e-learning and online tutoring.

In Chapters 12 and 13 we turn to assessment, firstly to the assessment of learner needs and ways in which we can support access and progression, and then to the practice and theory of assessing learner achievement. Chapter 14 looks at the very practical issue of ways in which we can motivate learners who appear disengaged or even antagonistic towards learning and at strategies we can use to encourage positive behaviour. It illustrates in practice some of the uses we can make of the learning theory we covered in Chapter 7 in order to reward, support and encourage learners and get them enthused. And in Chapter 15 we turn the spotlight on to some of the younger learners currently entering FE: the 14–16 year olds. We discuss the specific learning needs of this group and look at ways in which we can best address them.

The final two chapters take us back to the concept of the reflective practitioner and the value base with which we began the book. Chapter 16 offers extracts from recent key texts and encourages the reader to engage critically and analytically with these in order to identify areas for reflection appropriate to their own practice. And in Chapter 17, we discuss how you can draw on your knowledge about practice in order to plan, teach and evaluate a successful observed session as part of the process of achieving your teaching qualification in the Lifelong Learning sector.

Finally, a word about the language employed in this book. You'll find the term *learner* used in preference to *student* or *trainee*. There are two reasons for this. One is that it serves for both in a sector where we still have not resolved the question of whether there is a distinction between the two, nor, if there is, whether it simply reflects that old debate about whether we can or should distinguish between education and training. This is an issue explored in some depth in Chapters 4 and 16. The other reason is that *learner* describes what we are there to help them become. That our learners are learning is the one sure way to evaluate our own effectiveness as teachers, tutors and trainers. And this leads us to another point: you'll also find the word *teacher* used in most contexts, rather than, for example, *tutor* or *trainer*. This is simply to reflect the language used in the QTLS Standards. There was, we know, a great deal of debate at policy level about which terminology to employ, and we'd probably all agree that the right decision was made. Where the role of tutor is specifically referred to (for example in Chapter 2), this is in the specialised sense of that aspect of the teacher's role which involves them in working closely with individuals or small groups. Apart from specific examples such as this, *teacher* should be taken generally to encompass the roles of teacher, trainer and tutor.

When it comes to describing the sector, however, the terminology is a little more flexible. You'll find it referred to here variously as PCET (Post-compulsory Education and Training), Lifelong Learning, FE (Further Education), and Learning and Skills. The first two are the most all-encompassing, in that they include work-based learning, sixth forms and so on. FE tends to be used now to refer specifically to provision available in colleges of general or specialised further education, while Learning and Skills is a familiar term for the sector in England, Wales and Northern Ireland, but does not apply in Scotland.

However you use this book – whether to support your development towards a teaching qualification or as a source of ideas and information – I hope you find it useful and I hope you also find it – in some places at least – fun. After all, if we can't smile at ourselves now and again it would be a great shame. Enjoy your teaching!

1
The reflective practitioner

The objectives of this chapter

This chapter is designed to address the areas of essential knowledge, skills and values which will help you to reflect upon your professional practice and use what you learn from this to enhance your performance as a teacher. It links closely to the Professional Standards for QTLS, particularly in helping you to:

- **evaluate the impact of your own teaching skills on learner performance and identify ways in which you could improve them (AS4; AK4.2; AP4);**
- **evaluate the impact of your own practice on promoting equality, diversity and inclusive learning (AP3.1; AS3);**
- **evaluate the effectiveness of your own communication skills (AK5.1; AP5.1);**
- **reflect upon and evaluate your own contribution to organisational processes such as quality assessment (AK7.2; AP7.2);**
- **reflect upon and evaluate the effectiveness of your lesson planning (DK3.1; DP3.1; DK3.2; DP3.2);**
- **reflect upon the uses you make of assessment and feedback in order to improve your own performance (EP4.2; EK4.2).**

Introduction

In this first chapter we shall look at ways in which we can reflect upon and learn from our professional practice in order to further develop the skills and knowledge we need to support our learners. We shall look at the advantages of keeping a reflective journal, and how reflection on our practice links to action research and to evaluation.

Why keep a journal?

Socrates claimed that, *'The unexamined life is not worth living'*. All very well for Socrates, you might think. Perhaps he had more time on his hands than a teacher. But the principle is an important one, particularly when we are engaged in teaching and learning. If we don't examine our experiences and reflect on them in a constructive way, how will we learn from our successes and our mistakes? This is why reflective practice is one of the core values informing the QTLS Standards. When our working lives are crowded with incidents and we are constantly hurrying on to the next class, the next meeting, the next project, our focus is usually on planning (or worrying about) what's happening next. This gives us little opportunity or inclination to examine, in any constructive way, what has just passed. During the morning you may have prepared and taught a lesson which succeeded in every way: you enjoyed it, the students enjoyed it and they achieved the required learning outcomes. Or you may be trying to put behind you one of those lessons which – although it was with a similar group of students – felt like a disaster: mobile phones ringing, students coming in late, the big lad with the nasty sense of humour making sure no one stays on task for long. How do you improve the chances of reproducing more lessons like the first and take measures to avoid more going the way of the second?

This is where keeping a reflective journal can help. You ask yourself: what were the factors that made that first lesson a success? Was it simply that the students were in a positive mood? If so, how could I recreate that? If not, was it something I did that I could do again? And if I had that second lesson to teach again (perish the thought!), is there anything I could do differently – something I did in the first lesson – in order to keep the students more focused on achieving the learning outcomes?

It isn't for nothing that the QTLS Standards place particular emphasis on reflective practice. As professionals in the field of teaching and learning, we can't improve our practice as teachers unless we set ourselves constantly to learn from it. The reflective journal will help us to do this.

What's the difference between a log, a diary and a reflective journal?

A log is usually a factual record of events. A ship's log, for instance, will give a brief day-by-day account of position, weather, speed and heading, with an occasional mention of significant events: another ship sighted or the ship's cat dies. If you were to keep this sort of factual account of your activities it wouldn't qualify as 'reflection'. It would describe the framework of your day, perhaps, but provide no analysis of your experiences and no reminder to yourself of what you think about them and what you might have learnt from them. Even Captain Kirk, whose starship's log is less terse and infinitely more eventful than most, gives only an account of events. His moments of introspection are rare. His log would be of little use to him as evidence of meeting the QTLS Standards of professional reflective practice.

A diary, on the other hand, can serve many purposes. At one extreme it may be used as an outlet for creative writing; at another it may simply be used to record appointments. It may be used to capture or express powerful emotions, or – as in the case of my cousin, whose diary entry for one week read: 'Went to Egypt. Saw pyramids' – it may not.

A reflective journal may be used for all these purposes – to log events, to describe circumstances, to vent feelings – but it will also, *and primarily,* be used to record and reflect upon incidents and experiences from which something useful can be learnt that will help us to develop and enhance our professional practice.

So what does being 'reflective' really mean?

The best way to explore this question is to look at some extracts from journals of teachers in the Lifelong Learning sector.

TASK TASK TASK TASK TASK **TASK** TASK TASK TASK **TASK** TASK

- Read the three following extracts taken from teachers' journals.
- Identify those passages you would describe as reflective and those you judge to be simply descriptive.
- Decide which of these teachers is providing evidence he or she is learning from his or her professional practice.

- Further, specific questions and tasks follow each extract. All the answers will be discussed after the final journal entry.

Extract one

This is from the journal of a full-time learner on a PGCE FE course.

Monday 11 November

My mentor said this morning's lesson was okay. The content was good and that all I need to do is to slow down a bit when I'm talking – and I agree with that.

I'm not sure how nervous I looked, but I felt like the students would be taking more notice of my signs of nervousness than of anything I was saying. I felt I'd planned the content okay, but I'm not sure I made myself understood very well. I did talk too fast, and I didn't put things in a very good order. I need to be surer about what I want to say. And I need to relax a bit instead of trying to drag the lesson along.

I found myself talking to the whiteboard a lot, but then maybe I wouldn't do this if the overheads worked better. I ought to write them in permanent marker next time – or get them typed and photocopied on to the transparency. But I did feel that I got as much response to my questions as [my mentor] usually does. Very difficult to tell whether they're listening, though, or whether they couldn't care less. I suppose at the end of the day there's nothing I can do to make them pay attention or write things down. Next time I might allow more time for them to ask questions.

Tuesday 12 November

I spent hours and hours getting my head round some of the theory last night ready for today's lesson. And I kept thinking, how am I going to be a teacher if I've got to teach the students to get their head round this and I can't even do that myself? But it's strange really because [my mentor] told me that today's lesson is the best one I've done so far. And then I made the connection. Because by having to spend so much time struggling to learn something, I ended up in a better position to teach it because I knew the bits that caused difficulty, and I wouldn't assume any prior knowledge, so I wouldn't leave anything out. Actually, in terms of planning, I'd thought it would take a lot longer to teach this than it did, and I had time at the end of the lesson to go over it and ask questions.

All in all I think it was a success, and I feel really good about it. This is what I've heard some of the others describing – that you leave the lesson feeling a real buzz.

Wednesday 13 November

This is really strange. Taught the same thing to the other parallel group and it felt totally different. Yesterday's group are much more up for discussion, and were happy to take notes from the overheads, even though it took a long time. Today's group don't show the slightest interest in involving themselves in the lesson and are really slow and reluctant about taking notes from the OHP. Moaned every time a new one went up. The girl who usually gives me grief was worse than usual – never stopped – sighing and putting her head in her hands and all that sort of thing. But I've found that the best way to deal with this is to ignore her. She wants attention, I think, and maybe she'll just get bored and give up trying if I don't give her any. She's not malicious, really, so I don't think ignoring her would make it escalate.

But it's really weird how yesterday's group can focus and today's can't, even though it's the same lesson done in the same way.

Thursday 14 November

I'm going to have to be a bit more assertive. I'm going to have to tell [the reluctant group] to do things, rather than ask nicely, otherwise they're going to keep taking advantage. I think they need to know where the boundaries are and I ought to tell them outright, rather than leaving it to them to test them all the time. They're too used to being given leeway. I'm not sure I'm skilled or confident enough yet, though, to take a different line. Some of them just aren't learning. I give them plenty of opportunities to ask questions, and I go over the stuff several times, and so if they aren't taking the opportunity to learn I don't see there's a lot else I can do.

CLOSE FOCUS CLOSE FOCUS CLOSE FOCUS CLOSE FOCUS CLOSE FOCUS

Two additional points you might like to consider about this extract are:
- **What questions would you want to prompt this teacher to ask him or herself?**
- **Identify two points this teacher intends to incorporate into his or her action plan.**

Extract two
This is from the journal of a full-time lecturer who has been teaching for just over a year.

2 February
Am getting very stressed about the Advanced class. Seems like there's been no attempt to try and run this module correctly and there's no support and I'm finding it more and more difficult to find new material and assessment methods. I'm losing confidence about taking the class at all, and there's no support. Every time I approach [the section head] he doesn't seem to have any real advice (though he's always friendly). He just seems to leave it to me so I'm back at square one.

There never seems to be an end to it. You finish one class and you're worrying about the next and planning for the next. Though if I'm honest I have got some really good classes and a nice rapport with some of the students. It does help when you're all on the same side. I'm glad I've got the insight to sum people up fairly accurately and quite quickly. It lets me feel my way around how best to present things to the class. The Level Two group were brilliant today. Asked lots of questions and responded really well. I like it that I can make it seem easy.

8 February
Got into class this morning and only one student there! Another rolled in about 20 mins late. Should've been 15. I'm going to concentrate on disciplining the ones that miss lessons or turn up late. It's no good them being nice and treating me like a friend and then doing this. I had to change my plan when there were only two of them, so all that time spent planning was wasted. I just made them sit in silence and do their assignment. Then afterwards, when I saw [the section head] and told him, all he said was that the assignment should have been a report and not an essay. This wasn't explained before. It's the old familiar problem - I only find out afterwards when I've done something wrong. No support. And I'm also fed up about the register never being available – somebody not putting it back where it should be. And I know who. So it means I'm not keeping a proper record. I meant to ask [section head] about internal verification and also about me seeing the External Verifier, but he's always rushing away and I didn't get a chance.

CLOSE FOCUS CLOSE FOCUS CLOSE FOCUS CLOSE FOCUS CLOSE FOCUS

1. Take one of the incidents or experiences from this teacher's journal and rewrite it as a reflective rather than descriptive entry.
2. If you were this teacher, what questions would you be asking in your journal?
3. What plans of action would you be setting down?

Extract three

This is from the journal of an experienced teacher.

Monday

Took the Advanced students on their trip on Friday as planned. Briefing them several times before-hand seemed to work well, and the work sheets kept them busy on the coach, so that although they were exchanging answers and doing lots of talking they were most of them on task for most of the time. I'll certainly use this strategy another time.

They were pretty well behaved when we got off the coach – just a bit noisy, but I think that's to be expected. They calmed down as requested when we got into the building, and everything was going well until the guide took us up the tower. The spiral staircase is very dark – the windows are spaced at long intervals and they're only arrow slits really, so it's very dark. And it's narrow as well. And the steps narrow to nothing at the inside edge, so you have keep close to the outside wall to find a broad enough tread to get your whole foot on. The guide was at the front, and then about fifteen students, and then me in the middle and Malc at the back behind the other fifteen. I was feeling a bit hemmed in and not very comfortable. We'd been climbing for probably about five minutes when one of Malc's students, about three behind me, started panicking. He was trying to turn round and go down and he was thrashing about and shouting that he had to get out. He was setting some of the others off and there was some squeaking and screaming. I had to let three students go past me before I could get to him, and that meant balancing right on the inside where the step was narrowest so that they could get past safely on the wide bit. Scary! But I couldn't show it. I got down to this lad and tried to calm him down, but he was hysterical, flapping about all over the place. I decided the best thing was to get the others safely past us so that I could take him back down to the bottom. I pulled him to the inside so they could get past and I stood a couple of steps below him, holding him up so he didn't feel as though he could fall off the narrow bit of step, and I told him if he held on for a couple of minutes while they all got past, I'd take him back down. When Malc got up to us, he offered to do it, so I let him because the lad knew him, and I went on with the others, because one of us had to.

What a drama. And now that poor lad's got to live it down. So what have I learnt from this about planning visits?

1) Think ahead to what we'll be doing and identify anything likely to trigger phobias like this.

2) Tell them again, before we do whatever it is – like climbing the tower – that if anyone would rather not, that's OK because one of us teachers will be staying at the bottom (or wherever) anyway to give them an alternative activity.

3) Take an extra member of staff so that we can do this. And make sure at least one of us is a First Aider.

4) Put something in the letter and permission slip we send to parents/carers explaining the proposed activities in detail and asking whether there's any problem. And make sure the insurance covers us for incidents like this.

Otherwise it was all OK and they got lots of stuff for their assignment and seem quite fired up about it.

CLOSE FOCUS CLOSE FOCUS **CLOSE FOCUS** CLOSE FOCUS **CLOSE FOCUS**

Does this qualify as a reflective piece of writing? If so, why? If not, why not?

Discussion of the three journal extracts

Let's look at the three extracts in terms of the general questions posed at the beginning. You were asked to pick out the reflective passages from the purely descriptive ones and to identify the journal writers who provide evidence they are learning from their professional practice.

Extract one

There are three entries from the first journal. The first one, dated 11 November, begins with a flurry of self-criticism. You could call it 'reflective' in the sense it's going over what happened in a critical way, but it's not particularly useful or productive. It's a record of the teacher's self-doubts rather than a measured reflection and plan of action arising from what went well and what did not.

By the third paragraph, however, the writing has become more analytical. It begins to follow a structure that is a basic model for reflection on practice and goes something like this:

- **What problems were there with the lesson?** (*'I found myself talking to the whiteboard a lot.'*)
- **Why did they arise?** (*'... but then maybe I wouldn't do this if the overheads worked better.'*)
- **How can I avoid it happening like that next time?** (*'I ought to write them in permanent marker next time – or get them typed and photocopied on to the transparency.'*)

The fourth paragraph is reflective because it records a real insight into what it was about the teacher's preparation and planning that had made the difficult content of the lesson so accessible to the students. The teacher is focusing on a success here rather than a problem and so, although the written reflection follows the same basic structure, this time the questions have a positive emphasis:

- **What succeeded?** (*'But it's strange really because [my mentor] told me that today's lesson is the best one I've done so far.'*)
- **Why?** (*'And then I made the connection. Because by having to spend so much time struggling to learn something, I ended up in a better position to teach it because I knew the bits that caused difficulty.'*)
- **How can I increase the chances of repeating this success?** (*'....and I wouldn't assume any prior knowledge, so I wouldn't leave anything out.'*)

The fifth and last paragraph for 11 November is in direct contrast to the first. By moving beyond the simple record of self-doubts, the teacher has found that, on reflection, a lot has been learnt from the lesson and there is much to say about it that is positive.

The entry for 13 November provides a comparison of two groups which is largely descriptive. It identifies a problem, certainly; but it doesn't yet pursue a solution. The entry becomes reflective, however, when it turns to the troublesome student. It's reflective because it sets out what the teacher intends to do to remedy the situation and gives the reasons for trying this particular strategy. Again, it follows the familiar structure:

- **What succeeded?** (*'But I've found that the best way to deal with this is to ignore her.'*)
- **Why?** (*'She wants attention, I think.'*)
- **How can I increase the chances of repeating this success?** (*'... and maybe she'll just get bored and give up trying if I don't give her any.'*)

On 14 November the teacher picks up again the problem of the reluctant student group, simply described in the previous entry, and now begins to reflect on what to do about it. The order of the questions is slightly different but the elements of the reflective structure are all there. On Wednesday 13th it only gets as far as: what problems were there with the lesson? (*'One group of students seems reluctant and undermotivated.'*) But on Thursday 14th we find the teacher is now considering a solution: how can I avoid it happening like that next time? (*'Be more assertive.'*) And finally hypothesising about the cause of the problem: why did the problem arise? (*'The students are too used to being given leeway.'*)

There is clear evidence in the extracts from Journal One, therefore, that this teacher is learning from his or her professional practice. You may not agree with all the analyses or solutions this journal-keeper comes up with but, nevertheless, his or her journal is evidence he or she is a reflective practitioner. And so, having read his or her entries and reflected on them yourself, are there any questions you feel this teacher has left unasked? Consider, for example, this sentence from the final paragraph of the entry for Monday 11th:

> *'I suppose at the end of the day there's nothing I can do to* **make** *them pay attention or write things down.'*

Could this be phrased in a more useful way? How far do you think the teacher's resolve – to allow more time for questions – might go towards solving the problem?

Extract two

As you will probably have identified at first reading, this teacher's journal entries are very largely descriptive. In his or her first entry there is a brief reflection on how a difficult topic can be made accessible to students by relating it to something within their experience. Useful as this is, however, it appears to be something the teacher has realised already rather than an insight gained by current reflections. In the second entry the teacher resolves to 'discipline' late-comers and non-attenders. Again, this is reflective in the sense it is taking a problem and planning a strategy which may solve it. On the whole, however, this teacher appears to be using the journal more as a diary in which to record frustrations and let off a little steam than as a method for reflecting upon practice and learning from it. The pattern of reflection is absent. Instead, the predominant structure in this extract seems to be:

- **What happened?**
- **How do I feel about it?**

The difficulties encountered are mostly attributed to the fault of others and, while this may well be an accurate assessment, there is little or no questioning of the teacher's own practice or consideration of alternative courses of action that might be taken. The extract, therefore, provides little evidence this teacher is a reflective practitioner.

So, if you were this teacher, what questions would you be asking in your journal? (You'll find some ideas in the next section of this chapter.)

Extract three

At first it seems this extract is purely descriptive. It relates a dramatic event in quite some detail, and is rather like reading a story. It is not until we come to the action plan at the end that we see this is a useful piece of reflective journal-writing. The teacher records what happened and then answers the key questions: what have I learnt from this? And, what will I do differently next time? There's no agonising internal dialogue here – perhaps I shouldn't have done such-and-such. Such agonising is not an essential part of reflection. In fact, the structure used here is simply an abbreviated version of our familiar model:

- **What happened? (The events described in the first two paragraphs.)**
- **How can I avoid it happening like that next time? (The plan of action that follows.)**

The middle step – Why did it happen? – is implicit in the clear and detailed action plan at the end. This teacher, like the first, is providing evidence in the journal of reflective practice.

What sort of things should I include in a reflective journal?

This will very much depend upon what you yourself consider to be critical incidents – incidents and experiences from which there is something to learn. We've seen some examples already in the opening paragraphs of this chapter and in the journal extracts. A careful look at some of the Standards related to reflection (listed at the beginning of this chapter) will also give you some useful pointers towards the sort of issues you could usefully reflect upon. If, for example, you realise on reading through your journal that you have never recorded your thoughts about the way in which the results of learner assessment have caused you to revise or rethink aspects of your teaching, you may choose to make this the focus of your next journal entry.

Your conclusion might justifiably be that poor assessment results were nothing at all to do with the quality of the teaching. On the other hand you might, on reflection, conclude the learners needed to be more actively involved in their learning or needed some help with their note-taking skills. You may then try out this solution when next planning for a similar group or topic. If it doesn't work, you can record this in your journal, reflect again and perhaps try another solution.

Some of you will recognise this process of action, reflection, revised action, reflection, as a simplified model of educational action research. In a sense, when you keep a reflective journal about your professional practice, this is what you are engaged in.

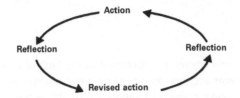

A simplified model of educational action research

You are asking yourself, among others, the following questions.

- **What happened?**
- **What would I like to change, and why?**
- **What action could I realistically take to change it?**
- **Did it work?**
- **If so, is there a general principle here I can use again?**
- **If not, what could I try next, and why?**

As long as you get beyond that first question, you are on your way to being a reflective practitioner.

Here are some further questions you might like to use to ensure your journal moves beyond the purely descriptive. They are intended as a guide only. As you become used to keeping a journal and discover its benefits, you'll find you don't need a checklist to help you to write reflectively.

✓ Why am I choosing to write about this particular incident or experience?

✓ How do I feel about it?

✓ What have I learnt from it about:
   - myself;
   - my subject knowledge;
   - my professional skills;
   - my students?

✓ What were the successes involved? What could I learn from it in order to do it again?

✓ If there was a problem, was it within my control to prevent it?

✓ If it was within my control, what could I have done differently?

✓ When might there be a practical opportunity to see whether this different strategy works better?

✓ If it wasn't within my control, are there nevertheless any measures I can take now to reduce the possibility of this happening again?

✓ Has this shown any gaps in my professional practice or subject knowledge?

✓ If so, how will I go about filling them?

✓ Did I enjoy teaching this lesson? If so, why? If not, why not?

✓ Did the students seem to enjoy their experience of learning? If so, why? If not, why not? If I don't know, how could I find out next time?

✓ Were the learning outcomes achieved? How do I know? If not, what can I change in order to make it more likely they are achieved next time? If I don't know, how can I revise my lesson plans to make sure I have this information?

✓ If I am writing about a lesson I participated in as a learner rather than as a teacher, what have I learnt in terms of dos and don'ts that will be useful for my own professional practice?

How much should I write, and how often?

Again, this will depend very much upon your circumstances. The key words here are 'ongoing' and 'sufficient'. If you are a part-time teacher the range and number of your teaching experiences may be limited, for example. The important thing is that you should not think of the journal as simply a hoop you are being asked to jump through. It's a useful tool for any teacher, particularly those who are actively involved in professional development – and ideally that should mean all of us. It would be a pity, therefore, to see the journal as a chore or as a purely instrumental step towards gaining your teaching qualification. You may not write in it every day – indeed, it would be remarkable if you had the time to – but you should aim at first to make at least one journal entry each week in which you record and reflect upon an aspect of your practice, an incident or experience that has occupied your mind. In an incident-filled week you may make several journal entries.

The number of words you write isn't crucial. What is important is that the emphasis is upon reflection rather than description. If you are asking yourself questions and attempting to answer them, this is an indication you are being reflective. As we saw from the journal extracts earlier in this chapter, some people's reflections can be quite succinct while others find it useful to 'think aloud' and express themselves at great length. It isn't the quantity but the reflective quality that counts.

If the process of reflection has been productive, it will usually end in an action point or an entire plan of action. In this sense your journal becomes an ongoing and discursive action plan, charting your concerns, your solutions, your professional needs and your successes. In other words, you are charting and planning your own professional development.

What if I'm a trainee teacher with no prior classroom experience to record?

First of all it has to be said that you almost certainly do have classroom experience – as a learner. And as learners we are constantly reflecting on how we are being taught (whether we do this consciously or not) and identifying which teachers or teaching styles or activities we learn from best, and why. Although the Standards require you to reflect upon your own practice, your experiences as a learner can be a useful starting point for this. As a full-time trainee teacher on an initial PGCE or Cert Ed programme, you will very quickly find yourself being given opportunities to teach, whether it is micro-teaching exercises to the rest of your group or under guidance at the college that hosts your teaching practice. Initially, you will have a limited range of teaching experiences to draw upon, but you will be expected to demonstrate the same capacity for reflection as a full-time teacher. The experiences you have to draw upon will be fewer and more limited in scope, but your depth of reflection and your ability to learn and plan from these experiences should be unaffected by this.

So, let's assume you are at the beginning of your initial teacher education and that so far you have only your experiences as a learner to reflect upon. Taking these as your starting point, here are some questions you could usefully explore in your journal pages.

Who would I identify as the best teacher I ever had, and why?
This might be Ms Plumpton at primary school, who showed a special interest in your artwork; or a college lecturer who made you realise for the first time that learning could be fun. When you've decided whom to nominate as your best teacher, write down a list of the qualities that made him or her so. It needn't be a very long list – two or three sentences would do – but take some time to think about it.

Now look at what you've written. The chances are the qualities you admired in your best teacher will be ones you are hoping to develop yourself. In other words, consciously or not, it's likely that, to some extent, you will take your best teacher as a role model or benchmark for your own classroom practice. If your best teacher was impressively authoritative about his or her subject, this is one of the main standards you'll measure your own success by. If he or she was a stern disciplinarian, you'll be drawing on his or her strategies for keeping order. Perhaps the qualities you identified in your best teacher were their enthusiasm for their subject and their ability to make students or pupils feel they cared about their learning. If this is so, it's no surprise. These are the qualities the majority of people associate with their best teacher. And that in itself is worth reflecting on.

Another question you could explore is: what am I most looking forward to about teaching, and what aspect, if any, is worrying me?

This will help you to identify what you perceive as your current strengths and weaknesses and will allow you to draft out a preliminary action plan. As you begin to gain some practical classroom experience as a teacher, you can refer back to this starting point to reflect upon how your perception of your strengths and weaknesses is changing, and to consider how new priorities might cause you to revise your plan of action.

You might also like to ask yourself: what do my current experiences as a learner tell me about what to do and what not to do when it's my turn to be up there teaching?
You can identify the teaching styles, the learning activities, the methods and strategies you would like to add to your own repertoire. You can observe and record the reactions of other student teachers in your group and consider why some will respond well to certain teaching styles and learning activities which you yourself may have found less enjoyable. You can observe your tutors making the occasional mistake and reflect that it isn't necessary always to be perfect. You'll relax and enjoy your teaching so much more if you keep this in mind. And if you're enjoying your teaching, that's usually a good indication that your students are too.

A SUMMARY OF **KEY POINTS**

In this chapter we have:
> discussed the usefulness of keeping a reflective journal;
> looked at what we mean by 'being reflective';
> evaluated some examples of teachers' writing to distinguish between description and reflection;
> considered what might be suitable issues or incidents for reflection;
> discussed the part reflection plays in the Action Research cycle.

Branching options

The following tasks are designed to allow you to apply or explore further some of the contents of this chapter. If you are using this book to support your professional development leading to a teaching qualification, or as part of a formal CPD programme, you may find it useful to choose a task according to the level at which you are currently working. These are indicated in brackets.

1. Reflection and self-evaluation (NQF level 5)

When drawing up the lesson plan for your next teaching session, include a column headed *Reflection.* Use it after the lesson to note down your reflections on each stage of the lesson, asking yourself questions such as:

Did this work in the way intended?
How successful was this activity in supporting learners' learning?
Did I leave enough time for this activity?
Could I have done more here to provide differentiated tasks according to learners' learning needs?

You may wish to discuss your answers to these and other questions with your mentor, tutor, or critical friend.

Now draw up an action plan for yourself, based on these answers, listing the aspects of your professional practice which you intend to address in your next session with this group of learners.

2. Evaluation: theory and practice (NQF level 6)

Consider now your own strengths and development needs as a teacher. On what do you base your evaluation? In the process of reflecting on your own practice, you will no doubt also take into consideration feedback from learners, colleagues, mentor and – perhaps – tutor.

Gregorc (1973) describes four stages of a teacher's professional development: 'Becoming' (in which the focus is on their methods, planning and resources); 'Growing' (a period during which these skills are consolidated); 'Maturing' (in which the teacher has gained the confidence to innovate and experiment); and 'Fully Functioning' (in which the teacher's skills of reflection and self-evaluation enable them to take responsibility for their own professional development).

- **Based on the feedback available, and on your own reflection, which of Gregorc's stages best describes your own current development needs?**
- **Drawing on your current teaching, what evidence would you put forward to support your answer to the previous question?**

3. Engaging critically with the literature (NQF level 7: M level)

> *... those engaged in the 'practice' of education must already possess some 'theory' of education which structures their activities and guides their decisions.*
>
> (Carr and Kemmis, 1986)

Based on your own reflections on your current teaching, how would you describe the 'theory' which informs and structures your own professional practice? What examples from your practice would you cite to support this?

REFERENCES AND FURTHER READING

Bolton, G. (2001) *Reflective Practice: Writing and Professional Development*. London: Paul Chapman.

Carr, W. and Kemmis, S. (1986) *Becoming Critical: Education, Knowledge and Action Research*. London: Falmer Press.

Gregorc, A. F. (1973) Developing plans for professional growth. *NASSP Bulletin*, Dec 1973, pp1–8.

Hillier, Y. (2005) *Reflective Teaching in Further and Higher Education*. London: Continuum.

2

Communication, tutoring and teamwork

The objectives of this chapter

This chapter is designed to address the communication skills necessary for effective teaching and tutoring, and the areas of essential knowledge, skills and values relevant to working as part of a team. As well as looking at some Minimum Core issues, this will also help you to:

- **develop, evaluate and adjust your own communication skills (BK3.4; BP3.4; AK5.1; AP5.1; AK5.2; AP5.2);**
- **communicate effectively, appropriately and ethically, including the use of different forms of written, oral and non-verbal communication in the interests of learners' achievement (BS3; BK3.1; BP3.1);**
- **develop a range of listening and questioning techniques essential for effective tutoring (BK3.2–BK3.5; BP3.2–BP3.5);**
- **promote effective and respectful communication between learners (BP1.2);**
- **demonstrate through your practice an understanding of the ways in which language and literacy skills are integral to learner achievement, and supporting learners in these areas (CK3.3; CP3.3; CK3.4; CP3.4);**
- **work collaboratively to share and evaluate best practice in order to improve your own performance and enhance learners' experience (AS5; BS4; AK5.1; AP5.1; BK4.1; BP4.1; FK4.2; FP4.2);**
- **demonstrate a knowledge of what constitutes good practice in teamwork, and evaluate the effectiveness of your own contribution to the team (DK3.2; DP3.2);**
- **demonstrate a clear understanding of the ways in which mentoring can enhance and support your professional practice, and make use of this support as appropriate (BK2.7; BP2.7);**
- **work as part of a team to establish valid, reliable, and fair assessment of learners (EK2.4; EP2.4);**
- **work collaboratively to contribute to organisational systems of communication and quality assurance (AP7.1; AK7.2).**

Introduction

No one would question that communication skills are essential if you're to be an effective teacher. To say that someone teaches well, or successfully supports and facilitates learning, is also to say that they're a good communicator. But it's important to understand what we really mean by *effective communication*. Here are some of the things that do NOT necessarily denote a good communicator.

✗ Being able to talk at great length without interruptions.
✗ Being fluent in polysyllables and/or specialist jargon.
✗ Always having something to say at meetings.
✗ Having no qualms about addressing very large groups.
✗ Always having the last word.

✗ Expressing complex ideas in a complicated and 'academic' style which is difficult to understand on first (or second or third) reading.

Now of course, people who do these things may very well also be effective – even excellent – communicators (apart from the final one!); but the point I'm making here is that when you come to evaluate your own effectiveness as a communicator and tutor, and set yourself action points for professional development, you will need to focus on a much more valuable set of skills, which include:

✓ listening to others;
✓ asking the right questions;
✓ presenting complex ideas or processes in a clear and straightforward way;
✓ making regular eye contact;
✓ using your body language effectively, and accurately interpreting the body language of others;
✓ writing (reports, student feedback, minutes, assignments, etc.) in a style that is clear and accessible to the intended reader/s;
✓ being able to adapt your language, register and style so that it is appropriate to the situation and the audience.

In this chapter we shall explore all of these and look at ways in which you can evaluate, develop and apply your own communication skills in order to improve your professional practice as a teacher and/or tutor.

Your own communication skills

So, how would you rate yourself as a communicator against that second list of criteria we've just looked at? It's often very difficult to gain an accurate idea of our own strengths and weaknesses as communicators. Our most helpful clues will come from those we interact with: our learners, our colleagues and others. But we have to be alert to those clues and reflect on what they mean in terms of their implications for our practice. For example, a good indicator that you're not communicating effectively would be if you regularly experience people's eyes glazing over while you're talking to them – but if you neglect to make eye contact or are unable to read body language accurately, you're not going to pick this one up!

TASK TASK **TASK** TASK **TASK** **TASK** TASK **TASK** TASK **TASK** **TASK** TASK

How effective a communicator are you?

You could start, however, by asking yourself a few questions. You might find it useful to jot down your answers – in your professional reflective journal if you keep one – and note particularly any areas for development. Then look at your answers again in six weeks' time to see whether you have changed anything about the way you communicate.

1. In the last session you taught, how much time (roughly) did you spend speaking, and how much time listening to what the learners had to say?

2. How appropriate was this to the methods and strategies you were using? (For example, if your chosen method was to 'lecture', you would expect to be speaking for more of the time than if your method was 'small group discussion' or 'role play'.)

3. In the room/workshop/studio you most often use for teaching, what are the seating/working arrangements? Do they allow you to make eye contact with every learner? If not, is there anything

you could change to make this possible? (For example, rearrange the seating or resources, change your own position, or move about more.)

4. Are you careful to use a vocabulary that your learners will understand? Do you carefully explain, and write on board or screen, any words or terms that might be unfamiliar to them?

5. How do you sit/stand/move about when you're teaching? Is it in such a way as to make you look enthusiastic and approachable? Do you look and act like someone who's got something interesting to say?

6. Think of the last lesson you taught. How much conscious notice did you take of the learners' body language? What was it communicating to you? Did you respond to it, and if so, how?

7. In your last one-to-one tutorial session, what proportion of the time, roughly, did you spend listening?

We hear a great deal in the post-compulsory sector about *constant improvement* in terms of provision, achievement and standards. It is a phrase all of us can very appropriately apply to our own communication skills. Whatever our role is in the organisation, we should never become complacent and assume that our ability to communicate is perfect. It is an area of our professional practice to which we should always give attention, since so much else of what we do depends upon it.

Effective communication

Let's have a look now inside a teaching room and see what we can learn from this brief glimpse of the communication between Kelly and her learners.

The learners are sitting in small groups around five tables, talking amongst themselves, and Kelly is seated behind a large table at the front of the class.

'Right!' she says. 'Are you listening?' (They are not.) 'This is what we're going to do. Er, I *said*, "Are you listening?"' (Actually, no, they still aren't.) 'What you're going to do is.............' She reads out quite a long list of instructions from a sheet of A4 which is lying on the table in front of her, and ends with, 'Okay? Got that?'

Without waiting for a reply, and without casting much of a glance in the learners' direction, she gets up and switches on the OHP. 'Right!' she says, gazing up at the screen. At least half of the learners, however, are sitting facing in some other direction. 'This is how I want you to set it out.' She describes several details, reading them from the screen, and finally says, 'Okay. You've got 20 minutes to get that done, and then I'm going to take it in.' She turns and walks back to her seat.

One of the learners raises his hand. He has to wave it around for a while before Kelly notices it. When she does, she frowns and folds her arms. 'What?'

'Say again,' says the learner, mildly. 'What is it you want us to do?'

'For goodness' sake!' snaps Kelly. 'When are you lot going to learn to pay attention and *listen*?'

TASK TASK **TASK** TASK **TASK** TASK TASK **TASK** TASK **TASK** TASK TASK

Barriers to communication
Answer the following questions and compare your answers with those in the discussion which follows.
1. How many barriers to communication did you identify in that brief scenario, and how did each arise?

2. Which of them could we reasonably expect Kelly to address, and how would we advise her to go about it?

3. Think now for a moment about your own professional practice. Is there anything you can learn from Kelly's mistakes that could improve your own classroom communication?

Discussion

You may well be thinking that Kelly was lucky to have such a mild-mannered group of learners. Indeed, you may be wondering how she would survive with a more confrontational group. This is a good question. Clear communication is absolutely essential to effective class management and motivation, as we shall see in detail in Chapters 14 and 15.

So, how many barriers to communication did you identify? Your list will probably include some or all of the following 12.

1. The learners are seated around small tables, which means some will probably have their backs turned to Kelly. One consequence of this is that she can't make eye contact.
2. Kelly sits behind her desk. She is therefore putting a literal and physical barrier between herself and her learners.
3. She begins her instructions without ensuring she has the learners' attention.
4. She reads the instructions from a piece of paper which is lying on the table. This means not only that she can't make effective eye contact with the learners, but also that her voice won't be directed towards them either.
5. The list of instructions is long. How will the learners remember them? Are they taking notes? Do they have the skills to do so? Kelly doesn't know, because she's not looking up.
6. She doesn't check their understanding of the instructions before moving on. Saying, 'Okay? Got that?' and not waiting for a reply, does *not* constitute checking their understanding.
7. She hardly glances at the learners as she moves to the OHP, so she can't pick up any clues about whether they have received and understood what she's been saying.
8. She keeps her eyes on the OHP screen. Again, this makes eye contact impossible, and also means that her voice will again be directed away from the class.
9. At least half the group are sitting facing away from the OHP screen.
10. She again fails to check the learners' understanding after this second set of instructions.
11. When she is asked a question, Kelly frowns (signalling disapproval) and folds her arms (signalling defensiveness, and forming a further physical barrier between herself and the learners), thereby sending a clear message that she does not welcome questions. This, ironically, is the first time we've seen her communicate anything clearly.
12. Her verbal response to the learner's question is: 'When are you lot going to learn to pay attention and *listen*?' This is misleading in that it misplaces the responsibility for the failure of communication on the learners. It also reinforces the message that questions aren't welcome.

Sadly, the overall message that Kelly is communicating to the learners is: *I don't particularly want us to communicate.*

Given a little help and advice, Kelly could reasonably be expected to address every one of these barriers, as follows.

- She could rearrange the tables into a horseshoe shape or open square. Or, if this is impractical, she could make sure that no learner is seated with their back to her. Persuading learners to move is not always easy, but we shall be looking at some strategies for doing this in Chapters 14 and 15.
- She could move her chair out from behind her desk so that she is no longer presenting a barrier between herself and her learners. Removing a physical barrier can send an important signal about your readiness to communicate.
- Kelly could wait until she has made eye contact with the learners, and has their attention. With some groups, certainly, this is far from easy; but we'll be looking at some strategies for gaining the learners' attention in Chapters 14 and 15.
- She could – and, indeed, with most groups should – avoid *reading out* instructions. It puts a distance between her and the learners, and makes it difficult for her to watch them for clues as to whether or not they've understood. If she's not confident of remembering the instructions in detail and doesn't want to use the board or screen, she could always write the main points on small cards which she can keep in her hand and glance at when necessary. This will allow her to address the learners directly most of the time.
- Most learners, particularly in the 14–19 age group, need help with note-taking. Kelly could produce a handout for them, summarising the main points; or she could give directive guidance, such as: 'This is important. Write this down.' She needs to be looking at them to see whether they are indeed making a note, and whether she's going too fast or too slowly for them. She needs to see who is *not* writing this down, discover why, and address it. All this and more. In other words, she needs to be interacting with the learners, not simply talking at them.
- She could check their understanding very easily with a short question-and-answer session: 'So, let's go over that again. What's the first thing you're going to do?' She won't get accurate feedback about their understanding if she simply says, 'Got that?' Even 'Any questions?' will not necessarily reveal gaps in learners' understanding, as those who do have questions may well not want to draw attention to themselves; and those who couldn't care less won't bother asking anyway.
- She could use the OHP (or the data projector) correctly. These devices are designed specifically to allow you to face front and still read the 'slide', so that you can both see and be clearly heard. But how often have you watched colleagues or presenters gazing as though mesmerised by their own words on the screen?
- She could make a conscious effort to adopt a body language that makes her more approachable and encourages, rather than discourages, learner-teacher communication.
- In her own verbal communication with the learners she could model good practice. This means speaking to them in the way that she would wish them to use in interacting with her and with each other; that is, in a way that both demonstrates and earns respect.

So, from analysing Kelly's mistakes we are able to draw the following rules of thumb for effective communication in a learning and teaching situation, whether with a large group or in a small tutorial. They are:

- arrange the furniture or seating for maximum teacher-learner eye contact;
- avoid putting barriers such as tables between yourself and the learners;
- don't start giving instructions until you have learners' attention;
- speak to the learners directly where possible, rather than reading from notes;
- be alert to learner needs in terms of note-taking skills, and offer support where necessary;
- regularly check learners' understanding, for example through question-and-answer;
- maintain eye contact whenever possible;

- be aware of your body language and the non-verbal signals you are communicating;
- be aware of learners' body language and what it's telling you;
- model good practice in the way you communicate with learners.

Communication and the Minimum Core

This last point – about modelling good practice – is part of what we mean when we talk about communicating *appropriately*. (The Minimum Core refers to a set of skills and underlying theory in literacy, language and numeracy introduced by FENTO in August 2003 and fully implemented as an integral part of FE teacher training programmes from September 2004.) The way we communicate with our learners, our colleagues, our managers and other stakeholders is an important aspect of our professional practice. And this applies to written communication and non-verbal communication as well as simply the way we speak to people. For example, there would be no point in giving a learner lengthy and detailed written feedback on their work if you were employing a vocabulary which was not meaningful to them. Similarly, you wouldn't talk to an employer about college provision with the same informality and vocabulary that you'd use to talk about *The X Factor* with your friends in the pub. To most of us, this is simply common sense. But the distinction between formal and informal, appropriate and inappropriate, may well not be so self-evident to some of our learners; and yet these are distinctions they'll need to understand if they are to gain the social skills that will allow them to succeed in relationships and in their work. We can *explain* to them what is appropriate and what is not; but we can also make sure we always provide a clear example in our interactions with them and others.

TASK TASK **TASK** TASK **TASK** TASK **TASK** TASK **TASK** TASK **TASK** TASK

Communicating appropriately

Ask yourself the following questions, and answer as honestly as you can. When you speak to learners, do you:

1. make a conscious effort to model clear and appropriate communication?
2. avoid swearing?
3. avoid use of slang?
4. avoid joining in with inappropriate discussion (e.g. of a racist or sexist nature)?
5. avoid joining in with discussions or criticisms of the competence of other members of staff?
6. try to communicate not by emulating the learners' informal vocabulary and mode of speaking, but by encouraging them to acquire skills in a more formal mode of address where possible?
7. provide a glossary of technical or subject-specific terms to help familiarise them with the vocabulary appropriate to the course of study?
8. ensure your spelling is correct and your writing legible on hand-outs, data projections, OHPs, flip charts and boards?
9. point out the different registers necessary for communicating appropriately in our complex world, and provide them with opportunities for extending their range?
10. ensure that all hand-outs, PowerPoint displays, OHTs, etc. employ a vocabulary and syntax appropriate to the learners' level of understanding?

Discussion

The ideal answers here would be YES to all ten questions.

As a professional, your role requires you to enter into communication with a whole range of people besides your learners. In relation to some of these – for example, colleagues, line managers, employers, parents – you can usefully ask yourself many of the same questions, particularly 1–6. In some cases your answers may differ. You may judge it perfectly appropriate, for example, to discuss colleagues with your line manager (5), or to employ slang when speaking informally with colleagues in the staff workroom (3). But would you consider it appropriate to discuss the sexual attractiveness of a learner (4) with colleagues, or to discuss the competence of other members of staff (5) with local employers? Almost certainly not.

Ethics and confidentiality

As professionals, we need to bear in mind the importance of ethics and confidentiality in our communication with learners, colleagues and others. The final two questions in the discussion above are questions about ethics and confidentiality respectively. It would be a breach of ethical and professional conduct to discuss learners in an inappropriate way. This would be an abuse of the position of power you occupy in relation to your learners. Similarly, to disclose confidential information about students or colleagues to others who do not need to know, would be to act unethically and unprofessionally.

There is another aspect to confidentiality, however, which it is important for all teachers to bear in mind. If a learner asks to speak to you in strict confidence, you should always make him or her aware that you cannot promise confidentiality if you judge that what they tell you needs to be passed on to an appropriate authority or source of help for the sake of the learner's safety or the safety of others, or for your own legal protection.

Vocabulary, syntax and register

CLOSE FOCUS CLOSE FOCUS **CLOSE FOCUS** CLOSE FOCUS **CLOSE FOCUS**

1. Is the way you speak to local employers different in any way from how you speak to your learners? If so, how?
2. Is the way you speak to a group of learners exactly the same as the way you speak to one individual learner, for example in a tutorial? If not, how does it differ?

Vocabulary, syntax and register are useful terms when talking about appropriate communication. Our *vocabulary*, as teachers, is extensive. When we speak or write, we draw on that vocabulary in order to say what we mean. However, one of our criteria for choosing which words to use will be whether the person we are talking or writing to will be familiar with and understand them. You might, therefore, use a very much wider vocabulary when speaking to your Head of Faculty than when speaking to your three-year-old niece; and similarly, the vocabulary you use when teaching on a Foundation Degree may well be slightly different from the one that you employ when teaching 14–16 year-olds.

The same can be said of your use of *syntax* – the way you order your words and construct your sentences. Complex sentence structure can impede communication with some learners, but may be entirely appropriate when you're writing a report for your line manager or an assignment for your professional development course. *Register* is perhaps the least familiar term of the three. It refers to the language we employ as it is defined by its social use: chatting with friends at the gym and attending a formal interview would usually involve two different varieties of talking, two different registers. This variation is to do with the level of formality or informality as expressed through vocabulary, syntax, and even accent (think of Auntie Mabel's 'telephone voice'). Many learners come to us able to communicate in one register only – the informal, casual way of speaking they use with their friends and family. In order to help extend their social and employment opportunities, we need to help them to extend this repertoire so that they can communicate confidently in more formal situations. Part of this process requires us to set an example in the common social courtesies – the *pleases* and *thank yous* – which facilitate formal (and informal) social interaction. We shall explore this further in Chapters 14 and 15.

Non-verbal communication

We saw very clearly from Kelly's example earlier in this chapter that non-verbal communication is very important in a learning and teaching situation. Indeed, it was estimated long ago that what we actually *say* only accounts for about 10 per cent of our communication (Mehrabian, 1972). As teachers, we need to be able both to use non-verbal communication effectively, and to read accurately the body language of others, particularly that of our learners. There are many contexts in which you can apply these skills. To illustrate how central they are, here are some of the most obvious.

1. Using non-verbal communication effectively
- **Signalling you're in charge: smiling, shoulders back, taking opportunities to move forward towards the learners.**
- **Signalling you're relaxed: smiling, avoiding sitting or standing with arms and/or legs crossed, perching on (or leaning against) desk.**
- **Signalling that the subject or topic is really interesting: smiling, using energetic movements and expansive gestures (within reason!).**
- **Making learners feel valued: smiling, making lots of eye contact, looking interested and nodding when they ask questions or contribute to discussion.**

As we see – and not surprisingly – smiling is the single most effective way of communicating positive signals to your learners.

2. Reading non-verbal clues
- **Watch the facial expressions of your learners. Is someone frowning? Perhaps they don't understand what you're saying, or perhaps they don't agree with it. Either way, it's time to pause and find out by asking or inviting questions.**
- **Still watching facial expressions, does one of the learners want to say something? Are they leaning forward, making eye contact, raising their heads? These are all clues for you to stop and invite their contribution.**
- **Are the learners interested and engaged? Are they leaning forward, looking at you, looking animated? Or are they disengaged, bored, resistant, leaning back, looking away, crossing their arms?**

If you aren't focusing your attention on the learners, looking from face to face, you'll miss the opportunity to pick up these obvious signals.

If we had to pick out from these the two elements of non-verbal communication most important to effective teaching, they would almost certainly be:

- **make frequent eye contact with the learners;**
- **smile.**

Listening skills

When we talk about 'communication skills', we can all too easily forget that listening attentively is just as important as speaking clearly. This can be particularly important in tutorials. In communication theory, *transmitting* and *receiving* are of equal importance. Communication will not take place if either one of these fails.

And how do we know that someone has heard what we've said to them – or, in communication parlance, that the communication has been received? Well, we know that from the feedback. When we use the word *feedback* in learning and teaching, we're borrowing the terminology from communication theory. In diagram form, it looks like this:

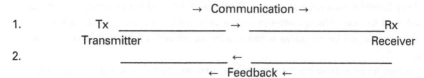

What we need to remember is that the feedback can be intended (conscious) or unintended (unconscious). For example, if someone is telling you about their holiday at great length with the help of 200 photographs, you might find yourself at some stage stifling a yawn or glancing about the room for some means of escape. If you're lucky, this unintended feedback will be picked up and correctly interpreted by Ms or Mr Holiday-snaps, who will quickly put the photos away. On the other hand, if you have a very low tolerance of other people's holiday tales, things will never have got this far, because your feedback will have been given openly and with intent: 'No thanks'.

The first of these, the non-verbal feedback, depends for its effectiveness on the original communicator's ability to notice and interpret your signals. The second is crystal clear, but risks causing offence. There's a third option, too: the hint. 'Well, I've only got a few minutes before the next meeting,' or, 'Love to, but I've lost my glasses.' This sort of feedback still requires some interpretation, and – as most of us know to our cost – some people are incapable of understanding what's being communicated by this sort of evasion. When we put all this into the context of our professional practice, it becomes clear that we need to pay close attention to what our learners are really saying, by the way they respond or don't respond, the way they sit, the words they choose and the expressions on their faces. We need to interpret the feedback and *demonstrate that we have understood it correctly*. This gives us a third line in our diagram:

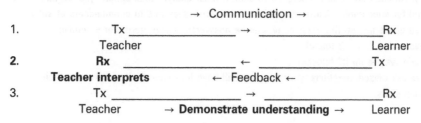

This means that we have to develop our skills of *active listening.*

Active listening means paying close attention to what someone is saying, and showing them that you have heard them and understood them correctly. This can be particularly important in a one-to-one interaction with a learner, such as in a tutorial situation. There are few better ways to encourage learners to engage actively with their learning than to show them you are interested in, and actively listening to, what they have to say. Active listening means:

- not turning away while the learner is talking to you. If you need to summarise or write out what they're saying on the board, wait until they've finished;
- summarising what you've heard the learner say, and checking with them that you've understood them correctly;
- using your body language to give encouragement – for example, nodding, leaning forward;
- trying not to interrupt. If the learner is in error, you don't necessarily have to cut them off mid-sentence, as this may discourage them from speaking up again. If possible, thank them for answering (or asking a question or contributing) and then use the error as an opportunity to accurately recap for the whole group;
- tolerating a delay between question and answer. (Sometimes this is about tolerating a short and apparently awkward silence, although silences – even short ones – are not frequent in most classrooms and workshops!) When you've posed a question, allow the learner or learners some thinking time;
- cheering the learner on by making encouraging noises, such as: Really? – uh-huh – okay – right – yes – I see;
- not allowing your mind to rush on to the next step in your lesson plan or tutorial so that you're not giving your full attention to what the learner is saying.

By demonstrating the skill of active listening you are modelling good practice for your learners, with the intention that some of this skill will rub off on them and help them to become active listeners, too.

Questioning skills

The skilful use of questions is an important part of any teacher's or tutor's communication repertoire. We can use questioning to assess learners' current state of knowledge and skills; to encourage them to think something through; to show them they already have the answer if they think about it carefully enough. And we can use questioning to draw learners into the lesson, to get them actively involved, to give them a sense of ownership over the body of knowledge or range of skills that they are engaging with. But effective use of questioning is not as easy as some people make it look. There are, however, some basic guidelines we can follow, so let's remind ourselves of them here.

- *Open questions serve a different purpose to closed questions*, and so it's important to choose appropriately. An open question is designed to elicit a fuller answer than simply 'yes' or 'no'. They're useful for encouraging learners to think, to explore issues and to communicate at some length. Closed questions, on the other hand, can be answered in one word. For example:
  In what ways would........? (open)
  Is this the right way to do it? (closed)
  If you always ask closed questions, your learners will have less opportunity to practise their communication skills.

- *Hypothetical questions are useful for encouraging learners to consider new ideas and possibilities.* They are the 'What if...?' questions, and the 'Just imagine if this were the case, what would happen to...?' They provide opportunities for using the imagination and for elaborate problem-solving.
- *Leading questions should be used with care.* They can be useful in helping learners express their ideas by providing them with a form of words. For example: 'So do you mean...?' But the obvious danger is that you might be simply putting words in their mouth because you can't wait any longer for them to articulate clearly whatever it was they wanted to say, and they simply nod agreement, relieved to be let off the hook. They won't improve their communication skills that way.

Promoting effective and respectful communication between learners

We shall be looking in detail, in later chapters, at ways in which we can establish positive interaction between learners and encourage respectful communication in our classroom and workshops. The key point to take from this chapter is the importance of teaching by example. Every interaction with our learners provides us with an opportunity to model for them the communication skills we would wish them to develop for themselves, whether it's about adopting the appropriate register, showing respect and observing social courtesies, or correctly employing a specialist vocational vocabulary.

Written communication

In this chapter we have focused very much on oral and non-verbal communication. Most of our interaction with learners is of this nature. Obvious exceptions are in online tutoring, where communication will be in written form; and, of course, the written feedback we provide for learners when we assess their work. We will also communicate in writing with our colleagues, our managers, and outside agencies in the form of reports, emails, returns and so on. Many of the issues we've looked at so far in this chapter are equally applicable to written modes of communication. For example, when writing an email to learners, we should observe the rules of syntax and register as well as the rules of ethics and confidentiality, just as we would if we were talking face to face.

Communication and teamwork

Teaching, like most professions, depends a great deal on effective communication not only with learners but with colleagues, employers and other stakeholders. To be a teacher is to be part of a team and one of the functions of a team is that it encourages cooperation and collaboration. Cooperation is about 'pulling our weight', helping to achieve common goals – which in our case are usually about helping learners to achieve *their* goals and, in the process, enhancing their experience of learning. It is also about working within the rules, whether these be the formal contractual issues that regulate our profession, or the unwritten rules of courteous social interaction. Being cooperative is about choosing to behave in a way that is helpful to colleagues, wherever this is possible. Collaboration, on the other hand, can be used to describe a more proactive process of working together with others to create something specific or achieve a finite goal. A collaborative project might involve planning a scheme of work, drafting a policy, or writing a book. It usually suggests a fixed timescale and a pre-planned, specific outcome. We may collaborate frequently or only from time to time; but cooperation is something we, as professionals, will be practising every day.

An effective team usually needs a range of expertise and professional qualities. A team consisting entirely of 'ideas people' might never get a project off the ground, and a team made up exclusively of 'action-takers' might find themselves short of ideas to act on (Belbin, 1993). What is important is that we should be clear about what we, as individuals, can contribute to the teams to which we belong, and the ways in which we might want to draw on the expertise and support of our team to sustain our own professional development. Is someone in our team really good at motivating disengaged learners? Then let's ask for some tips; or, even better, ask whether we can observe one of their lessons. Or perhaps there's a technophobe on the team who's having trouble with the data projector. That's our cue to take them through it step by step. It is cooperation of this kind within teams that helps develop a culture of collegiality. This sense of belonging and mutual support can be vital to our motivation, particularly during tough times. So, in this chapter we're going to look at what skills and qualities we need to be a good team player, and how we can best use these for the benefit of our learners.

Being a good team player

Let's begin by looking at one team in action and asking ourselves some questions about how teams function in pursuit of their goals and how individual team members identify and play out their role.

TASK TASK **TASK** TASK **TASK** TASK TASK TASK **TASK** TASK **TASK** TASK

Read through the scenario below and, as you do so, consider the following questions.

1. What is this team's declared goal?
2. Do all individual team members share this goal?
3. What examples can you find of team cooperation?
4. Does everyone cooperate? If not, why not?
5. What distinct roles can you identify as being played out within this team?
6. What would you identify as the barriers to teamwork in this situation?
7. What are strengths of this team, and how would you, as a team member, build on them?

There is to be an inspection next term of the Construction and Trowel Trades provision at Ashleigh College. Nat, the Head of School, has called a team meeting to discuss what actions need to be taken in the run-up to the inspection. Four team members attend the meeting, including Nat. Two are absent.

Nat: *Okay, guys. Thanks for being here. We've got apologies from Jez, who's teaching. The only other person not here is . . .* [looks around the table] *. . . Pete.*

Alex: *Pete's gone home.*

Raj: *Surprise, surprise.*

Nat: *So let's get down to business. We've got an inspection coming up* [there are groans around the table]. *Aren't we the lucky ones? So what we need to sort out in the next 40 minutes or so is: what actions do we need to prioritise to get ourselves ready for this?*

Raj: *I think we're pretty much on track. Retention and achievement are good. We're recruiting well. . .*

Alex: *Yeah, but this is Ofsted, remember. All those things'll impress the boss, but Ofsted are going to be looking at the quality of teaching, and the procedures for assessment, and how we evaluate what we're doing, and all that stuff.*

Bo: *And the quality of our teamwork.*

Raj: *Our teamwork's good.*

Alex: *But what about Pete?*

Nat: *Let's just focus on what we need to do. Let's not get into personalities.*

Alex: *But he's dead weight, boss. He's going to bring us down.*

Raj: *Quality of teaching. We've been doing that peer assessment project. We need to make sure they know about that, and get all the paperwork looking presentable.*

Nat: *Okay. Thanks. Got that. What about assessment? Moderation procedures?*

Bo: *What moderation procedures?*

Alex: *Oh come on. Get a grip. Moderation procedures. You've been here longer than I have. Internal moderation?*

Raj: *Well, obviously we've got a problem here.*

Alex: *You can say that again. Ever seen Pete's marking?*

Nat: *Bo, can you get the assessment and moderation paperwork sorted out. Records, spreadsheets, examples . . .*

Bo: *Why me?*

Nat: *Well, Alex then. Okay? And, Raj, I want you to make sure all the documentary evidence is sorted out from the peer assessments.*

Raj: *Okay.*

Alex: *But what about Pete? He's not been assessed and he's not done any assessing, so how's that going to look?*

Raj: *Well how about if Bo sorts that one out? Bo, you can arrange to observe Pete and get him to observe you, okay? And make sure the paperwork's all done and passed on to me.*

Bo: *Hey, that's a bit unfair. That's mission impossible, that is.*

Nat: *I agree. We can't really ask Bo to do that. I'll sort that one out. And all the retention and achievement figures, obviously. And I'd better do the stuff about liaison with employers as well.*

Alex: *So that gets Pete nicely off the hook yet again, then.*

Bo: *Yeah. That's not fair. He always gets away with it.*

Raj: *Just a minute, Bo. I don't see you contributing much here either.*

Discussion

The news of a forthcoming inspection can often put people into a bit of a flap, so we can probably make some allowances for what's happened in this team meeting. But what's happening here in terms of teamwork?

The team's declared goal (that is, the reason the meeting was called) is to draw up a preliminary action plan for the inspection. This is the goal the team leader, Nathalie, is trying to steer them towards. But do all team members share this goal? What about Alex? If we look carefully at her contributions we can see that she's largely concerned with pointing out Pete's shortcomings, perhaps even trying to get him into trouble. And what about Bo? His agenda seems to be about avoiding being allocated tasks if at all possible. In any joint venture, individual team members will, of course, have their own preoccupations and personal goals. But effective cooperation requires that we shuffle our priorities for the duration of the task, and focus on team goals. We could use the analogy of a football team here. If individual members decide to show off or sulk or worry about keeping their kit clean, instead of focusing on defending their own goal and attacking their opponents', the team as a whole will be unlikely to achieve its (literal) goals.

So Nat's team does not, as a whole, cooperate well. Raj perhaps provides the only example of wholehearted cooperation, but his contributions to the meeting could be seen as more reassuringly enthusiastic than helpful. For example, at one stage he declares that, *'Our teamwork's good'*, when quite patently it's not. And we could argue that this bright-eyed enthusiasm, if misplaced, is counter-productive to the drawing up of a realistic action plan. Those who don't cooperate will have their own various reasons for this. We don't know what makes Pete tick, but can infer from what's said here that he's uncooperative about practically everything, and is not a team player. Alex doesn't cooperate fully because she resents Pete always 'getting away with it'. Bo withholds his cooperation in order to avoid increasing his workload. But a key underlying factor here is Nat's apparent willingness to step in and do it all herself: (*I'll sort that one out. And all the retention and achievement figures, obviously. And I'd better do the stuff about liaison with employers as well.*) Team members don't need to volunteer or comply if they know that eventually the team leader will give in and carry the entire burden. Over-zealous, over-managing, or over-generous team leadership will have just as detrimental an effect on teamwork as isolates like Pete or shirkers like Bo; and those of us who lead teams need always to bear this in mind.

So what distinct roles are being played out here? Well, first there is the over-conciliating leader, who takes on the work herself rather than press others to do it; and who avoids confronting non-compliance (Bo's and Pete's) and failure to meet professional standards (Pete's). Then there is Raj, the enthusiast, who can be a real asset to a team, but whose over-optimism and unrealistic evaluations – if unchecked – may present problems. We also have Alex, the watchdog, who is more concerned with distributing work fairly and bringing retribution down on poor performers than in achieving the team task. And there's Bo, the avoider, who will dodge and weave and keep his head down, and do everything possible to avoid contributing to the team effort while, on the face of it, appearing to comply by showing up at meetings. Pete, a team member in name only, is the fugitive: he doesn't do what he's supposed to do, and they can never get hold of him.

We can summarise those team roles like this:

- **over-conciliatory leader;**
- **unrealistic enthusiast;**
- **watchdog who monitors workloads;**
- **avoider;**
- **fugitive.**

The characteristics and behaviour of the team members, therefore, present the most serious barrier to teamwork in this situation.

So, what are the strengths of this team, and how would you, if you were a team member, build on them? We've only talked about the negative aspects of this team so far, and yet most of the characteristics and behaviours we've seen could be turned around quite easily to become strengths and assets. Nat, for example, although over-conciliatory, is at least not confrontational and overbearing. She consults her team. She listens to them. She is keen – in theory – to encourage teamwork. She would not have to adjust her behaviour very far in order to behave as a supportive member of her team who will give firm direction where necessary. Raj's optimism and enthusiasm will be an asset if he's able to counter-balance it with an ability for realistic evaluation. It will then work effectively to help motivate and enthuse the team. And Alex's focus on fair distribution of work will also be a strength if she is able to stop obsessing about bringing retribution down on Pete. Even Bo could be considered an effective team player if he put his listening and problem-solving skills to better use than to simply spotting and dodging incoming tasks. All teams need listeners and thinkers as well as talkers and motivators. And what about Pete? Well, who knows? We've probably all worked at some time in a team which has a fugitive among its ranks. Unless you fall into this category yourself (in which case you probably wouldn't be reading this book), there's not a lot you can do about it. It's a problem best left to managers.

So, let's summarise these positive roles.

- **Supportive leader who both directs and consults, as necessary.**
- **Realistic enthusiast and motivator.**
- **Watchdog who monitors workloads.**
- **Listener and thinker/strategist.**

CLOSE FOCUS CLOSE FOCUS **CLOSE FOCUS** CLOSE FOCUS **CLOSE FOCUS**

We've discovered a number of roles here, both positive and negative. From your own experience of teamwork, what other typical roles can you identify? If you identify further roles that hinder teamwork, how could these be turned around?

Evaluating your own effectiveness as a team member

So, how effective are you as a team player? What roles do you play? What do you contribute to the working and achievement of your team or teams, and how could you improve your effectiveness?

TASK TASK **TASK** TASK **TASK** TASK **TASK** TASK **TASK** TASK **TASK** TASK

Ask yourself the following questions and try to answer as honestly as you can. It will be useful to think back to the last couple of team meetings you attended, and to your professional practice over the past couple of weeks. If you are a student teacher, you may choose to think about your contribution to, and behaviour in: a) small group activity, and b) larger group interactions, on your teacher training programme.

Question 1: When working on a group task do you:
a) tend to take the lead?
b) wait to see what everyone else thinks and then join in?
c) watch the group dynamics and let others take the strain?
d) do as you're told?

Question 2: When you've produced some useful learning materials, do you:
a) make them available to the team as a whole?
b) tell the team leader about them but not distribute them unless asked?
c) keep them to yourself and for your own learners?

d) you've never actually made your own materials; you've always used others'.

Question 3: If your team needs a volunteer to collect information or compile a report, do you:
a) volunteer straight away?
b) volunteer, but only after you've waited and seen whether someone else would like to do it?
c) keep your head down and wait for someone else to step forward?
d) find an excuse if asked?
e) volunteer someone else for the job?

Question 4: If you're told you're to be peer observed by another member of your team, do you feel:
a) pleased that you'll be able to show off your expertise?
b) pleased you'll be able to get some feedback on your teaching?
c) anxious?
d) resentful?
e) determined to get out of it somehow?

Question 5: If you are newly appointed to your team – and sometimes for other reasons, too – you may be allocated another team member as a mentor. How would you make best use of this mentor? As:
a) someone to discuss your professional performance with?
b) someone to give you practical advice on your teaching?
c) someone to watch and assess your teaching?
d) someone to advise you on your specialist subject and how to teach it?
e) someone to give you support and encouragement and help you to get to know the place?

Question 6: If work you have marked is moderated by another member of your team and changes are made to your assessment decision, do you:
a) feel it as a professional insult?
b) get angry and defensive and ask for it to be changed back?
c) discuss the assessment decision with the moderator and come to an agreement?
d) shrug and bide your time, and wait until you're moderating *their* work so you can pay them back?

Question 7: Of which of the following could you draw a clear and accurate diagram or flow chart:
a) the Quality Assurance processes within your institution?
b) the chain of command within your institution as it relates to your role?
c) the lines of communication you (or your team leader) would have to follow in order to get a decision on whether you can develop a new programme or provision?
d) the lines of communication you (or your team leader) would have to follow in order to get a decision on a fees or funding issue?

Discussion

1. *Working as part of a group*

As we discussed earlier, a team needs a range of strengths within it: careful listeners as well as people quick to action; followers as well as leaders. Whatever your answer in response to this question, what really matters is that you contribute in some way towards achieving the group goal. Only (c) doesn't do this, unless the team has specifically agreed to appoint an observer in order to monitor and evaluate their teamwork.

Reflect for a moment on the answer you gave to question 1. Does the role you play within your team accurately reflect your strengths? Is it the role you *want* to play? If not, what is preventing you from contributing as you would like? Is there an action point here for your professional development, or an issue it would be useful to discuss with your team leader or mentor?

2. *Sharing or hoarding*
Being an effective team member means sharing resources for the benefit of the team (a), rather than hoarding (c) or freeloading (d). Seeking credit for your hard work (b) is perfectly understandable, because we all need positive feedback and praise to keep us motivated, just as our learners do. If everyone else in your team is a freeloader, however, you may well feel disinclined to share the results of your hard work quite so freely. However, a collection of freeloaders will never really constitute an effective team – so that's one for your team leader to sort out!

Do you actively seek credit for your hard work? To what extent is your own motivation dependent upon the praise and approval of those who lead or line manage you? To what extent are you motivated simply by knowing yourself that you're doing a good job, without having to be told? Take some time to reflect on this, and perhaps discuss it with your mentor or a trusted colleague. Understanding your own motivation will help you to be a more effective team player.

3. *Being an active team member*
Some people volunteer for everything that's going (a). We joke about them collecting 'Brownie points' – and sometimes, indeed, their enthusiasm is rewarded with promotion or projects. We probably all know, too, people who never volunteer for anything (b), avoid being 'volunteered' (c), and even load the job on to someone else (d). These last three don't really deserve to be called team players. But we could also argue that (a) *might* not be a good team player either – always wanting to do everything themselves. So we're left here with (b) as perhaps the most sensible approach: willing but not pushy, cautious but not work-shy. To volunteer for *everything* is unwise unless you are extremely gifted at managing your workload. How well do you manage yours?

4. *Peer evaluation and assessment*
The great advantage of peer assessment or peer evaluation is that it provides a way of sharing good ideas and best practice. There's always something to be learned from observing the professional practice of our colleagues, even if it's only how *not* to do something. And it can be a useful and enlightening experience to get feedback on our own practice from a colleague who has had the opportunity to observe us teaching and interacting with our learners. Because peer observation and/or assessment should be seen as a positive step towards sharing *best* practice and encouraging *reflective* practice within a team, the most appropriate response will be (b), although you will probably inevitably feel a little of (a) and (c) into the bargain!

If you were to be observed by another member of your team, what would you hope to demonstrate as examples of best practice? And if you yourself were to be the observer, what skills or qualities would you be hoping to learn more about by watching your colleague in action? It's worth taking time to reflect on these two questions, as your answers will help you to formulate your own skills audit and professional action plan.

5. *How would you make best use of your mentor?*
Did you answer 'yes' to all those questions, (a) – (e)? If you did, you are absolutely right. Your mentor can fulfil all those functions; although mentors, being only human, will have their own strengths and weaknesses. Some might be more skilled than others at the caring side of mentoring (e), or particularly good at giving you constructive feedback on your teaching. But to make best use of the mentoring arrangement in enhancing and supporting your professional practice, you should expect your mentor to discuss, advise on, and assess your teaching; provide subject specialist support; and offer encouragement, care, and practical help.

CLOSE FOCUS CLOSE FOCUS CLOSE FOCUS CLOSE FOCUS CLOSE FOCUS

If you would like to explore this further, you can read more about making the most of your mentor in Chapter 2 of *Mentoring in the Lifelong Learning Sector (Wallace and Gravells, 2007)*, entitled, 'How to be a good mentor and mentee'.

6. *Assessment as a team activity*
We should all, of course, welcome feedback on our assessment decisions, just as we should welcome feedback on our teaching. It's only through careful moderation and verification procedures that we can ensure that our assessment decisions are reliable and consistent with team, institution, or national standards. We shall look at these issues in detail in Chapters 12 and 13. If a mark or assessment decision you have given is later adjusted, clearly the only appropriate response is (c). As professionals, we should resist viewing such judgements as a criticism or an affront.

CLOSE FOCUS CLOSE FOCUS CLOSE FOCUS CLOSE FOCUS CLOSE FOCUS

Are you familiar with the moderation procedures within your team? Is there an institutional policy on double marking or the moderation of assessment? To what extent are procedures dependent upon the requirements of the awarding body? These are all questions to which you need to know the answers if you are to take an active part in team assessment.

7. *Using organisational systems*
In your professional capacity, you are a member not only of your immediate team within your Section, School, or Department, but also of the wider organisational team. It's important, therefore, that you understand how this Big Team operates, in terms of its practices and procedures, and its lines of communication. In a Big Team – such as a college or other training organisation – systems such as these can be complicated and take time to learn. Whether you are a student-teacher, a newly qualified or newly appointed teacher, the sensible thing, therefore, is to find out, ask questions, read organisational policies and structural charts. The answer to Question 7 is that you should be familiar enough with each of these (a – d) to be able to draw up an accurate flow chart illustrating systems and procedures.

A SUMMARY OF **KEY POINTS**

In this chapter we have:

> discussed what makes a good communicator;

> looked at how you can evaluate and develop your own communication skills as a teacher and a tutor;

> explored ways to remove barriers to communication in a learning and teaching situation, whether classroom-based or tutorial;

> emphasised the importance of communicating appropriately and ethically;

> discussed the parts played by vocabulary, syntax and register in ensuring we are communicating appropriately;

> identified ways in which non-verbal communication contributes to the learning process;

> presented a range of listening and questioning techniques which can be used to support learning, particularly in a tutorial situation;

> looked at how our own communication skills can encourage effective and respectful communication between learners;

> examined the importance of being a good team player;

> looked at some of the different roles that can be played within a team;

> encouraged you to evaluate your own effectiveness as a team member;

> discussed peer evaluation and assessment;

> considered ways in which you can make best use of the mentoring arrangement in enhancing and supporting your professional practice;

> explored some of the issues around assessment as a team activity;

> considered the importance of understanding and using organisational systems;

> explored how far theory about team values is reflected in your own experience.

Branching options

The following tasks are designed to allow you to apply or explore further some of the contents of this chapter. If you are using this book to support your professional development leading to a teaching qualification, you may find it useful to choose a task according to the level at which you are currently working. These are indicated in brackets.

1. Reflection and self-evaluation (NQF level 5)

a) When drawing up the lesson plan for your next teaching session, include a column headed *Communication*. Use it to note down the opportunities for improving and consolidating communication at each stage of the lesson, whether this is about organising the teaching environment so as to optimise eye contact, or a reminder to yourself to consciously observe your use of vocabulary or body language.

b) When you come to evaluate the lesson afterwards, highlight these communication issues for discussion with your mentor, tutor, or critical friend.

2. Evaluation: theory and practice (NQF level 6)

Tuckman (1965) suggested that most teams go through a series of developmental stages before they begin to work effectively. These stages have become known as:

- **forming;**
- **storming;**
- **norming;**
- **performing.**

This suggests that, following its initial formation, a team will usually go through a turbulent period where individual members are not only jostling to establish their specific roles, but also to establish their points of view, aims, or values. The stage at which these are being resolved, accepted or agreed is the 'norming' stage – where the team reaches towards a shared understanding of what is the 'norm'. Only then will the team go on to 'perform' effectively.

Using Tuckman's theory as a starting point, analyse either the performance of your professional team at work, or the dynamics of the next group you find yourself in as part of your professional development programme. How convincingly is this model reflected in your own experience? Are you able to add to it in any way? For example, what happens if the team loses one of its members? What factors might lead a team to under-perform, and why?

3. Engaging critically with the literature (NQF level 7: M level)

We can, for our purposes, divide communication theory into four fields.

1. Semiotics (the use and interpretation of signs).
2. Mass media.
3. Psychological uses and interpretations.
4. The technology of communication (e.g. e-learning; data projection).

Choose which ever of these you consider most relevant or useful to your own subject specialism, and, with reference to one or more articles from an academic journal, critically analyse the extent to which the theory can help illuminate your own professional practice.

Is there anything about the way you communicate with learners or others that you'd like to change, having worked through this chapter?

REFERENCES AND FURTHER READING

Belbin, M. (1993) *Team Roles at Work.* London: Butterworth-Heinemann.
Bess, J. L. (2000) *Teaching Alone, Teaching Together: Transforming the Structure of Teams for Teaching.* San Francisco: Jossey-Bass.
Briggs, A. (2001) Academic Middle Managers in Further Education: reflections on leadership. *Research in Post-Compulsory Education*, Vol 6, No 2, pp. 223–239.
Davies, P. (1999) *70 Activities for Tutor Groups.* Aldershot: Gower.
Exley, K. and Dennick, R. (2004) *Small Group Teaching: Tutorials, Seminars and Beyond.* London: RoutledgeFalmer.

Hargie, Owen (2004) *Skilled Interpersonal Communication: Research, Theory and Practice*. London: Routledge.

Hoggart, R. (1992) *The Uses of Literacy*. Harmondsworth: Penguin Books.

Levin, P. (2004) *Successful Teamwork!* Maidenhead: Open University Press.

Mehrabian, A. (1972) *Silent Messages: Implicit Communication of Emotions and Attitudes*. Belmont CA: Wadsworth.

Pease, A. and Pease, B. (2005) *The Definitive Book of Body Language*. London: Orion Books.

Tuckman, B. (1965) Development sequences in small groups. *Psychological Bulletin*, Vol 63, pp. 384–399.

Wallace, S. and Gravells, J. (2007a) *Professional Development in the Lifelong Learning Sector: Mentoring* (Second Edition). Exeter: Learning Matters.

Wallace, S. and Gravells, J. (2007b) *Professional Development in the Lifelong Learning Sector: Leadership and Leading Teams*. Exeter: Learning Matters.

West, M.A. (1994) *Effective Teamwork*. Oxford: BPS Blackwell.

3
Recognising diversity and supporting equality

The objectives of this chapter

This chapter explores issues about social justice, and looks at how we, as teachers, can recognise diversity and support equality through our professional practice. It addresses the areas of essential knowledge, skills and values which relate to these issues in the Professional Standards for QTLS. These include helping you to:

- **value equality and diversity and promote inclusion at college, in the workplace and in the wider community (AS3);**
- **be aware of and adhere to current legislation relating to equality and diversity, and the protection of the vulnerable; and understand how it relates to your own specialist area (AK6.1; AP6.1; AK6.2; AP6.2);**
- **promote equality, diversity and inclusion through your own practice (BS1; BK1.2; BP1.2; BK5.2; BP5.2; DS1; DK1.1; DP1.1; EK2.1; EP2.1);**
- **evaluate your own practice in terms of equality and diversity (AP3.1; AS4).**

Introduction

Let's agree first of all that the promotion of equality and diversity is not an aspect of our professional practice that we can view in isolation. It's not something separate that we bolt on to our teaching in order to tick the right boxes. It is central to our professional values; and it should underpin all our planning and teaching, as well as being evident in our interactions with learners and colleagues and others. That's why you'll find issues about equality, diversity and inclusion appearing throughout this book as we explore Assessment, Planning, Motivation, and so on. In fact, we've already encountered these issues in Chapter 2 in relation to Communication. So why a separate chapter on them?

The answer is: because they're so important. If we want the promotion of equality and diversity to underpin everything we do, it's helpful if we take some time to focus in on it, both in terms of how it fits with our personal and professional values, and of what it means in practical terms for our professional practice. What does the promotion of equality and diversity *look* like? What strategies and attitudes does it require in our classrooms or workshops, and in our organisations as a whole, in order to succeed? How do we evaluate our own success as individual teachers in terms of promoting inclusiveness? Exploring these questions is essential if we are to understand the values on which we base our practice.

What is social justice?

One of the terms we use to talk about equality and diversity is *social justice*. Implicit within that phrase is the aspiration to create a just society, one in which everyone is treated fairly. It's unlikely that any of us would disagree with this as a worthwhile goal. But if we want to do our bit towards achieving it, we need to think carefully about what we take this to mean. What, for example, do we understand by a *just society*?

Philosophers will tell us that a just society could mean one of two things, and the interpretation you opt for will depend on whether you value individual rights more than the rights of the population as a whole. The claim for the rights of the individual – to freedom from oppression, to justice, to education – is sometimes traced back to the philosopher Kant (1724–1804), who argued that no individual should be treated as a means by any other or others in pursuit of their own ends. This would mean, for example, that if I could save my entire college from closure and all my colleagues from redundancy by kidnapping the Head of Resources and forcing him to take a crash course in accounting, I could not, given this interpretation of social justice, do so without compromising my principles. If, however, I were to take the alternative view of social justice – the view that the good of the many is more important than the good of the few – I might feel fully justified in infringing the Head of Resources' individual rights in order to save the jobs and livelihoods of the entire college staff. The good of the many – or the greatest good for the greatest number – is an argument advanced by Bentham (1748–1832). It's known as the *utilitarian argument* (utility being in this sense a synonym for good), and can be used to justify any course of action which increases the overall happiness of the many, even if this means overriding the individual rights of the few.

So, what do we mean by a just society? Do we mean one in which every individual has inalienable rights which must be respected? Or do we mean one in which the welfare of the population as a whole must sometimes take priority over the rights of the individual?

TASK TASK TASK TASK TASK **TASK** TASK TASK TASK TASK **TASK** TASK

Consider the following situations and decide on the best course of action. Identify which philosophical position underpins your decision in each instance. Is your position consistent? If not, why not?

1. You have a disruptive and demanding learner in your class. She doesn't actually break any rules, but her constant attention-seeking prevents all the other learners from concentrating. You have tried every strategy to cope with this, but failed. She still demands almost all your attention. If she was removed, the others would be able to fulfil their potential and achieve their qualification. If she stays, many of them undoubtedly will not.

Question: Whose rights are paramount here? Would you recommend the disruptive learner be excluded for the greater good of the many? Or would you respect the individual's right to education and training and resign yourself to the other learners achieving poor results?

2. One of your learners is, for some reason, unpopular with the rest. When you organise group work, none of them wants to work with him.

Question: Do you persevere, on the grounds that he has a right to be included in group work? Or do you let him work alone or with you in the interests of keeping the rest of the class happy and onside?

3. Your college is facing the possibility of a merger with a larger, neighbouring college. At least 20 jobs will be lost if this goes ahead; but you have received absolute assurance that yours will be safe. On the other hand, if the merger doesn't go ahead, the college will reorganise and four jobs will be under threat, including your own.

Question: You are staff representative on the Board of Corporation. How will you vote when the question of the merger comes up?

4. One of your learners has a hearing impairment which also affects the clarity of her speech. Your next lesson plan, which you've used successfully for three years now, involves learners making and taking simulated phone calls and taking accurate notes of the conversation. It specifically covers one of the objectives of the course specification. The learner who has a hearing impairment insists she wants to join in the activity, and doesn't want to be singled out in any way.

Question: Do you re-think and re-plan the lesson around that one learner's needs? Or do you stick to your plan on the grounds that the majority of the learners will benefit greatly from the exercise? Or do you devise an alternative activity for the learner in question, despite her request, because you know she can't do herself justice in a phone exercise?

5. One of the pieces of coursework which goes towards your learners' summative assessment is a group task. It has to be assessed based on overall final product and not on individual contributions to the task. In allocating the groups for this task you have the opportunity to put one of the weaker but hard-working learners in with a very able group. This will have a good chance of bringing up his overall grade, but could – and in fact almost certainly will – adversely affect the grade of the others slightly. You feel the less able student deserves this chance. If you put him with his usual group it is quite possible that they will fail the task and this would keep his overall mark down to just below a pass.

Question: How will you manage the learning here? Whose rights are the most important? Does the less able student have the right to be put in the group where he'll be enabled to do as well as he possibly can? Or should you uphold that same right for the more able group?

Discussion

1. So, would you recommend the disruptive learner be excluded for the greater good of the many? If so, you are taking a utilitarian standpoint in which the right of the individual to this particular course of training or education is abrogated – withdrawn – in favour of the good of the many (the good in this instance being the freedom to take full advantage of their learning opportunity). If, on the other hand, you decided that the rights of the individual here are sacrosanct, you'd be deriving your position from the Kantian argument that no individual should be treated as a means to an end (in this instance, exclusion of that one learner would be a means to improve the learning opportunities of the others). As we've seen, either course of action could technically be justified on the grounds of social justice.

2. And what about the isolated learner? Do you let him work alone or with you in the interests of keeping the rest of the class happy and onside? This would be the utilitarian answer. Or do you persevere until you have facilitated his inclusion? I know which I would do. One of the difficulties, though, that faces us all as teachers is the degree to which we are constrained by lack of time. Facilitating inclusion in a sensitive and supportive way is not a quick or easy process, and there will always be the temptation to take the easier route. However, it seems to me that this particular scenario presents us with additional moral issues. The other students may well be 'happier' if the isolate is excluded. But what sort of 'happiness' is that? If the happiness or 'good' involved in the utilitarian argument is of the morally dubious sort – enjoying someone else's pain or unhappiness, for example – then we will probably want to question the application of the utilitarian approach in such circumstances. These learners don't want to include this particular learner? Including him will make them unhappy? Tough! They have a lot to learn about social justice, and learning to be inclusive and tolerant is a good place to start.

3. How will you vote when the question of the merger comes up? This is a nasty one, isn't it? It raises yet another complication to the philosophical debate – and again it's a moral one. It seems to me that if you were not personally involved in this situation, you would be able to vote against the merger on purely utilitarian grounds and with a light heart. Fewer job losses mean (in this simplified scenario) the greater happiness of the greater number. But wait a minute! If I'm one of

the few whose job is being sacrificed for the good of the many, I'm almost certainly going to feel rather differently about it. The complication which this scenario invites us to think through is *self-interest*. Self-interest isn't something we can just ignore. We have to be aware of the way it operates to influence our judgements. In the context of the previous two scenarios, for example, we might have felt a personal dislike of the attention-seeking learner and wanted her off the course for our own selfish reasons (scenario 1), or have decided in our own interests to opt for a quiet life and let the isolated learner continue to work on his own (scenario 2). Taking a wider view of this, it's important to remember that, in the context of diversity and inclusion, we may often identify ourselves as one of the many with a shared self-interest. In this position it behoves us, as teachers, always to remember the interests of the few.

4. Did you decide to go ahead and teach the lesson as planned; or did you re-think and re-plan the lesson around that one learner's needs? At first sight this would appear to be an obvious example of the need for differentiation. With ingenuity you can easily devise an activity that will meet the individual learner's needs and at the same time satisfy the course specifications. One class, two alternative activities to teach and assess the same outcomes: this is what we mean by differentiation. However, in this case the learner in question has made it clear that she doesn't *want* to be treated *differently*. She wants to participate in the same activity as the other members of her class. So now you have a rather different kind of dilemma. Do you respect the individual's right to be included without being made to feel 'different', or do you have a duty to ensure she receives her full entitlement as a learner, which includes learning activities and assessment strategies which meet her individual needs? Suddenly this has become a question about who makes the decisions about what's best for the learner. And if it isn't the learner herself who is allowed to make those decisions, then how does that square with her 'rights'? This is a question of some significance as we shall see later in this chapter. Whatever course of action you decided upon in this case, you will certainly have discovered that the answer is not straightforward.

5. The final scenario asks us, whose rights are the most important? Can we be justified in supporting the less able learner towards a 'pass' grade at the cost of the more able learners losing a few marks? *'Why not?'* you may ask yourself. *'After all, that way the more able ones will still pass, and there's the added advantage that he will too.'* And yet I find this one the most difficult dilemma of the lot. In a sense we make decisions like this all the time. We teach classes where there is a mix of ability and a range of learning needs, and inevitably some learners will demand more of our time and attention than others. We could argue – though I hope we don't – that every minute we give to less able learners is a minute that could have been spent further improving the chances of the more able ones. But that isn't a good reason to withdraw our attention from those who need it most. In fact most of us would find such an argument distasteful if not downright offensive. It should logically follow, therefore, that we would be happy to help this less able learner along by managing the learning in such a way that he is able to pass his course. But, given that position, we could as easily argue that we could probably achieve a pass even for the less motivated group of learners with whom he usually works if we were to devise groupings with a balance of low and high achieving learners. Obviously this will have the effect of levelling the marks, and some learners will come out of it with a lower grade than they would have had if they'd been allowed to work with other high achievers. But the advantage would be that some learners who would otherwise have failed will all have been given a chance now of passing. So that would perfectly well justify the strategy. Or would it?

Individual rights, or the good of the many?

How consistent was your position in responding to those scenarios? Did you find yourself taking a utilitarian stance, defending the good of the many; or did you take a Kantian view and stand up for the rights of the individual? If you're like most people you will have applied whichever seemed best to fit the specific case. In practice, it would seem, we – by which I mean not only you and me but also our political and social infrastructure in the UK – choose which of these positions to apply, depending on the circumstances. We don't operate to a hard and fast philosophical position. We apply a certain pragmatism. Or, as philosophers would say, the stance we take is *contingent* on the case in point. For example, the rights of the individual are respected in law. But if that individual becomes a danger to others – by breaking the law, say – their individual right to freedom is overridden by the right of the many to be protected from them, and so they find themselves imprisoned on what are basically utilitarian grounds. To some extent we can see that same principle operating in our classrooms and workshops. As teachers we will defend individual rights – up to a point. And that point is contingent on all sorts of other circumstances, including and especially the welfare, rights and happiness of other learners.

Equality and equal opportunity

Let's look now at two further related concepts: *equality* and *equal opportunity.* The QTLS Standards, quite rightly, place a great deal of emphasis on *equality.* They refer to *'Equality,* diversity, and the need for inclusion' (AS3); and 'promoting *equality* and inclusive learning and engaging with diversity' (AP3.1); and so on. So what is meant by 'equality' in this context?

There are at least two ways we can answer this question. We could answer that equality is about fairness and even-handedness; that it requires us, as teachers, to ensure that we show no favouritism or antipathy towards any learner and that we are entirely non-partisan in our dealings with them. In other words, this understanding of equality requires us to *treat them all the same.* Whether they are keen and motivated or bored and disengaged; or whether they are friendly and sociable or morose and threatening, they are nevertheless *equal* and should be treated *equally.*

The other way we can interpret equality is in terms of value. If this is what we mean by equality, our focus is not on what we *do* (show no favouritism, treat them equally, and so on), but on what we *believe. We value* all learners equally. The way in which we interact with them will follow from this, and will be pretty much indistinguishable from that which arises from our other interpretation of equality. So we now have two ways of understanding what we mean by equality. It can be about how we *act towards* our learners, or it can be about how we *value* our learners. Now, it will be immediately evident to you that only one of these is observable. If I come to assess your practical teaching, I'll be able to observe and assess how you behave towards your learners, but how can I know whether this way of interacting arises from genuinely held values, or whether it is a set of behaviours adopted in order to ensure that your practice is in line with the QTLS Standards? And does it matter that I don't and can't know? After all, the accurate assessment of attitudes and beliefs is always problematic, as we shall discover later in this book when we come to discuss the domains of learning. To help answer our question about whether it does really matter, let's look at a practical situation.

Darren's teaching is being observed by his subject specialist mentor. He knows he's being assessed against the QTLS Standards. He takes great care to treat all his learners equally, paying particular attention to a group of female students who usually sit quietly and isolate themselves from the lesson and the rest of the class. Usually he leaves them to it. It's too much of an effort to coax them to join in, because they don't respond; and he doesn't expect them to achieve very much anyway. But today he makes a special effort to draw them in. They look a bit surprised and show their usual reluctance, but Darren's mentor is satisfied with what he's seen, and writes on the report that Darren is meeting the standards, including AS3, AK3.1, and DS1.

CLOSE FOCUS CLOSE FOCUS CLOSE FOCUS CLOSE FOCUS CLOSE FOCUS

So does it matter that Darren's engagement with equality is limited to this one occasion? Does it matter if it extends as far as his behaviour but not his values?

My answer to both questions would be that yes, it does matter. But then, in terms of the Standards, how are we to assess the values that a teacher holds, other than through their observable behaviour? This is not just a dilemma for teacher trainers; it is one which all of us will confront in our teaching if part of our professional responsibility is that we should positively promote equality. Will it be enough if we simply achieve a change in learners' *observed behaviour*? Or should the goal be one of addressing their *values?* And, if the latter, how will we know if we have been successful?

Entitlement and equality of opportunity

Language-watchers among us will have noticed a recent change of phraseology in relation to equality. The most often-used expression ten years or so ago was *equal opportunities* or equality of opportunity. Colleges had their Equal Opportunities policies and Equal Opportunities committees, and so on. Now, however, we tend to use the terms *social justice* and *equality*. We can see this development illustrated in the Equality Acts of 2006 and 2010, both in their title and the fact that they replaced, among others, the Equal Opportunities Commission (EOC) with the Commission for *Equality* and Human Rights (CEHR). And in the QTLS Standards there are, as we've seen, a number of references to equality, but no mention of equal opportunities. What might be the reason for this?

Part of the answer probably lies in the fact that *equal opportunities* is quite a slippery concept when we try to relate it to the practicalities of provision. For example, have a look at the following extract from the White Paper *14–19 Education and Skills* (DfES 2005).

TASK TASK TASK TASK TASK TASK TASK TASK TASK TASK TASK

Read the following extract carefully and make some notes on what you think it is saying about a) equality, b) entitlement, and c) equality of opportunity.

> ... this White Paper ensures that young people are able to pursue qualifications pitched at the right level for them, whatever that might be. QCA and the LSC already plan to develop a range of units for those working below level 2. These would cover functional skills, vocational and general learning and personal and social development. We intend that every young person should be supported and challenged to achieve the most of which they are capable. The new proposal for stretch in the White Paper achieves that for some young people; the new proposals for better progression at foundation level achieve it for others.
>
> (DfES 2005, para 9.11)

Discussion

What is proposed here is about equality, in the sense of the government acknowledging an equal duty of care for all young people, and also in the sense of acknowledging that they all have an equal right to education and training. As young citizens they all have an entitlement to the level of education and training that meets their needs. But do these proposals offer them all an equal opportunity? You would probably have to conclude that they do not, although you may well feel there are valid reasons for this. So, an equal value may be placed on all these young people, and they may all be equally entitled to education and training; but this will not necessarily provide them with equal opportunities – for career progression, earning potential, higher education, and so on. They may all be entitled to education and training, but they are not all automatically entitled to the *same* education and training. This is one of the reasons that *equal opportunities* is a problematic term to apply in practice. In the next chapter we shall see that much of the recent legislation on education and training has been about establishing and revising differentiated provision for learners.

Diversity

What do we mean by diversity? In very simple terms it expresses the fact that not all our learners are the same. They may be diverse in terms of their cultural background, their physical or learning abilities, their age, their 'race', their religion, their gender and sexual orientation. We will encounter some level of diversity in most educational or training orga-nisations; but we could argue that it is in the Lifelong Learning sector where we will find the greatest diversity of all. This is because the provision of the sector is not aimed at a specific group of learners – in terms of age, for example, as schools do; nor in terms of level of qualification, as universities do. The range of courses in the Lifelong Learning sector is the underlying reason for the diversity of our learners. But the sense in which we use the term *diversity* in this chapter, and in relation to the Standards, is not simply descriptive. It implies the very set of values which we have been examining here. It conveys not simply difference, but difference coupled with equality. In our teaching we are likely to encounter a wide and diverse range of learners, and it is part of our responsibility to demonstrate through our professional practice that we *value and respect all learners equally.*

Current legislation

Let's go back now to the *Equality Act* of 2006. The single commission it established (the Commission for Equality and Human Rights (CEHR)), as well as replacing the Equal Opportunities Commission (EOC), also replaced the Commission for Racial Equality (CRE) and the Disability Rights Commission (DRC). The 2010 Act now requires public authorities to promote equality between men and women, and to explicitly prohibit sexual harassment. It also makes it unlawful for anyone or any body or organisation to discriminate against anyone on the grounds of religion and belief; and it also enables provision for the prohibition of discrimination on the grounds of sexual orientation.

As a teacher, you need to be conversant with current legislation, not only in order to under-stand what the law requires of you, personally and professionally, but also to enable you to clarify such requirements for your learners when necessary. Some sorts of offensive beha-viour which previously would have been discouraged by college or organisation rules or policies are now prohibited by law. These include discriminatory behaviour, or bullying, by learners on the grounds of a fellow learner's sexual orientation or beliefs.

Other key legislation over the past 30 years includes:

- **1975 Sexual Discrimination Act;**
- **1976 Race Relations Act;**
- **1995 Disability Discrimination Act;**
- **1999 Sex Discrimination (gender reassignment) Regulations;**
- **2000 Race Relations Act (1976) Amendments;**
- **2002 Sexual Discrimination (Election Candidates) Act;**
- **2003 Race Relations Act (1976) Amendments;**
- **2003 Employment Equality (Sexual Orientation) Regulations;**
- **2003 Employment Equality (Religion or Belief) Regulations;**
- **2003 Employment Equality (Age) Regulations.**

The 2002 legislation relating to election candidates may not seem at first sight to be particularly relevant to ourselves as teachers. But, in fact, this Act made provision for positive measures to be taken in order to address the disparity between numbers of men and women chosen to stand for parliament. It may be useful to draw an analogy here with the way we recruit learners onto programmes that traditionally have been gender-specific, such as nursery nursing or construction. The 2002 legislation provides a precedent for 'positive action' – that is, taking active measures to redress the imbalance. This could mean, in theory, offering a place on a programme to a male applicant rather than a female applicant who might be equally or even better qualified for admission, in the interests of a more even gender balance. Inevitably, this sort of thing remains controversial.

CLOSE FOCUS CLOSE FOCUS **CLOSE FOCUS** CLOSE FOCUS **CLOSE FOCUS**

In terms of the two conflicting interpretations of social justice which we considered earlier in this chapter, how would you evaluate the practice of 'positive action'? It may help here to think about means and ends.

Applying the legislation to our professional practice

You can access all this legislation in full through the internet, using most search engines. A useful key phrase for your search is *Anti-discrimination legislation.* You can also access very useful summaries through, amongst others, the ACAS website, *teachernet*, and the website of the Metropolitan Police Authority (MPA).

TASK TASK **TASK** TASK **TASK** TASK **TASK** TASK **TASK** TASK TASK

Choose two pieces of legislation which, in your view, have the most relevance to your own professional practice, and use your ICT skills to access both these and the Equality Act of 2006, either in full or in the form of summaries of their main points. When you have read and reflected on these, consider the following questions.

1. How effectively do your own institutional policies (for example, on Equality or Diversity) reflect current legislation? (You should be able to acquire copies of all college policies through your Human Resources or Personnel department.)

2. What specific issues in relation to this legislation are raised by, or particularly relevant to your own specialist subject area?

You may find it useful to address these questions with the help of a critical friend or mentor, or with a group of colleagues who share your subject specialism.

A SUMMARY OF **KEY POINTS**

In this chapter we have:

> emphasised that the recognition of equality and diversity is central to our professional values;

> discussed what we mean by 'social justice' and the tension between individual rights and the greatest happiness of the greater number;

> explored some of the issues surrounding 'equality' and 'equal opportunity';

> discussed the relationship between beliefs, values and observable behaviour;

> summarised the Equality Act (2006) and other relevant legislation, and considered how these apply to our professional practice.

Branching options

The following tasks are designed to allow you to apply or explore further some of the contents of this chapter. If you are using this book to support your professional development leading to a teaching qualification, or a formal programme of CPD, you may find it useful to choose a task according to the level at which you are currently working. These are indicated in brackets.

1. Reflection and self-evaluation (NQF level 5)

Choose one class or group which you currently teach, and reflect on the following questions, giving examples and making notes, where appropriate, in your professional journal.

- How do you promote equality and diversity to these learners?
- How do you ensure, in your planning and teaching, that you don't discriminate against any learner on the grounds of gender, race, religion, disability, sexual orientation or age?

2. Evaluation: theory and practice (NQF level 6)

Employing your research skills, use the internet or library to identify which pieces of anti-discrimination legislation have been informed by, or are relevant to, the following milestone reports in the field of inclusive education and training.

- 1996 Tomlinson Report (Report of the FEFC Learning Difficulties and/or Disabilities Committee chaired by Prof. John Tomlinson).
- 1999 Kennedy Report (*Learning Works*).
- 1999 Moser Report (*A Fresh Start – Improving Literacy and Numeracy*. Report of working group chaired by Sir Claus Moser).
- 2002 LSDA's *Access for All*.

3. Engaging critically with the literature (NQF level 7: M level)

Consider the following questions.

- In what sense can we argue that education is a 'right'?
- What do you understand by 'equality' in the context of education and training?
- To what extent might there exist a contradiction between inclusion and diversity on the one hand, and the raising of standards of achievement on the other?
- In your view, is the promotion of equality and diversity a practical issue or a moral one, and how would you distinguish between the two?

REFERENCES AND FURTHER READING

Cole, M. (ed.) (2006) *Education, Equality and Human Rights: Issues of Gender, 'Race', Sexuality, Disability and Social Class.* London: Routledge.

Department of Education and Employment (1999) *A Fresh Start – Improving Literacy and Numeracy.* London: DfEE (Moser Report).

Kennedy, H. *et al.* (1999) *Learning Works.* London: HMSO.

Learning and Skills Development Agency (2002) *Access for All.* London: LSDA.

Davis, L. (ed.) (1997) *The Disabilities Studies Reader.* London: Routledge.

DfES (2005) *14–19 Education and Skills.* London: HMSO.

Disabilities Rights Commission (2002) *Code of Practice for Providers of Post-16 Education and Related Services.* London: DRC.

Hughes, C., Blaxter, L., Brine, J. and Jackson, S. (eds) (2006) *British Educational Research Journal special issue: Gender, Class and 'Race' in Lifelong Learning.* London: Routledge/Taylor & Francis.

McNary, S. (2005) *What Successful Teachers Do in Inclusive Classrooms: 60 Research-based Teaching Strategies That Help Special Learners Succeed.* London: Sage.

Ostler, A. (ed.) (2005) *Teachers, Human Rights and Diversity: Educating Citizens in Multi-cultural Societies.* Stoke-on-Trent: Trentham.

Vincent, C. (ed.) (2003) *Social Justice, Education and Identity.* London: RoutledgeFalmer.

4
Lifelong Learning: the organisational, local and national context

The objectives of this chapter

This chapter is designed to provide you with a clear picture of what is happening in the Lifelong Learning sector today, and why. It focuses particularly on post-compulsory education and training (PCET), its structures, processes and qualifications, and the policy decisions over the past two decades or so which have created the context in which we find ourselves now working. It also addresses values, skills, and essential knowledge set out in the Professional Standards for QTLS. These include helping you to:

- **recognise and adhere to agreed codes of practice (AS6; AK6.1; AP6.1);**
- **recognise the role that the Lifelong Learning sector plays locally and nationally (AS2);**
- **use organisational, local and national systems and networks effectively in the interests of raising the quality of the learning experience (AS5; AK5.1; AP5.1);**
- **be familiar with relevant legislation and statutes relating to the sector (AK6.2; AP6.2).**

Introduction

A sound knowledge and understanding of the sector's operational context is of vital importance to the teacher in the Lifelong Learning sector. This includes:

- **the purpose, accountability and funding of the sector;**
- **the vocational-academic divide and issues about parity;**
- **the status of the sector and its learners;**
- **the role of its teachers;**
- **the development of the vocational qualification framework over the past few decades;**
- **how all of these are reflected in your own institution and its working practices.**

One of the purposes of this chapter, therefore, is to set out this context as straightforwardly as possible. It is designed to help you to find your bearings if you are new to the profession; or, for those of us who have been involved in it for some time, to fill in the gaps and provide what we might call a 'helicopter's eye view' of the significant milestones which created the Lifelong Learning sector as we know it today.

Recent developments in the sector have been complex. In order to find our way clearly, we shall take a chronological route, with short stops here and there to get a close up view of essential issues and key turning points. You'll be asked from time to time to reflect on ways in which national developments in policy and practice can be illustrated by, or be seen to have had an impact on, policy and practice in your own organisation. Our exploration in this chapter will provide an overview, and although it cannot aspire, in the space available, to cover every development in detail, it should help to point you in the right direction to follow up themes of particular professional interest or concern. To help you with this, you'll find suggested reading at the end of the chapter.

The vocational-academic divide

In England two centuries ago, education usually concentrated on the classics. It was the grammar of Latin and Greek that gave grammar schools their name. The purpose of education, in the eighteenth and early nineteenth centuries, was to produce the cultured gentleman – women were rarely educated outside the home – and, although there was a recognition that a wider understanding of, for example, science, was essential to the country's industrial progress, this sort of education was considered as something for the artisan class. Science was *useful*; and *useful* smacked of industry and labour – quite unsuitable pursuits for the gentlefolk of the day. *Their* education – classical education – was often referred to as a *liberal* education, in the sense of broad and life-enhancing; while, in contrast, a scientific or *vocational* education was considered to be narrow in purpose and outcome, equipping the learner only with the skills to earn their living. The rewards of a liberal education were a high social standing and a passport to positions of power; while what we would call now a vocational education was seen as lower status, a provision for workers rather than gentlefolk.

We don't have to look much further than this to see how we have arrived at a position where vocational qualifications are still often held in lower esteem – even with some employers – than traditional 'academic' qualifications such as A levels and degrees. But how has this been perpetuated to the present day, despite successive policy statements about raising the status of vocational education? This is the question we'll focus on in this chapter, and will return to again in Chapter 16.

CLOSE FOCUS CLOSE FOCUS **CLOSE FOCUS** CLOSE FOCUS **CLOSE FOCUS**

We've said that, historically, an 'academic' education was considered a *broad* education, while education for work was thought of as *narrow*. In your view, how does this compare to the sense in which *broad* and *narrow* are used today in discourses about the 14–19 curriculum?

Rapid industrial expansion during the nineteenth century made it necessary to provide some form of relevant training for industrial workers. This further reinforced the rigid link between education and social class, as vocational education became inextricably associated with the artisans and workers. This was reinforced by the suspicion, expressed by radical educators of the time, that the 'education' being offered to artisans was little more than indoctrination designed to produce a workforce capable of producing profits for the owners of capital, but not capable of questioning why they themselves earned so little for their efforts. The education provided for the artisan was sometimes referred to as *useful knowledge*; and the debate over what really constituted useful knowledge became a debate also about the purposes of education; about what it means to be educated. There was even at the time a *Society for the Diffusion of Useful Knowledge,* whose acronym, SDUK, is a only a letter away from a more recently formed body in the field of post-compulsory education. No prizes for identifying that one!

Vocation versus *vocational*

At this point we might want to ask ourselves why, in this case, does the perception of low status not apply to *all* vocational education. Training for medicine, law, and the Church, for example, while still spoken of as 'vocational' (in the sense that those entering these professions are said to have a 'vocation' for them), are all routes which are accorded high status. What reasons would you suggest to account for this? You may like to jot down some notes and compare your answers with the discussion that follows.

Discussion

There are a number of reasons we could put forward. One is that all three vocations – law, medicine and the Church – imply positions of authority within society. All three have traditionally involved a substantial degree of classical learning – a knowledge of Latin, for example, traditionally associated with a high status education. And, of course, the training for all three pertains to a body of knowledge largely independent of commerce and industry, and therefore free of the historical association between 'trade' and low status education.

The status of vocational education

So history tells a story of two kinds of education: education for the development of the individual (general/liberal/academic), and education for work (vocational/skills), each traditionally associated with a different social stratum and differing thereby in status. Echoes of this differentiation have remained apparent in policy and provision throughout the twentieth and into the twenty-first century. For example, to take a major milestone, the Education Act of 1944 (sometimes known as the Butler Act) introduced a system of selection whereby children were tested at the age of 11 to determine whether they would go to a grammar school for an 'academic' education, or to a secondary or technical school which would provide a more 'practical' curriculum. Despite claims that both types of provision would be held in equal esteem, those who secured a place in a grammar school were referred to as having *passed* the 11+ exam, and those who did not were spoken of as having *failed*. Fifty years later, the policy of introducing some 14–16 year-olds into PCET on the grounds that they will respond better to a vocationally-oriented provision than to the National Curriculum could be seen as repeating this same ' horses for courses' argument (in this case, 'courses' being the operative word).

This difficulty with the status of vocational education should not blind us, however, to PCET's valuable role as the sector of the second chance, providing an opportunity for learners to re-engage with learning, whether after a long absence or whether following a negative experience of school. We should also remember that, whatever the apparent status of vocational education, it is absolutely essential in creating, sustaining and updating a skilled workforce.

In the next section we shall see how successive policy initiatives have been launched with the declared purpose of addressing the status issue and establishing 'parity of esteem' – that is, a recognition that both should be valued equally – between the vocational route and the general or academic one. And we shall reflect on the question of why, so far, none appears to have completely succeeded. But before we do, let's say something about language. We all know that the language we use not only reflects our value judgements, but also reinforces them. So, for example, when we read or hear of someone having 'academic' qualifications, we may find ourselves making certain assumptions about that person, their abilities and their social status, which are different from those we would make if we heard instead that they had 'skills training'. And our own choice of words will reflect and reinforce these assumptions, whether we are aware of it or not. For this reason, for the rest of this chapter we'll use the less value-laden term *general* rather than *academic*, to describe the non-vocational route and non-vocational qualifications. And we shall also pay particular attention to the language used in the White Papers and other policy documents, in order to identify the ways in which it could be said to reflect or reinforce the status and the role of the PCET sector.

Milestones and turning points

The direction which vocational education has taken over the last quarter of a century is marked out for us clearly by the White Papers, statutes, and policy documents which stand as milestones along the way. By taking a fairly long perspective on this – twenty-five years or so – we shall be able to see how initiatives, themes and ideas recur over time. You'll be given fuller details on earlier documents which are not so readily accessible, while later ones, which you are asked to visit for yourself online, will be more briefly summarised.

TASK TASK **TASK** TASK **TASK** **TASK** TASK **TASK** TASK **TASK** **TASK** TASK

Reading the White Papers
As you read through this section, look out particularly for how successive White Papers present the following:

- **the purpose of education and training;**
- **the reason for unemployment among young people;**
- **the purpose of general vocational qualifications;**
- **the idea of competition.**

If you would like to read any of the following documents in more detail – and it's certainly very interesting to do this – the full text versions of earlier White Papers are probably most easily accessed in hard copy through your college or local library. Most later documents can be accessed online through the DfE site: www.education.gov.uk

1. 1981: A New Training Initiative

We start with this White Paper because so many subsequent developments originated here. The paper introduced three major initiatives. Firstly, there was the reform of the apprenticeship system in order to introduce standards-based qualifications rather than qualifications based on time served. This was the beginning of the wholesale change to **competence-based training**, where the emphasis shifted to what a candidate could do, rather than what courses they attended or what written exams they passed. This set off a number of debates, including the following.

- **Given the competent/not competent mode of assessment, how do we differentiate between a learner who is barely competent and a learner who is extremely competent?**
- **Is competence enough? What about experience and theoretical understanding?**
- **How many times should a candidate be required to show they can successfully complete a task before being judged 'competent'?**

The other two initiatives included in this White Paper were the introduction of training schemes for school leavers (two years later this would become the Youth Training Scheme (YTS)), and the development of training for adults wishing to acquire or update their skills. The central argument of this paper was that a more highly skilled workforce would mean more jobs and a stronger economy (DoE 1981, p11). The argument also suggested that because people lacked skills there were no jobs for them. This is known as the **deficit model** of the learner. In other words, it suggests that it is a deficiency in the learner as an individual (in this case their lack of skills or training) which prevents them from finding employment.

CLOSE FOCUS CLOSE FOCUS **CLOSE FOCUS** CLOSE FOCUS **CLOSE FOCUS**

a) What, in your view, might be the limitations of using this deficit model in policy discussions about post-compulsory education and training?

b) As you go on to read about subsequent White Papers in this chapter, look out for other instances of this deficit model being used, and make a note in each case of how effectively, in your view, it supports the policy argument.

This 1981 White Paper also suggested the setting up of:

general vocational courses in schools and colleges for those with modest examination achievements at 16-plus who are not looking towards higher education.

(DoE 1981, p5 para 16)

This concept of the general vocational course eventually re-emerged in 1992 as the GNVQ. By that time it was no longer presented, as it is here, as a route for the lower achiever with no prospects of going on to university. On the contrary, the general vocational qualification was, by 1991, hailed in White Papers as the long-awaited alternative route into higher education, as we shall see below.

2. 1986: Working Together: Education and Training

This next landmark White Paper moved the competence-based policy forward by introducing National Vocational Qualifications (**NVQs**). In this sense it is a pivotal document in the development of the sector as we know it today. It explains that hitherto the field of vocational qualifications has been over-complex and confusing, with employers and learners alike unable to ascertain the level of one qualification in relation to another, or to identify clear routes for progression. We must have a clear vocational qualifications framework, it tells us, in order to build a skilled workforce which will strengthen the economy. Its opening paragraph has a Darwinist ring to it, telling us that we are living:

in a world of determined, educated, trained and strongly motivated competitors

(DES, 1986, para 1.1)

who are threatening our 'survival'. It attributes the country's poor record on qualifications and training to wrong attitudes, arguing the necessity for 'people to acquire the desire to learn' (ibid. para 1.4); and to a deficiency in the teaching profession which makes it necessary to 'raise teaching quality and teacher motivation' (ibid.). Two questions which are not asked are: *Why are people reluctant to learn? Why are teachers poorly motivated?*

CLOSE FOCUS CLOSE FOCUS **CLOSE FOCUS** CLOSE FOCUS **CLOSE FOCUS**

Turn for a moment to the 2006 White Paper, *Further Education Reform: Raising Skills, Improving Life Chances* (available on www.dfes.gov.uk*)*, and compare what that has to say about the current vocational qualification framework. What parallels do you see? Twenty years on from the introduction of NVQs, why do you think the same arguments for change are being made?

3. 1991: Education and Training for the 21st Century

3. 1991: Education and Training for the 21st Century

Let's move on now into the 1990s, and to a White Paper which introduced a whole raft of innovations that have helped shape the sector we work in today. Among other things, it signals the reform of the careers service and begins the removal of colleges from local authority control. It also encourages vocational education in schools and introduces GNVQs. It states quite clearly, however, that all its reforms of education and training will be achieved

> *without the need for radical change to a highly regarded, tried and tested examination system.*

(DES 1991 para 3.15)

What is being referred to here is the A level system; and it is interesting to see how repeated attempts to introduce revisions to the system of 16–19 qualifications – including that of the Dearing Review, as we shall see below – carry the proviso that the *gold standard* of A levels must not be tampered with.

In providing an alternative route into higher education, GNVQs were essential to the government's declared policy of strengthening the economy by creating a better educated workforce. Up until this time, A levels had provided almost the only route into higher education (exceptions were the BTEC National, accepted as the equivalent of two A levels by some universities; and Access programmes for adult entrants). But A levels provided a very narrow route, in the sense that it did not allow for many learners to pass through it. Only a minority of 16+ learners chose, or were chosen, to take A levels. This created a bottleneck which had to be by-passed somehow if the government of the day was to succeed in raising the numbers of graduates entering the workforce. The introduction of GNVQs would achieve this only if the new qualification:

a) appealed to learners who would not previously have chosen advanced level study;
b) was accepted by higher education institutions (HEIs) and learners themselves as being the 'equivalent' of A levels for the purpose of progression.

To some extent, these two conditions worked against each other. Keeping A levels as 'the gold standard' inevitably implied that any alternative was second best. Moreover, the emphasis on continuous assessment was a characteristic of GNVQs which many found difficult to see as comparable to the rigorous assessment model of A levels, which at that time was largely based on end exams. And in addition to this, the name chosen for this new general qualification sounded so much like the more familiar 'NVQ' that there was an assumption by many in the public at large that GNVQs were a practical and vocationally-specific qualification. This, of course, was not the case. In fact it could be argued that the high level of written reportage required in GNVQ assessments gave it more in common with the GCSE than with the NVQ.

In introducing the idea of GNVQs, *Education and Training for the 21st Century* declares that they will have **parity of esteem** with general education qualifications such as A levels. It uses a number of terms to emphasise this idea, including:

- **equality of status (para 1.2);**
- **equal esteem (para 1.5);**
- **equally valued (para 3.1).**

It does not, however, develop this claim in terms of how such parity or equality might be achieved, nor does it identify any of the obstacles that must be overcome to bring this about.

Read again through this section on the 1991 White Paper and identify what some of these obstacles to parity of esteem might have been. Are there more you can think of from your reading of this chapter as a whole?

4. 1992: Further and Higher Education Act

This Act marks the point at which Colleges of FE were finally separated from local authority control and funding. It was implemented on 1 April 1993 – the beginning of the new financial year. Colleges were now independent corporations, responsible for their own budgets and funded through a newly established Further Education Funding Council (FEFC). From this point on – referred to as **Incorporation** – colleges found themselves operating within a **market** in which they had to **compete** with other colleges, and with schools, to recruit learners.

Previously, Local Authorities had exerted a strategic control over post-compulsory provision, encouraging cooperation and specialisation rather than competition between colleges. Following Incorporation, the emphasis on marketing and competition brought with it a number of major changes in the working lives of professionals in FE. The market mechanism – that the most effective organisations will thrive and their less effective competitors will be put out of business – led to college closures and mergers. Staff were required to sign new contracts affecting their salaries and conditions of service. Managers at all levels, from principal to team leader, found their focus shifting from pedagogical and curriculum issues to matters of funding, recruitment and cost-savings. This in turn had an effect on the role of the teacher in almost every aspect of their work, from class sizes to the amount of paperwork and admin required of them.

You and your organisation in the marketplace
Consider the following two questions. Discuss your answers with your mentor, tutor or colleagues.
1. What policies and procedures are in place in your own institution for marketing its provision?
2. How does your own role as teacher involve you in marketing courses or competing for students?

5. 1996: The Dearing Review of Qualifications for 16–19 Year Olds

Sir Ron Dearing and his team of reviewers were given the task of reviewing post-16 qualifications and making recommendations for ways to improve the system. Many reformers in the early 1990s hoped for the recommendation of a unified system of qualifications to replace the three existing routes of NVQ, GNVQ and A level. Sir Ron's brief, however, discouraged any major change to the A level system; and the recommendations contained in his 1996 report were not as radical as some had hoped. They included however:

- **introducing key skills into all three routes, rather than confining them to GNVQs as previously;**
- **changing the name of Advanced GNVQs to 'Applied A levels'.**

CLOSE FOCUS CLOSE FOCUS **CLOSE FOCUS** CLOSE FOCUS **CLOSE FOCUS**

To what extent do you think the two recommendations of the *Dearing Review* referred to above could be considered as a move towards **parity of esteem** between A levels and the other two post-16 routes?

6. 1996: *Tomlinson Report: Inclusive Learning*

We have encountered this report already in Chapter 3. Not to be confused with the more recent (2004) Tomlinson Report into post-16 qualifications, you will recall that the 1996 Report focused on **inclusive education**. The report's proposals were aimed at improving FE's response to learners with disabilities or learning difficulties, and at matching provision to a wider range of individual learning needs. It **challenges the deficit model** of the learner, and stresses the responsibility of the college or other educational institution to take into account the requirements of each individual. A useful summary of this report can be found at: http://inclusion.uwe.ac.uk/csie/tmlnsn.htm – you may find it useful to read this before continuing to the next section.

CLOSE FOCUS CLOSE FOCUS **CLOSE FOCUS** CLOSE FOCUS **CLOSE FOCUS**

In what ways does the provision offered by your own college or institution conform to the model of inclusive education as defined in the *Tomlinson Report (1996)*?

TASK TASK **TASK** TASK **TASK** **TASK** TASK **TASK** TASK **TASK** **TASK** TASK

What's in a name?

Below is a table showing revised namings, mergers and 'marriages' between key organisations since 1988. Look at it carefully and then consider the questions which follow.

Date	Organisations which have merged, or been replaced or re-named...	...to become
1988	Manpower Services Commission (MSC)	Training Commission (briefly) and then: Training Agency
1990	Training Agency	TECs (Training and Enterprise Councils)
1995	Dept for Education + Dept for Employment	Dept for Education and Employment (DfEE)
1996	Awarding bodies: BTEC + London Examination Board	Edexcel
1996	Awarding bodies: AEB (Associated Examining Board)+ NEAB (Northern Examinations and Assessment Board)	Assessment and Qualifications Alliance (AQA)
1997	NCVQ (National Council for Vocational Qualifications) + SCAA (School Curriculum and Assessment Authority)	QCA (Qualifications and Curriculum Authority)
2001	DfEE (Department for Education and Employment)	DfES (Department for Education and Skills)
2001	FEFC (Further Education Funding Council)	LSC (Learning and Skills Council)
2001	TECs	Regional LSCs (Learning and Skills Councils)
2005	FENTO (Further Education National Training Organisation)	LLUK/SVUK (Lifelong Learning UK/Standards Verification UK)
2007	DfES (Department for Education and Skills)	DCSF (Department for Children, Schools and Families
2008	QCA (Qualifications and Curriculum Authority)	QCDA (Qualifications and Curriculum Development Agency)
2010	DCSF (Department for Children, Schools and Families)	DfE (Department for Education)

Questions to consider
1. How might these changes, mergers and re-namings be interpreted as a move towards parity between the vocational and the general education routes?
2. How might we see evolving assumptions about patterns of work and about the role of PCET reflected in these developments and re-namings?

7. *1998: The Learning Age*

This was the Green Paper which proposed the target that all teachers in FE should possess, or be working towards – a professional teaching qualification. With its emphasis on lifelong learning, it also proposed the introduction of learning into the workplace and into people's home environment. You can read a summary of this paper at: www.lifelonglearning.co.uk/greenpaper (accessed 21.3.11).

8. 1999: *Learning to Succeed*

This White Paper signalled the establishing of the central and regional LSCs, which would replace the FEFC nationally as a source of funding for FE, and replace the TECs as a local body for the strategic distribution of that funding to colleges and other providers in the Learning and Skills sector.

TASK TASK **TASK** TASK **TASK** TASK **TASK** TASK **TASK** TASK **TASK** TASK

Implications of *Learning to Succeed*
Consider the following questions and discuss your answers with a colleague, mentor or tutor.
1. To what extent might the requirement for all FE teachers to have or be working towards a recognised teaching qualification be seen as part of the drive towards parity of esteem between vocational and general education?
2. In what ways does your local LSC have a strategic impact on the training provision offered by your own institution?

9. 2002: *Success for All*

This document set out a strategy of reform, designed to enable FE and other providers in the Lifelong Learning sector to become more responsive to national and local training needs. This included the need to work more closely with employers; to streamline access by tackling bureaucracy; to ensure that provision supports and encourages diversity and equality (see Tomlinson, *et al*. 1996); and to encourage the development of e-learning in order to provide wider access to education and training. You can see this paper at: www.globalgateway.org.uk/pdf/PZ-Success-2002.pdf (accessed 21.3.11).

10. 2003: *Every Child Matters*

This Green Paper was aimed at every sector of education, including FE. Its themes include reform of the workforce, the need for accountability and integration between agencies, services and organisations in terms of support for young people, and particularly those at risk; and support for parents and carers, including early intervention, where necessary, for the protection of young people. You can access this paper at: www.publications.parliament.uk/pa/em200405/cmselect/cmeduski/40/40.pdf (accessed 21.3.11).

CLOSE FOCUS CLOSE FOCUS **CLOSE FOCUS** CLOSE FOCUS **CLOSE FOCUS**

What impact have *Success for All* (DfES 2002) and *Every Child Matters* (DfES 2003) had on your own college or organisation, in terms of its provision and its procedures?

10. 2005: *14–19 Education and Skills*

This is the White Paper which sets out the argument for motivating 14–16 year-old learners by disallowing parts of the National Curriculum and allowing them instead to undertake part of their learning in colleges of FE. It also sets the target that all young people should have a mastery of functional English and mathematics by the time they leave full-time education; and proposes that vocational diplomas, designed to meet the specified needs of employers should be introduced in 14 broad vocational areas. This paper can be accessed at: www. education.gov.uk/publications/eOrderingDownload/CM%206476.pdf (accessed 21.3.11).

11. 2005: *Realising the Potential: A review of the future role of further education colleges* (often referred to as the *Foster Report*)

This report marks a significant point in the history of FE because it sets out to define the *purpose* of the sector. The vision which this publication puts forward is of FE as the corner- stone of skills training. It also presents us with a new metaphor. Instead of being referred to as the *Cinderella sector*, FE is now re-presented as the *Middle Child*, equally valued but sometimes over-looked or taken for granted.

TASK TASK **TASK** TASK **TASK** **TASK** TASK **TASK** TASK **TASK** **TASK** TASK

Consider the following questions and discuss your answers with your mentor, tutor, or colleagues.

1. What has been the response of your own institution to *14–19 Education and Skills* (DfES 2005)? What provision has been made for 14–16 year-old learners, and what issues has this raised?

2. What do the two metaphors used to describe FE (*Cinderella sector* and *Middle Child*) tell us about common perceptions of the sector? How does this relate to the arguments around 'parity of esteem'?

12. 2006: *Further Education: Raising Skills, Improving Life Chances*

This White Paper was part of the government response to the Foster Report (2005), and proposes the implementation of its major recommendations. As well as confirming the role and purpose of the FE sector as one of skills training, it proposes new entitlements for 19–25 year-olds who are undertaking their first level 3 qualification. It also sets out the proposal that all new college principals should have, or be working towards, a relevant qualification in leadership. The **four targets** set by this White Paper are:

1. Participation rates by 16–19 year-olds to rise by 15 per cent by 2015.
2. Apprenticeship completion rates to increase by 75 per cent by 2008.
3. The number of adults gaining a level 2 qualification to reach 3.6m by 2010.
4. 50 per cent of all 18–30 year-olds to be participating in Higher Education by 2010.

Its **six 'key areas of reform'** are as follows.

1. Strengthening the focus of FE as a sector specialising in skills training (thus endorsing the *Foster Report*).
2. Developing the system to meet the needs of employers and of learners.
3. Raising the quality of teaching and learning, and introducing from September 2007 a regulatory CPD (continuing professional development) requirement for all 'lecturers' (i.e. teachers) in the sector.
4. Addressing poor provision and extending the market in skills training to more providers. (This is based on the theory that market competition will drive up standards, which we discussed earlier in relation to the 1992 Further and Higher Education Act.)

5. The reform of funding for 14–19 year-olds' learning, so that each institution involved can be funded proportionately.
6. Adjusting the relationship between colleges and their LSC, to give colleges more autonomy and the LSCs a more strategic and supervisory role.

The current context of PCET

As we saw earlier, the Standards were designed as part of the initiative to raise standards in PCET. It is important, however, we do not lose sight of the overall context in which teachers within this sector operate. If we do so, we risk falling into the trap of assuming that the quality of teaching is the only problem that needs to be addressed if we are to raise standards of achievement. However reasonably it is expressed, this assumption presents a deficit model of teachers and teaching which serves to perpetuate what Ball (1990) has called a 'discourse of derision'. Setting and acknowledging high standards for the teaching profession in the Lifelong Learning sector is to the benefit of everyone, not least us professionals ourselves. But it would be foolish to assume this alone is the answer to raising standards of learner achievement.

If we put teacher performance aside for a moment, what other factors might depress levels of achievement? Or, to put it another way, what factors, other than the quality of teaching, would tend to affect learners' motivation detrimentally? We shall consider three possible culprits here and, in doing so, will take the opportunity to explore some of the policy frameworks within which PCET currently operates.

It has been argued, for example by Reeves (1995), that the dominance of the work-related qualification system has served to make the PCET curriculum less stimulating and enjoyable for the students. The imperative to repeat and acquire skills in a routine very much like that of the workplace may lead learners who assume no pleasure is to be gained from work to apply that assumption equally to their education. The expectation is that their effort will be rewarded by accreditation, but not by any enjoyment of the learning itself. This is compounded by the knowledge that, in the current employment market, even if they gain their qualification this will not necessarily give them access to a job. Some researchers, like Ainley and Bailey (1997), claim the expansion of post-16 education and training may be seen as a means of occupying young people who are not in employment. The corollary of this is that some learners may be staying on in education not by choice but because it is their last resort. It can also mean that learners who are perfectly aware their prospects of employment are poor may find themselves on 'vocational' courses preparing for a job they know they are unlikely to be offered. These are brutal arguments. But they are arguments of which the teacher needs to be aware. In this context, the question the professional must ask is: given all this, how do I go about motivating these learners to engage with, and take pleasure from, their learning? To do this they must be clear that lack of learner motivation is not always the teacher's fault.

Another contextual issue which may impinge upon learner motivation and achievement is the growing emphasis in PCET upon competition and market forces. As we have seen, since the Further and Higher Education Act 1992, the sector has shifted from the strategic regional planning of its provision to a purchaser-provider model. Indeed, it would appear the effects of a policy of free market competition can be more readily observed in the Lifelong Learning sector than in any other sector of education (Ainley and Bailey, 1997). Although the declared purpose of introducing competition is to bring about a raising of standards (the college must ensure its provision is good if it is to compete successfully for students), this market model may have other effects too. One of these is that the concerns of college senior managers and of college teachers are likely to diverge, the teachers focusing on learners and curriculum while their managers are obliged to focus increasingly upon competition and matters of finance (Ball, 1994). The policies necessary to ensure survival in a competitive market may include increased class sizes, increasing use of resource-based learning and a consequent reduction in the quantity, if not quality, of teacher–learner contact. This may well affect the quality of the learners' learning experience and consequently their level of motivation and engagement with their learning. If we add to this the financial pressures the market exerts upon colleges to recruit and retain high numbers of learners, we can recognise the possibility that some learners at least may find themselves recruited onto courses which do not necessarily meet their needs. We can recognise that it could also – although we would hope it does not – lead to tolerance of learners who disrupt the learning of others because of pressure to retain viable numbers.

A third factor, which links the work-related qualification system and the pressures of the market, is the use of performance indicators (PIs) as part of the funding mechanism for colleges. PIs are a measuring of 'input' and 'output'. In simple terms, this means the student enrolments and the qualifications gained – one way of assessing whether the college is giving value for money. But an emphasis on input and output leaves out the middle of the equation – what we may feel to be the important bit – the process of teaching and learning, other than to decide whether it is cost-effective. Now clearly, enrolment, retention and qualification rates will not tell us everything we need to know about the quality of learning provision. PIs can be applied only to what is easily measured. Teaching and learning represent a complex process. Embedded in that process are the factors which may encourage or discourage learner motivation and engagement. These cannot be assessed by PIs. Moreover, there may be contradictions inherent in the pressure on colleges to attain both high retention and high achievement rates, because learners who find a course too difficult would normally drop out. Similarly, there may be difficulties in simultaneously raising achievement and widening participation because widening participation implies the recruitment of, among others, learners who may experience difficulties with learning (Perry, 1999).

Since the 14–19 Education and Skills White Paper (DfES 2005) the decision to open up FE provision to 14–16-year-olds has had a profound impact on the working lives of many teachers in colleges. Tasked with teaching and supporting the learning of an age group that had hitherto been accommodated within compulsory education and working to the National Curriculum, some teachers have understandably felt concern not only at their lack of previous training or experience with Key Stage 4 pupils, but also at their continuing lack of parity with teachers in schools working with similar groups. This is an issue which is not likely to go away. In the 2005 General Election all three major parties declared in their manifesto the intention to incorporate the option of vocational education into the curriculum of all 14-year-olds for whom it might be appropriate. We shall explore the implications of this in Chapter 16.

A programme of teacher education or CPD for the Lifelong Learning sector, at whatever stage of teacher development it is aimed, will require that the teacher or student teacher has a clear grasp of the current topography of the PCET sector and the ways in which policy impinges upon and shapes practice. To this extent the issues we have just explored are critical in that they form part of the context within which the aspiring professional will be operating.

Reflecting on theory

Let's have a look now in detail at a section from one of the key documents we have discussed in this chapter: *Realising the Potential: A Review of the Future Role of Further Education Colleges*, usually referred to as the *Foster Report* (2005).

TASK TASK **TASK** TASK **TASK** **TASK** TASK **TASK** TASK **TASK** **TASK** TASK

Read carefully through the passage below, paying particular attention to the choice of vocabulary; and then answer the questions which follow. You may wish to make some notes so that you can discuss your answers with others.

The fundamentals: skills

55. The potential value of the FE sector should arise from its contribution to the success of the economy, employers and individual learners. Only secondarily is it about the success of FE providers and those who manage and regulate them. We need a simple revisitation of purposes and values, and clear priorities, so that the system may be re-engineered around them.

56. Amongst the three broad categories of FE activity mentioned earlier (building vocational skills, promoting social inclusion and advancement, and achieving academic progress), where should the emphasis be placed?

57. Although the diversity of the FE offer is often celebrated, it became clear during the review that many stakeholders believe the unique core focus of FE should be in skill building for the economy. This is the tradition from which much of FE developed, but it is a tradition that has been diluted in recent years. We therefore propose that skills, and economic mission, is the route for FE, but interpreted in line with values of opportunity and inclusion which matter so much to those who work in FE. A focus on vocational skills building is not a residual choice but a vital building block in the UK's platform for future prosperity. It gives FE colleges an unequivocal mission and the basis of a renewed and powerful brand image. Recent reviews of FE in Northern Ireland and Ontario, Canada, have come to similar conclusions. . .

58. It is not suggested that skills development is the only thing that FE colleges should pursue. The other pillars of social inclusion and advancement, and academic progress, are not invalid. The important thing is to recognise and focus on the core purpose and have declared, clear priorities. In any event it is absolutely clear that an emphasis on skills development will itself turn out to be a huge driver for social inclusion and improved personal self-esteem, achieving a valuable synergy between societal and personal need.

(Taken from: Foster (2005) *Realising the Potential: A Review of the Future Role of Further Education Colleges* pp. 22–23; paras 55–58.)

Questions

1. What arguments are identified in this extract for defining the purpose of FE as one of skills training?

2. The Report refers to *'skill building for the economy'* and links this to *'the tradition from which much of FE developed'* (para 57). In your own view, and based on what you have read so far in this chapter, what implications does this focus on skills building have for the status of the FE sector?

3. What do you understand Foster to mean when he asserts that the tradition of skills building has been *'diluted in recent years'* (para 57)? What examples do you think he would cite to support his argument?

4. How is the economic argument and the market philosophy reflected in the language of this extract?

5. Can you think of circumstances in which the *'core purpose'* of FE might be at odds with *'the other pillars of social inclusion and advancement'* (para 58)? Why do you think social inclusion and advancement are referred to as *'the other pillars'*?

6. What do you understand the report to mean by *'a valuable synergy between societal and personal need'* (para 58)? How would you evaluate the argument that leads up to this statement?

A SUMMARY OF **KEY POINTS**

In this chapter we have:

> **examined the significance and origins of the vocational-academic divide;**

> **considered some of the major milestones and turning points in policy and practice in the Learning and Skills sector;**

> **explored the origins of the vocational qualification framework;**

> **considered the importance of Incorporation and the growth of market competition;**

> **charted the changes in name and/or function of key bodies;**

> **explored the issue of parity of esteem;**

> **provided opportunities for you to identify how national policy is reflected in the working practices of your own organisation.**

Branching options

The following tasks are designed to allow you to apply or explore further some of the contents of this chapter. If you are using this book to support your professional development leading to a teaching qualification or other CPD certification, you may find it useful to choose a task according to the level at which you are currently working. These are indicated in brackets. Or, if you're really keen, you may choose to work through each of the tasks in turn.

1. Reflection and self-evaluation (NQF level 5)

Consider how *at least three* of the policy initiatives and national developments charted in this chapter have contributed to the shaping of your own institution's curriculum, structure and mission, and how they have influenced your own professional practice.

2. Evaluation: theory and practice (NQF level 6)

This chapter has offered a summary of selected key documents. There have been others, however, which have had considerable impact on the FE sector. These include, for example:

• **1994 White Paper: *Competitiveness: Helping Business to Win/Forging Ahead* (proposes improved careers guidance);**
• **1997: *The Kennedy Report* (widening participation);**
• **1998 Green Paper: *The Learning Age (*taking learning outside institutions).**

Using your research skills, access *at least three* publications (White Papers, Green Papers, Reports) from the last decade which have not been discussed in this chapter but which have been relevant to the FE sector. Consider how they:

a) reflect the recurring themes of parity, market competition, the mission and purpose of FE;
b) have helped shape provision and processes within your current institution and your own working practices within it.

3. Engaging critically with the literature (NQF level 7: M level)

a) Taking one of the themes we've explored in this chapter – parity, market competition, or the mission and purpose of FE – show in detail how this is presented in *at least three* key documents (White Papers, Green Papers, and Reports) from the past ten years. You needn't restrict your choice to the documents summarised in this chapter.
b) To what extent do the three documents you've chosen address the two questions left unasked and unanswered in the 1986 White Paper, *Working Together: Education and Training:*
   - **Why are some people reluctant to learn?**
   - **Why are some teachers poorly motivated?**

REFERENCES AND FURTHER READING

Ainley, P. and Bailey B. (1997) *The Business of Learning: Staff and Student Experiences of FE in the 1990s*. London: Cassell.

Ball, S. *Politics and Policy Making in Education*. London: Routledge.

Ball, S. (1994) *Education Reform: a Critical and Post-structural Approach*. Buckingham: Open University Press.

Ball, S. *et al*. (2000) *Choice, Pathways and Transitions Post-16: New Youth, New Economies in the Global City*. London: RoutledgeFalmer.

DES (1986) *Working Together: Education and Training*. London: HMSO.

DES (1991) *Education and Training for the 21st Century*. London: HMSO.

DfEE (1998) *The Learning Age: a Renaissance for a New Britain*. London: HMSO.

DfES (2005) *14-19 Education and Skills*. London: HMSO.

DfES (2006) *FE Reform: Raising Skills, Improving Life Chances*. Norwich: TSO.

DoE (1981) *A New Training Initiative*. London: HMSO.

Foster, A. *et al*. (2005) *Realising the Potential: A Review of the Future Role of Further Education Colleges*. Annesley: DfES.

Green, A. and Lucas, N. (eds) (1999) *FE and Lifelong Learning: Realigning the Sector for the Twenty-first Century*. London: Institute of Education.

Perry, A. (1999) Performance indicators: measure for measure or a comedy of errors? Paper presented to FEDA Research Conference, Cambridge, 9 December 1999.

Reeves, F. *The Modernity of Further Education*. Bilston: Bilston College Publications.

Smithers, A. and Robinson, P. (eds) (2000) *Further Education Reformed*. London: Falmer Press.

5
Professionalism and scholarship 1: values and ethics

The objectives of this chapter

This chapter explores what we mean by professionalism. It examines how professionalism is demonstrated in our day-to-day practice, and encourages you to identify and reflect upon some of the key philosophical issues as a means to examining your own professional values. It is designed to address the areas of essential knowledge, skills and values relevant to your professional development as a teacher and subject specialist, as set out in the Professional Standards for QTLS. These include helping you to:

- **recognise and take opportunities for professional development and the updating of your own professional expertise (AS7; AP4.3; CS1);**
- **value the importance of reflecting on your own practice against the values base of QTLS (AS4);**
- **recognise and apply agreed codes of practice (AS6; AP6.1; AK6.1).**

Introduction: what do we mean by professionalism?

The Standards draw our attention to two aspects of professionalism: one is about applying a set of values; the other is about conforming to a code of practice. Central to both is the ability to recognise, and take responsibility for supporting, the rights and needs of learners. One of the things this chapter sets out to do is to encourage you to identify and reflect upon your own professional values. We began this process in Chapter 1 when you were asked to think about your 'best teacher'. In a sense, your best teacher will embody a set of values about teaching and learning you yourself believe to be both important and valid. You may never have articulated those values, even to yourself, but they are implicit in the very fact you see this teacher as 'The Best'. Perhaps he or she showed genuine concern for his or her learners. Or perhaps he or she kept excellent order in the classroom. Whatever his or her virtues, in choosing him or her you are recognising that these represent values you approve of and share. But of course, a set of professional values is more complicated than this. Another way to think about it is to ask yourself:

- **What is my philosophy of teaching and learning?**
- **What do I believe is the purpose of education?**
- **What is the teacher's role in the process of learning?**
- **What is my understanding of the power relationships involved?**
- **Where does my responsibility begin and end?**

These are some of the questions we shall be considering as this chapter proceeds.

Conforming to a code of professional practice is, by comparison, rather more straightforward. For while our values represent something internal to us – a part of our own moral and ethical guidance system – the code of practice to which we conform is external, embedded in the framework of the college's rules, regulations and duties of care to learners and to others. Such a code will require us, for example, to conduct ourselves in an appropriate and professional manner while carrying out our duties. In this instance our internalised set of values (if we have ten grams of common sense) will be telling us exactly the same. If we have chosen the right profession or the right institution, our own value base will generally support the agreed codes of professional practice within which we have to operate.

Working within a professional value base

In Chapter 1 we encountered a range of teachers whom we have come to know through the pages of their reflective journals. As you were reading those journal extracts, it is likely you were drawing inferences about the teachers' individual philosophies or value systems from the way they prioritised their concerns or the manner in which they wrote about their learners, or the degree to which they were able and willing to reflect on their experiences.

CLOSE FOCUS CLOSE FOCUS **CLOSE FOCUS** CLOSE FOCUS **CLOSE FOCUS**

Looking back at your last journal entry (or at the last lesson you taught or attended), you should begin to identify (if you have not done so already) some of the beliefs or values that inform your own teaching.

The professional values you hold will not relate exclusively to your teaching. They will inform the way in which you interact with colleagues and other professionals; your engagement with your specialist subject; and your relationship to the institution in which you teach (and learn). We shall consider this wider context in the later part of this chapter. For the time being, however, we will focus on identifying the values we bring to our teaching. We don't have to read philosophy books to do this – although it's interesting to do so and reading what philosophers have to say is an extremely useful way of reflecting on our own values and beliefs. In fact, as the philosopher Richard Rorty (1989) points out, we can look at literature of all kinds, including fiction, in order to trigger our thought processes into examining what we do or do not believe – in our case, about teaching, learning and learner motivation.

TASK TASK **TASK** TASK **TASK** TASK **TASK** TASK **TASK** TASK **TASK** TASK

Read the following extracts carefully and consider these questions. They require quite lengthy answers and so you may find it useful to make notes.
1. What theories or philosophies about education are implicit in each extract? (You don't need to come up with 'official' names for them – just describe them.) In other words, what is being suggested here about the nature and purpose of education? What underlying values are suggested?
2. What is your personal view about these theories and values?
3. What arguments would you construct if you wished to disagree or agree with each or any of them?
4. Just out of interest, can you identify the sources of the extracts? (There are lots of clues in the texts themselves.)

'Now, what I want is, Facts. Teach these boys and girls nothing but Facts. Facts alone are wanted in life. Plant nothing else and root out everything else. You can only form the minds of reasoning animals upon Facts; nothing else will ever be of any service to them. This is the principle on which I bring up my own children. Stick to facts, sir!'

The scene was a plain, bare, monotonous vault of a schoolroom, and the speaker's square forefinger emphasized his observations by underscoring every sentence with a line on the schoolmaster's sleeve.

'In this life, we want nothing but Facts, sir; nothing but Facts!'

The speaker, and the schoolmaster, and the third grown person present, all backed a little, and swept with their eyes the inclined plane of little vessels then and there arranged in order, ready to have imperial gallons of facts poured into them until they were full to the brim.

'Girl number twenty,' said Mr Gradgrind, squarely pointing with his square forefinger, 'I don't know that girl. Who is that girl?'

'Sissy Jupe, sir,' explained number twenty, blushing, standing up, and curtseying.

'Sissy is not a name,' said Mr Gradgrind. 'Don't call yourself Sissy. Call yourself Cecilia.'

'It's father as calls me Sissy, sir,' returned the young girl in a trembling voice, and with another curtsey.

'Then he has no business to do it,' said Mr Gradgrind. 'Tell him he mustn't. Cecilia Jupe. Let me see. What is your father?'

'He belongs to the horse-riding, if you please, sir.'

Mr Gradgrind frowned, and waved off the objectionable calling with his hand.

'We don't want to know anything about that here. You mustn't tell us about that here. Your father breaks horses, don't he?'

'If you please, sir, when they can get any to break, they do break horses in the ring, sir.'

'You mustn't tell us about the ring here. Very well, then. Describe your father as a horse-breaker. He doctors sick horses, I dare say?'

'Oh yes, sir.'

'Very well, then. He is a veterinary surgeon, a farrier and horse-breaker. Give me your definition of a horse.'

(Sissy Jupe thrown into the greatest alarm by this demand.)

'Girl number twenty unable to define a horse!' said Mr Gradgrind, for the general behoof of all the little pitchers. 'Girl number twenty possessed of no facts, in reference to one of the commonest of animals! Some boy's definition of a horse. Bitzer, yours.'

The square finger, moving here and there, lighted suddenly on Bitzer, perhaps because he chanced to sit in the same ray of sunlight which, darting in at one of the bare windows of the intensely white-washed room, irradiated Sissy. For, the boys and girls sat on the face of the inclined plane in two compact bodies, divided up the centre by a narrow interval.

'Bitzer,' said Thomas Gradgrind. 'Your definition of a horse.'

'Quadruped. Gramniverous. Forty teeth, namely twenty-four grinders, four eye-teeth, and twelve incisive. Sheds coat in the spring; in marshy countries, sheds hoofs, too. Hoofs hard, but requiring to be shod with iron. Age known by marks in mouth.' Thus (and much more) Bitzer.

Now girl number twenty,' said Mr Gradgrind. 'You know what a horse is.'

There are plenty of clues in this passage which tell us the scene described happened a long time ago. But we would be foolish to dismiss it simply on those grounds as irrelevant. There are theories of education and of learning implicit in this passage which are still alive and well today. You may have recognised some of them.

Let's look first at Mr Gradgrind's contention that education is about instilling facts. Whether you agree or disagree, this is certainly an idea worth unpicking. Defining education as the transmission of facts has many practical advantages. It is very easy to measure student achievement because the outcomes are completely straightforward – the learner either knows the facts or doesn't. Similarly, it is a simple matter to judge whether the teacher has succeeded – whether his or her teaching has been effective – by whether the learners know the facts or not. This idea of the teacher as a transmitter of facts, or that extension of facts we call 'knowledge', is still current. Consider the metaphor, widely used today but seldom heard thirty years ago, of the teacher as someone who *delivers*: delivers a lesson, delivers the curriculum, delivers the facts. Most teachers accept this metaphor without a second thought. But what if it is telling us something very important about how the role of the teacher is currently construed? Lakoff and Johnson (1980) argue that the metaphors we use reflect the way we see things. So, as a profession, do we simply deliver the curriculum or do we help shape and develop it? Do we just deliver lessons or do we carefully plan, implement and reflect upon how we facilitate learner learning?

Did you notice that Gradgrind's learners are described, on two occasions, as 'vessels' or 'pitchers'? This idea of the learner as an empty vessel waiting to be filled up by knowledge or 'facts' is certainly still with us. The South American educator, Paulo Freire (1972), described this as the banking model of education in which learners come to the teacher and 'withdraw' a body of knowledge they can then take away with them and consider themselves 'educated'. (We shall read more about Freire in Chapter 7.) Freire argues this model is fundamentally flawed. A close reading of the passage about Mr Gradgrind's teaching may lead us to agree.

For example, if we were to accept that learning is simply about the transmission of knowledge – about filling up empty pitchers – we would want to ask: who defines knowledge? Who decides what is going to be included in that body of knowledge and what will be left out? According to what criteria will such a decision be made? And to what ends? It's quite clear from the passage we've just read that only Gradgrind's definition of what constitutes knowledge is allowed in his classroom. Sissy's experiential knowledge of horses – which may include the intelligence with which they respond to humans or how it feels and sounds to watch them race at a gallop – is inadmissible. It is not counted as knowledge because knowledge is only what Gradgrind defines it to be. And this is extended even to reconstructing the learner's reality. Sissy's father is a performer: he rides horses in the ring. But this is unacceptable to Gradgrind, who insists the man must be described as a vet, farrier and horse-breaker. Thus redefined, the man's real occupation – too frivolous for Gradgrind's taste – becomes invisible. There is a very important issue here, and it is about power. Who defines what is legitimate knowledge? You? Mr Gradgrind? The awarding body? The Department for Education? Who decides what you teach and what you leave out? On what grounds is that decision made? Is legitimate knowledge that which will qualify the learner to serve the needs of the economy? Is it also that which allows the learner to develop his or her creative or artistic potential for purely personal ends? Who decides? And are these two purposes equally important? Would legitimate knowledge include the skills to question the purposes of education itself? These questions are slippery; which is to say they are hard to get a grip on and difficult to answer definitively, without feeling some degree of ambivalence. But they are questions which, as professionals in education, we need to engage with, discuss and reflect upon.

As well as a theory about what constitutes education, we also learn something from the extract about Gradgrind's theories of classroom practice. When he picks on Bitzer, he provides us with a classic example of what I have heard some trainers describe as the Pose, Pause and Pounce:

- **he poses the question:** *'Some boy's definition of a horse'*;
- **he pauses** – *the square finger moving here and there*;
- **and then he pounces:** *'Bitzer, yours.'*

The idea here is to seize every learner's attention. All are struggling to come up with an answer in case they are the ones pounced on. All eyes will be on the teacher. Everyone will be a little on edge, wondering, 'Will it be me?' and possibly hoping very much it won't be. The 'trick', so I'm told, is to pick on someone who's avoiding your eye, because if he or she is looking straight at you, that probably means he or she knows the answer. So you pick some poor soul who looks as though he or she doesn't know it and then, so the reasoning goes, he or she will make pretty sure they know the answer the next time in order to avoid humiliation. Now, although it may have its occasional uses, I'm not very keen on this idea, and not just because it's one Gradgrind uses. It seems to me that it's based on the theory that learners can be motivated by fear – of embarrassment, failure or humiliation – and, of course, they can. But there are much better ways of motivating them, as we've seen from some of the journals we've dipped into; and a personal theory of teaching which is not underpinned by values of concern for, and care towards, the learner, will limit rather than enhance the teacher's professional practice. However, such values are clearly not a part of Gradgrind's philosophy, as evidenced by the fact his learner is a number to him rather than a name. He only engages with Sissy's name in order to correct it.

So how well do you know your learners' names? How quickly do you learn them? Do you make an active effort to learn names when you first encounter a class? (We shall look at some interesting ways to do this in Chapter 10.) Addressing learners by name, and getting it right, may sound too obvious a thing to mention. But if you've ever encountered a teacher who doesn't, you'll have first-hand experience of how that makes a learner feel.

You may well have identified other ideas and theories from this passage you'll want to discuss or reflect upon and, if you are working alone, you can use your journal to do this. As we leave Mr Gradgrind, however, I will, out of deference to him, point out one interesting *fact*. The inclined plane of boys and girls, which is twice mentioned, refers to the custom, common in the nineteenth century, of seating pupils in a 'gallery' of raised tiers rather like a lecture theatre so the teacher, down at the front, could see all of them clearly at all times. You may like to reflect on what that tells us about the educational theories and values of the time.

'"All of you in this city are brothers," is what we shall tell them. "But the gods as they were making you, put gold in those of you with the capacity to rule; and so those are deserving of most respect. They put silver in those who are auxiliaries, and iron and copper in the farmers and craftsmen. In most cases your children are of the same nature as yourselves, but because you are all closely related, sometimes a silver offspring will come from gold, or a gold one from silver, and so on. Therefore the primary and most important command of the gods to the rulers is that they should be good guardians and watch carefully over their offspring, seeing which of those metals is mixed in their souls. And if their own offspring has a mixture of copper or iron, they must make no exception, but must do what is proper to its nature, and set it among the artisans or the farmers. If, on the other hand, in these lower classes children are born with a mixture of gold and silver, the rulers must do the right thing and appoint the first to be guardians and the second to be auxiliaries. For it is prophesied that the city shall perish if it is defended only by iron or copper." Is there any trickery we can use to persuade them to believe this story?'

'No,' he said, 'it cannot hope to succeed with your original citizens. But possibly their sons and grandsons, and future generations, might believe it.'

'Very well,' I said. 'That would still be advantageous if it made them loyal to the city and to each other.'

This passage, sometimes known as the *Myth of the Mixed Metals*, is a famous one. Considered in the context of a philosophy for education, it can appear to us today quite chilling. The citizens are to be told they are born with particular qualities that determine their position and role in the social hierarchy. They are to be told this is the way it was meant to be. This fiction is a conscious lie, designed to maintain social stability. Even so, it isn't too difficult to relate this to some of the ideas about education which were prevalent even in the last century. As we saw in Chapter 4, the tripartite system of secondary education introduced by the Education Act 1944 (sometimes called the Butler Act) was based on the premise that, by the age of 11 years, it would be possible to judge whether a child was best fitted for a grammar, a secondary modern or a technical education. Despite rhetoric at the time about parity of esteem, these three routes were never in reality accorded equal status. The subsequent debate about the relative merits of selective and comprehensive education has never gone away, and seems currently to be gaining a new impetus. GNVQs have become vocational A levels, but many issues about status remained largely unresolved.

This extract also describes the possibility of 'children of silver' being born from 'parents of gold', and vice versa. It is a discussion we still have today when we wonder about how much of our behaviour and ability is inherent when we are born, and how much is learnt. This is often referred to as the Nature-Nurture debate and, despite the continuing growth of research into genetics, it, too, has not been definitively resolved.

Within these contexts, then, some of the questions the passage may have raised for you are these.

- **Are learners' innate abilities fixed?**
- **Is it useful to group learners according to their level of ability?**
- **How can their level of ability be reliably judged?**
- **Who sets the criteria?**
- **What is the conceptual difference between grouping learners according to 'ability' and grouping them according to 'need'? (In other words, how might it change our thinking – and our practice – if we used the word 'need' instead of 'ability'?)**
- **What is the nature of the link between academic assessment and maintaining the social structure?**
- **To what extent is the purpose of education to serve society and strengthen the economy?**
- **Does education have any other purpose?**

- Is there any difference, perceived or apparent, within your institution between the status of GCE A-level and Vocational A-level students, or NVQ candidates and those enrolled on Access to HE courses?
- How do we, as teachers, judge a learner's potential and provide appropriate guidance?
- To what extent does your knowledge of learners' backgrounds and home circumstances affect the initial judgements you make about their needs, abilities or potential?
- How do these issues link with those we explored in Chapter 4?

Although Mr Bonnycastle was severe, he was very judicious. Mischief of all kinds was visited but by slender punishment, such as being kept in at play hours, &c.; and he seldom interfered with the boys for fighting, although he checked decided oppression. The great *sine qua non** for him was attention to their studies. He soon discovered the capabilities of his pupils, and he forced them accordingly; but the idle boy, the bird who 'could sing and wouldn't sing', received no mercy. The consequence was, that he turned out the cleverest boys, and his conduct was so uniform and unvarying in its tenor, that if he was feared when they were under his control, he was invariably liked by those whom he had instructed, and they continued his friends in after life.

Mr Bonnycastle at once perceived that it was no use coaxing our hero, and that fear was the only attribute by which he could be controlled. So, as soon as Dr Middleton had quitted the room, he addressed him in a commanding tone, 'Now, boy, what is your name?'

'Johnny.'

'And what is your other name, sir?'

Jack, who appeared to repent his condescension, did not at first answer; but he looked again in Mr Bonnycastle's face, and then round the room; there was no one to help him, and he could not help himself, so he replied, 'Easy.'

'Do you know why you are sent to school?'

'Scalding father.'

'No; you are sent to learn to read and write.'

'But I won't read and write,' replied Jack, sulkily.

'Yes, you will; and you are going to read your letters now directly.'

Jack made no answer. Mr Bonnycastle opened a sort of bookcase, and displayed to John's astonished view a series of canes, ranged up and down like billiard cues, and continued, 'Do you know what those are for? They are to teach little boys to read and write, and now I am going to teach you. You'll soon learn. Look now here,' continued Mr Bonnycastle, opening a book with large type, and taking a capital at the head of a chapter, about half an inch long. 'Do you see that letter?'

'Yes,' replied Johnny, turning his eyes away, and picking his fingers.

'Well, that is the letter B. Do you see it? Look at it so that you may know it again. That's the letter B. Now tell me what letter that is?'

Jack now determined to resist, so he made no answer.

'So you cannot tell; well, then, we will try what one of these little fellows will do,' said Mr Bonnycastle, taking down a cane. 'Observe, Johnny, that's the letter B. Now, what letter is that? Answer me directly.'

'I won't learn to read and write.'

Whack came the cane on Johnny's shoulders...

'What letter's that?'

'I won't tell,' roared Johnny; 'I won't tell – that I won't.'

Whack – whack – whack, and a pause. 'I told you before that's the letter B. What letter is that? Tell me directly.'

Johnny, by way of reply, made snatch at the cane. Whack – he caught it, certainly; but not exactly as he would have wished. Johnny then snatched up the book and dashed it into the corner of the room. Whack, whack! Johnny attempted to seize Mr Bonnycastle with his teeth. Whack, whack, whack, whack! and Johnny fell on the carpet and roared with pain. Mr Bonny-castle then left him for a little while to recover himself, and sat down.

At last Johnny's exclamations settled down in deep sobs, and then Mr Bonnycastle said to him, 'Now, Johnny, you perceive that you must do as you are bid, or else you will have more beating. Get up immediately. Do you hear, sir?'

Somehow or another, Johnny, without intending it, stood upon his feet.

'That's a good boy; now you see, by getting up as you were bid, you have not been beaten. Now, Johnny, you must go and bring the book from where you threw it down. Do you hear, sir? Bring it directly!'

Johnny looked at Mr Bonnycastle and the cane. With every intention to refuse, Johnny picked up the book and laid it on the table.

'That's a good boy; now we will find the letter B. Here it is: now, Johnny, tell me what that letter is.'

Johnny made no answer.

'Tell me directly, sir,' said Mr Bonnycastle, raising his cane up in the air. The appeal was too powerful. Johnny eyed the cane; it moved, it was coming. Breathlessly he shrieked out, 'B.'

'Very well indeed, Johnny; very well. Now your first lesson is over, and you shall go to bed. You have learnt more than you think. To-morrow we will begin again. Now we'll put the cane by.'

* Something that cannot be done without. (Literally, in Latin: 'without which not.')

Appalling as this now sounds to us, this passage was probably originally intended to strike the reader as amusing. Today it will strike many readers as distressing – indeed, I've omitted some of the more extreme parts for that very reason. It illustrates very vividly, however, that theories and values associated with education are far from fixed. One hundred and fifty years ago – only five generations of pupils or students – this manner of 'teaching' was seen as perfectly acceptable. In fact, we don't need to go nearly as far back as that. Some teachers teaching today will have encountered corporal punishment as a part of their 'education'. Mr Bonnycastle's pupils, we are told, rather like him and see him afterwards as a friend. For us, it is hard to see him as anything but a monster engaged in the breaking of a child's will. But a hundred and fifty years ago – and less – breaking a child's will was considered by many to be a perfectly acceptable part of what education was about. However, although values change, the challenges to the teacher remain the same. We will still encounter learners who don't appear to want to learn, who appear unmotivated or truculent. Of course, we find Mr

Bonnycastle's solution morally repugnant. So what strategies do we, in the twenty-first century, turn to, which are consistent with our values and our professional code of conduct?

What Mr Bonnycastle is up to in this extract is behaviour modification – although he wouldn't call it by that name. He uses punishment, and the subsequent fear of punishment, to make Johnny adjust his behaviour, to bring it in line with what Mr Bonnycastle requires in a pupil. This is an approach still used by some today, in the training of animals, for example.

The feared punishment need not be physical. It might be verbal – a lot of aggressive shouting, for example. This is an approach used in the armed services. And not only in the armed services. Most of us will have experience of a teacher, manager or parent who has resorted to this approach, if not systematically, at least from time to time. The frightening thing about it, of course, is that it works. If you hurt and scare any of us enough, eventually we'll conform. But this is why we need our code of conduct, why we need to be clear about the values that attach to our professional practice; because the fact that a strategy works does not necessarily mean it's an acceptable or proper thing to do. If this were not the case we would be unable to point to the defining line between what is teaching and what is indoctrination.

Behaviour modification is based on behaviourist theories of learning. These are certainly not, however, all about using punishment, and there is a lot the teacher can usefully learn from neo-behaviourist theories, as we shall see in Chapter 7, such as how learning may be reinforced, how the learner can be motivated by achievement and reward, and so on.

But a very interesting question the behaviourist theories raise – and one which you may have identified from reading that third extract – relates to whether we can draw a distinction between education and training; and indeed whether such a distinction is useful. This debate was at its height in the 1980s, sparked by the growth of Youth Training Programmes and later by the introduction of the competence-based National Vocational Qualifications. It is a debate that is unlikely to go away, and it is one that is inevitably value-laden. Are you, for example, a teacher or a trainer? If you reply indignantly that of course you are the former, there is, implicit in your response, a value judgement that assigns a higher value or status to being a teacher. Why is this? And if you consider yourself to be a trainer, or if your role designates you as such, what is it about what you do that distinguishes you from a teacher? Is Johnny being taught by Mr Bonnycastle, or trained? When Mr Bonnycastle says to him 'You have learnt more than you think', is he talking about having taught him or having trained him? Presumably he means Johnny has not only been taught to recognise and name the letter B but has, more importantly, been trained to respond obediently to Mr Bonnycastle's command.

CLOSE FOCUS CLOSE FOCUS CLOSE FOCUS CLOSE FOCUS CLOSE FOCUS

An interesting way to analyse the learning which is going on in Mr Gradgrind's and Mr Bonnycastle's 'lessons' is to identify and write out what you infer to be their intended learning outcomes and their criteria for assessing whether those outcomes have been met. But whatever you do, don't muddle those up with your own lesson plans – you could be in real trouble!

You may also find it illuminating to assess these two teachers against the Standards. This will help you to familiarise yourself with the standards as well as providing a convincing argument for why such standards may be useful.

Working with others

Although our first concern is always for our learners, we should not overlook the fact that our behaviour towards colleagues and others should also reflect our professionalism. What, you may ask, if I am working alongside a Mr Gradgrind? Well, that's a tricky one. But first of all let's recognise that Mr Gradgrind isn't going to be a colleague for very long, unless he changes his ways; because the Mr Gradgrinds simply won't be meeting the required Standards. Establishing a good working relationship with colleagues is important, not just for your own peace of mind at work but for the students, too. We may not approve of the way a colleague does things, but we can still behave towards him or her with the appropriate social skills of politeness and professional co-operation. Just as children will occasionally try to play Mum off against Dad or vice versa, so learners will sometimes say to you: 'I wish we had you all the time. Mr Gradgrind's lessons are boring.' While this may feel very gratifying at the time, it shouldn't be encouraged. And neither should it go to your head because who knows whether they aren't saying exactly the same thing to Mr Gradgrind about you? If you find yourself teaching with Mr Bonnycastle, on the other hand, a bit of whistle-blowing would certainly be in order.

Stages of professional development

We've talked at length about values and professional responsibilities. Let's turn now to ways of thinking about your own professional development as a teacher. As those of you who worked through the Evaluation option at the end of Chapter 1 will have discovered, Gregorc (1973) suggests that teachers' training needs change in accordance with their developmental stage. Gregorc describes four stages of professional development. These are 'Becoming', 'Growing', 'Maturing' and 'Fully functioning'. The developmental needs he identifies for the first stage – focusing upon the use of methods and resources and the skills of planning – might be referred to as a 'survival kit' for teachers and roughly correspond in scope to the 'Passport' stage as set out by LLUK. In Gregorc's next phase, 'Growing', the teacher's development needs are for consolidation and expansion of these skills and strategies. In the third phase, however, which Gregorc labels 'Maturing' and which involves strong profes- sional commitment, increased willingness to experiment and an ability to tolerate ambiguity, the teacher's developmental needs move out of the purely operational sphere and into an area much more difficult to express in terms of knowledge and skills. This is what Gregorc says about this stage of a teacher's development:

> the teacher comes to realise...that humans learn from many sources and in many ways. When his students fail to attain valid objectives...he examines his objectives, and alters his techniques, materials, and attitudes about roles played in the education process.
>
> (Gregorc, 1973, p4)

For Gregorc, however, this need not be the final stage in the teacher's potential develop- ment. He suggests a fourth, 'Fully functioning', phase, where the teacher has developed a high level of self-direction and astute skills of self-evaluation based upon self-referenced norms. Here the teacher's needs move definitively into the area of self-development and will lead the teacher to seek continuing opportunities for personal and professional growth. This may serve to remind us – if indeed we need reminding – that QTLS should not be taken as the apex of the teacher's professional development but rather as a preparation for continu- ing professional development and growth.

Gregorc's phases provide us with a useful perspective on two important issues. The first we may refer to as the issue of 'bottom lines and ceilings'. A key aspect of Gregorc's stage theory is that each phase may represent the ceiling of a particular teacher's development. That is, the teacher may get 'stuck' there, for whatever reason, and never progress beyond it. The QTLS Standards are operating within a different paradigm, although on the surface this may not be immediately apparent. According to LLUK the only sense in which the teacher can become 'stuck' is if the range and scope of the teaching experience available to him or her remain limited. This is an important distinction to make.

The second issue Gregorc's theory may serve to illuminate is the danger of viewing the QTLS Standards as a set of competencies that can be used as a tick-list to assess whether or not a teacher's performance is adequate. Many of the qualities Gregorc identifies as integral to the Maturing and Fully functioning phases would arguably slip right through a net of competencies, however fine the mesh, and be lost. Qualities such as reflection, motivation, commitment and integrity, for example, are difficult to square with a skills-based qualification; and the danger, of course, is that the Standards do look like competencies.

There are three major arguments related to using 'tick-list' assessment in a teacher development context, and they may be summarised like this:

- teachers may be at different stages of development or involvement and have different needs and aspirations, of which a common programme of competencies might meet only the most basic;
- the NVQ model of competency statement is emphatically employer-led rather than allowing for self-evaluation, reflection upon practice or the setting of self-referenced norms;
- an emphasis on teacher 'performance' may distract from the importance of the teacher-learner relationship and encourage the concept of the passive learner.

The first two issues, of differentiation and reflective professional practice, we have touched upon already. In Chapters 7, 14 and 15 we shall look at the third – the issue of the teacher-learner relationship.

Reflecting on theory

TASK TASK **TASK** TASK **TASK** **TASK** TASK **TASK** TASK **TASK** **TASK** TASK

Read again the section above on Gregorc's theory of teacher development and answer the following questions.
1. How consistent do you find this to be with your experience of your own professional development?
2. In terms of the developmental stages, where would you currently place yourself, and why? What evidence would you present (for example, from your reflective journal) to support your answer?

A SUMMARY OF **KEY POINTS**

In this chapter we have:
> **examined the concept of professionalism in the context of teaching;**
> **looked at ways to explore and articulate our own values base;**
> **identified the values (or lack of them) implicit in others' accounts of teaching and learning;**

> explored the idea of professional development as a series of stages;
> considered the ethical responsibilities of professional practice.

Branching options

The following tasks are designed to allow you to apply or explore further some of the contents of this chapter. If you are using this book to support your professional development, either leading to a teaching qualification or other accredited CPD, you may find it useful to choose a task according to the level at which you are currently working. These are indicated in brackets.

1. Reflection and self-evaluation (NQF level 5)

Think about the last lesson you taught. In what ways were your own professional values reflected in:

- the planning?
- the strategies you used to motivate the learners?
- the nature of your interactions with the learners?
- your approach to accommodating the learners' assessment needs?
- the extent to which you reflected upon and learnt from the experience?

2. Evaluation: theory and practice (NQF level 6)

How would you describe the distinction between professional values on the one hand, and theories of learning on the other? How are these differentiated a) in the Standards for QTLS? b) in your own reflective journal? Give examples.

3. Engaging critically with the literature (NQF level 7: M level)

How can modernist preoccupations with the importance of individual 'choice' and the individual's prime responsibility towards themselves be reconciled with the idea of a fixed set of professional or ethical values? In constructing your argument, explain how you would support it with reference to relevant texts.

REFERENCES AND FURTHER READING

Ainley, P. (1993) *Class and Skill: Changing Divisions of Knowledge and Labour.* London: Cassell.

Ball, S., Maguire, M. and Macrae, S. (2000) *Choice, Pathways and Transitions Post-16.* London: RoutledgeFalmer.

Freire, P. (1972) *The Pedagogy of the Oppressed.* Harmondsworth: Penguin Books.

Gregorc, A. (1973) Developing Plans for professional growth. *NASSP Bulletin*, (Dec.) 1–8.

Hyland, T. (1994) *Competence, Education and NVQs: Dissenting Perspectives.* London: Cassell.

Lakoff, G. and Johnson, M. (1980) *Metaphors We Live By.* Chicago: Chicago University Press.

Maslow, A. (1987) *Motivation and Personality.* New York: Harper & Row.

Pring, R. (1995) *Closing the Gap: Liberal Education and Vocational Preparation.* London: Hodder & Stoughton.

Rogers, C. (1983) *Freedom to Learn for the 80s.* Columbus, OH: Merrill.

Rorty, R. (1989) *Contingency, Irony, and Solidarity.* Cambridge: Cambridge University Press.

Walker, S. (1984) *Learning Theory and Behaviour Modification.* London: Methuen.

Government publications

Current White Papers on education and training, as well as landmark ones such as:

DES (1986) *Working Together – Education and Training.* London: HMSO.
DfE and ED (1995) *Competitiveness – Forging Ahead: Education and Training.* London: HMSO.
DfEE (1998) *The Learning Age: A Renaissance for a New Britain.* London: HMSO.
DfEE (1999) *Learning to Succeed: A New Framework for Post-16 Learning.* London: HMSO.
DfES (2002) *Success for All: Reforming Further Education and Training.* London: DfES.

The sources

The first extract was from Charles Dickens's *Hard Times* (1854).
The second was from Plato's *Republic* (*c.* 370–390 BC).
The third was from Captain Marryat's *Mr Midshipman Easy* (1836).

6

Professionalism and scholarship 2: being a subject specialist

The objectives of this chapter

This chapter explores what it means to be a subject specialist in the Lifelong Learning sector. It offers some suggestions for ways in which to update your knowledge, understanding and skills within your specialist field, and discusses some of the issues around lesson planning which may confront the subject specialist. It also aims to get you thinking about how you can gain most benefit from being mentored by a specialist in your own subject. In the process, it addresses the relevant areas of essential knowledge, skills and values relevant to your professional development as a teacher and subject specialist, as set out in the Professional Standards for QTLS. These include helping you to:

- **maintain a confident and current grasp of your specialist subject (CS1; CK1.1; CP1.1; CK4.1);**
- **be clear about your own role and responsibilities as a subject specialist teacher (CS3);**
- **identify developments within your specialist field which are relevant to the needs of your learners (CK1.1; CS1; CK3.5; CP3.5);**
- **identify for your learners the ways in which your own subject relates to the wider social, economic and environmental context (CK1.2; CP1.2);**
- **provide information to learners about progression opportunities and transferable skills in your specialist subject (CK4-2; CP4.2; FK3.1; FP3.1);**
- **enthuse and motivate learners in your specialist area (CK2; CP2.1; CS3);**
- **develop good subject-specific practice (CS4; CP4.1);**
- **be aware of how the Minimum Core skills (language, literacy and numeracy) are relevant to your specialist area (CK3.4; CP3.4).**

Introduction

Traditionally, the PCET sector has been about preparation for work. This role has been reinforced, as we've seen, by the Foster Report (2005) which recommends that the sector's mission be seen unequivocally as focusing on skills acquisition. One of the consequences of this is that the sector needs to draw on teachers and trainers who possess these 'skills for work' in a way that other sectors – schools and universities for example – generally do not. The majority of the teaching staff of any FE college or vocational training organisation, therefore, will have dual identities. They are teachers, yes; but they are also experienced and skilled lawyers or hairdressers or nurses or engineers. The vocational identity which they bring with them is one of the factors that qualifies them to teach. It informs and gives credibility to their teaching. It is part of who they are as a teacher. One consequence of this is that the teacher in Lifelong Learning often has a dual professional identity. On the one hand is a broad area of professional expertise – teaching – which she or he shares with other teaching colleagues. On the other is another area of expertise which may be very much a part of their professional identity, but which they do not share with colleagues outside their own section or department. This part of their professional identity may have its own culture, norms and expectations (Spenceley 2006), which are different from those of colleagues in other parts of the organisation.

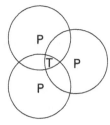

T=shared professional identity as teachers
P=professional identity arising from subject expertise

This dual identity also means we have to ask ourselves some important questions.

- **A hairdresser of many years' experience decides to become a teacher of hairdressing. How does he think of himself first and foremost now: as a hairdresser or as a teacher?**
- **How do others think of him? Is it the hairdresser they see, or the teacher?**
- **In terms of how the learners see him, where does his authority derive from: his successful vocational background or his role as teacher?**
- **Which set of professional skills will he prioritise: teaching or hairdressing?**

We could avoid addressing any of these questions by saying something like, *'Well, it's both, isn't it'.* But this would be a cop-out. The answer is highly unlikely to be 50 per cent in each case. Human nature doesn't work like that. If I have come into teaching from a successful career as a motor vehicle engineer, my answer to that first question isn't going to be, *'Exactly half one and half the other'.* Nor is it likely to remain constant over time. After 20 years of teaching I'll probably think of myself more as a teacher first and foremost than I did when I first entered the profession. As subject specialists, it's important that we explore these questions, because our answers will provide us with pointers for our professional development.

TASK TASK TASK TASK TASK **TASK** TASK TASK TASK TASK **TASK** TASK

What would be your answers to these questions in relation to yourself?

- **How do you think of yourself first and foremost now: in terms of your original area of vocational skill, or as a teacher?**

- **How do others (colleagues, learners, family, neighbours) think of you first: as a teacher, or in terms of your vocational background?**

- **In terms of how the learners see you, where do you think your authority derives from: your successful vocational background or your role as teacher?**

- **Which set of professional skills do you prioritise for development: your teaching or your specialist subject?**

If you have entered teaching without substantial vocational experience in your specialist field, you could try out these questions instead on a colleague or on your mentor. Make a note of your answers. You'll find them useful in the next section.

Updating and subject-specific development

We need now to look at the implications of some of our answers. Perhaps the best place to start is with the final question.

- **Which set of professional skills do you prioritise for development: your teaching or your specialist subject?**

You'll no doubt have realised, in trying to answer it, that it's a 'Catch 22' question. If you answer that teaching is your priority, you leave yourself open to this question.

- **If you give your teaching skills priority for professional development, don't you risk losing touch with current developments in your specialist subject?**

On the other hand, if you answer that your professional development priority is keeping yourself updated and up-skilled in your specialist subject, you're faced with this question.

- **If your professional development priority is your specialist subject, don't you risk letting your teaching skills slide and grow outdated? What's the point of being up-to-date in your subject if your teaching is not as effective as it could be?**

It's a tough life, isn't it?

In fact, the answer to this dilemma lies in our ability to operate as reflective practitioners and self-motivated professionals. As reflective practitioners we are able to identify for ourselves the areas of our practice which need development. Sometimes it will be an issue about *how* we teach; at other times it will be about *what* we teach. And, as self-motivated professionals, we should be expected to seek out the development we need, whether that is about classroom practice or about new developments in our subject area. It is not a matter of half this and half that. It's about being able to identify our development needs as they arise. In other words, the professional's answer to that 'Catch 22' question is:

- **it depends!**

However, unless we keep a watchful eye on what's happening in our specialist field, we won't be aware of whether it's overtaking us and leaving us behind. In some specialist subjects the risk of being overtaken by new developments is much greater than in others. In ICT (Information and Communication Technology) for example, the need for updating is likely to be more frequent than in Equine Studies. But no subject specialism is exempt, so we should all keep our eye on that rear view mirror. Let's look now at some ways in which we can do this.

TASK TASK **TASK** TASK **TASK** TASK **TASK** TASK **TASK** TASK **TASK** TASK

Think about the ways you could keep in touch with what's going on in your specialist subject; new developments, controversies, personalities and so on. List them as you think of them. You might like to do this as a member of a small group with people from different subject areas. This could trigger ideas to help you to expand your list. Then identify, with a tick, the ways you do already use to keep abreast with current developments.

Discussion

The sources you identified probably included some or all of the following:

- Talking to colleagues.
- Reading the general press.
- Reading subject specific journals or magazines.
- TV and radio news.
- Conferences and courses.
- A subject specialist mentor.
- School/section/department meetings.
- The internet.
- Observing an experienced teacher with current knowledge of your specialist field.
- Trade magazines.
- Going back into the field for a few days of updating.
- Curriculum, programme, or syllabus re-specifications.
- The educational press.
- Email bulletins from appropriate bodies.

How many did you tick? Did this task help you think of sources for updating which you hadn't considered before? If so, you might find it useful to incorporate these into your action plan for professional development.

Subject-specific teaching

Let's take one of those sources of updating now, and look at how you can use it most effectively.

Observing an experienced practitioner

You should take every opportunity to observe experienced and qualified practitioners in your own subject as they teach and support learning. To make the most of these learning opportunities, it is useful to record your observations. The following format suggests one way in which this can be done systematically.

Subject/level/year: ....

No. of learners: ....

1. Layout of room (draw diagram if appropriate)

2. Learner characteristics (age, gender, behaviour, etc.)

3. Methods and strategies (and how these relate to 1 and 2)

4. Patterns and styles of communication (teacher–learners/learners–learners) and how this relates to 1, 2 and 3.

---

5. How material was sequenced, presented and made accessible (relate to 2, 3 and 4)

6. Critical incidents – how they arose and how they were dealt with.

What you are particularly focusing on here is:

- **How does the nature of the subject specialism drive the planning and sequencing of the lesson?**
- **How does the subject specialism affect the choice of teacher and learner activities?**
- **What strategies are used to get the learners enthusiastic about the subject, and motivated to learn more about it?**

To give us an idea of the sort of things we might want to pick up on and incorporate into our own practice, we'll use as an example a passage from Theresa's journal which she wrote after observing a lesson taught by Shilpa, an Advanced Practitioner in her own subject area.

Planning

It's obvious – to me and to the learners – that Shilpa's had years of experience doing this stuff for real. She knows exactly what theory has to be covered, and in what order, to prepare the learners properly for doing the practical task. And she explains this to them, and says things like: 'In the workplace it's important to know what to do if this goes wrong. So before we pick up our tools, let's just go through some correction procedures we might have to use.' It's this sort of thing that makes her lesson plan look so logical. And I suppose it's also why it works so well in practice. The learners can see exactly how this would be happening for real, and they're being given the skills and knowledge they need in exactly the order that they need them.

Methods

She uses a lot of demonstration and practice. This is obviously really important, because she's teaching them how to perform skilled tasks and they have to get it right. No room for discovery learning here! That would be a health and safety nightmare. And she also has to make sure that they're clear about the theory side of things and have understood it correctly – otherwise they won't be able to correct procedures that go wrong. So she builds in short periods of exposition – no lengthy lectures, because the learners wouldn't be able to listen for too long – but just short bursts, followed by question and answer to check they've got it. And she also gives them research tasks to do on the internet between lessons, so they don't see this subject as something they can just passively learn on a one-off basis and then not think about any more.

Motivation

She talks a lot about her time in the business, and tells them funny stories, and about some of the really interesting things that happened to her. And she also – while she's doing her demonstration – tells them bits about current developments and the sort of interesting stuff they might end up doing if they work in this field. And she uses praise a lot. She says things like, 'I can see you're going to make a real success of your career at this.' And, 'That's just the sort of answer I'd expect from a real professional.' And even when she's presenting the theoretical stuff, she keeps up their interest and motivation by telling them how they'll be explaining this to someone one day in the workplace; or how listening skills are really important to the job and so this is an opportunity for them to practise. Watching her has given me lots of ideas I can use in my own planning and teaching – so I feel really motivated now, too!

CLOSE FOCUS CLOSE FOCUS **CLOSE FOCUS** CLOSE FOCUS **CLOSE FOCUS**

In her observation report, Theresa makes no mention of Shilpa's choice and use of resources and learning materials, nor of their appropriateness to the subject specialism. Think back now to the last lesson you taught and ask yourself these questions.

- **To what extent did your subject specialism drive your choice of learning resources and the use you made of them?**

- **To what extent did your subject specialism limit or dictate your design and use of learning materials such as handouts?**

Observing an experienced teacher in our own subject specialist area is something most of us can fairly easily arrange to do. If your subject is an unusual one – or if you are the only teacher of your subject in your organisation – this is obviously more difficult, but you'll probably find it well worth going to some trouble to set up an arrangement (perhaps a reciprocal one) with a fellow subject specialist elsewhere.

Another source of updating and expertise in subject-specific practice is – if you're lucky enough to have one – a mentor in your specialist subject. So let's look now at how you can make the most of having a mentor.

Making the most of mentoring

If you are fortunate enough to have a subject specialist mentor to help support your professional development, it's important that you do everything you can to make the most of this arrangement. Just as you wouldn't expect your learners to place all the responsibility for their learning on you, their teacher, neither would you expect your mentor to do all the work in a productive mentoring relationship. To summarise what we need to do in order to get the most from our experience of being mentored, Wallace and Gravells (2007) use the four Rs: Responsibility, Respect, Responsiveness and Reflection.

1. *Responsibility*: We need to accept responsibility both for the success of the mentoring arrangement and for identifying and addressing our own development needs. We don't leave it all to the mentor. We take the initiative and get actively involved.
2. *Respect*: We need to respect the time and effort the mentor is putting in, and make sure we keep appointments, turn up on time for meetings, and so on. Mentors on professional development programmes are often giving up their own time to fulfil this role, with no additional remuneration. If we're not happy with the way the mentoring is working, we need to talk this through with the mentor in the first instance.
3. *Responsiveness*: We need to remain open to new ideas, to listen and to take advice on board. This means not always saying, 'Yes, but...' And we need to make sure we incorporate the important learning points which come out of our conversations with our mentor into our professional action plan where appropriate.
4. *Reflection*: We mustn't expect our mentor to come up with all the answers. They're there to help us to think through for ourselves, to encourage us to reflect on our practice so that we can learn from it. We might very well value their advice, but that's not all they're there for. And sometimes we may not, on reflection, agree with what they say; in which case we shouldn't be afraid of challenging them and arguing our point – respectfully, of course!

Let's not forget there's also a great deal to be gained, too, from *being* a mentor. It, too, provides you with an opportunity to discuss your specialist subject and the ways it can be taught. It, too, can involve observing a colleague's teaching. We all appreciate opportunities to learn; and mentoring a colleague who has more recent experience of work in our specialist field than we do will probably provide us with valuable opportunities for updating as well as the pleasure of in-depth discussions about our subject.

Putting your subject in context

The QTLS Standards require us to *provide opportunities for learners to understand how the specialist area relates to the wider social, economic and environmental context* (CP1.2). So what do we mean by this?

The issues that we're looking at here are things such as:

- **the role this vocational area (or set of skills and knowledge) plays within the structure of society of a whole. What purpose does it serve? How does it contribute to our well-being?**
- **the contribution it makes to the health of the economy;**
- **how it contributes to the quality of life in general;**
- **what impact it has on the environment, and what environmental issues it might need to address;**
- **the opportunities it presents to improve our quality of life;**
- **the opportunities it presents to hard-working individuals for advancement and job satisfaction.**

One of our responsibilities as a subject specialist is making our learners aware of the wider implications, opportunities and significance of the subject they have chosen. This contextual background can serve to interest and motivate them, as well as helping them to understand the place of their subject in the scheme of things.

CLOSE FOCUS CLOSE FOCUS **CLOSE FOCUS** CLOSE FOCUS **CLOSE FOCUS**

What would be your own answers to those bullet points we've just looked at? To answer them all accurately, would you, yourself, need any specialist updating? Is there anything arising from this section that you'd wish to incorporate into your professional development action plan?

Applying the Minimum Core to your specialist subject

The Minimum Core refers to a set of skills and underlying theory in literacy, language and numeracy introduced by FENTO in August 2003 and fully implemented as an integral part of FE teacher training programmes from September 2004. The introduction of the Core was a strategy to ensure that all trainee FE teachers are themselves equipped to support learners' development of appropriate Functional Skills (see below). The teacher's ability to assess and develop learners' competence in the Functional Skills, particularly in Communication, is implicit throughout the Standards. The teacher's grasp of the Minimum Core – and particularly the language and literacy elements of it – is essential to this process.

The significance of your specialist subject, in terms of the Minimum Core, is the extent to which it provides opportunities for you to support learners' development in literacy and numeracy – essentials which we refer to formally as Functional Skills. Health and Social Care, for example, may well provide plenty of opportunities for developing learners' skills in communication, but may require some ingenuity if you are to build in corresponding opportunities for developing their numeracy. On the other hand, Trowel Trades will provide plenty of opportunities for developing learners' numeracy, but possibly fewer contexts in which to develop their communication skills. One of the ways we can help learners to develop these skills, as we saw in Chapter 2, is through setting an example and demonstrating competence in these skills ourselves. This is why it's important for us to identify the opportunities in our own subject area for modelling good practice for our learners in this way.

TASK TASK **TASK** TASK **TASK** **TASK** TASK **TASK** TASK **TASK** **TASK** TASK

Look at the following list of activities and interactions which provides examples of where the teacher's implementation of Minimum Core skills may be used to model good practice for the development of learners' Functional Skills.

a) Identify those which are relevant to your own practice.

b) List any additional activities and/or interactions where you think the Minimum Core fulfils this purpose.

Communication
- **Speaking to learners as individuals and as groups.**
- **Listening to learners as individuals and as groups.**
- **Writing on the board, flipchart, OHP.**
- **Pre-preparing handouts and other learning materials.**
- **Giving clear explanations.**
- **Summarising information.**
- **Using language appropriate to your audience.**
- **Using language appropriate to the situation.**
- **Spelling, punctuating and pronouncing correctly.**

Numeracy
- **Calculating marks correctly.**
- **Dividing learners into small groups efficiently.**
- **Calculating the correct number of resources needed for the group.**
- **Being confident and competent in making calculations related to your subject.**
- **Being able to handle statistical information correctly (e.g. in social sciences).**

Functional Skills-related activities

Discussion

This is a useful discussion to have with your mentor, or with a colleague from your own subject area. It should help you to identify what specific opportunities your specialist subject provides for you to demonstrate the requirements of the Minimum Core. If you identified any here which you are not currently using, you may wish to incorporate these into your professional development action plan.

Let's pick up now that idea of modelling good practice for our learners and evaluate some teachers' efforts to do this. We'll take Communication as our focus here and have a look at some handouts. The first handout is subject specific to Business Studies; but the teacher's application of Minimum Core requirements – which is what we're evaluating here – is applicable to any subject specialism.

TASK TASK TASK TASK TASK **TASK** TASK TASK TASK TASK **TASK** TASK

Evaluate this handout in terms of how good a model the teacher is providing of competence in communication.

Intermediate Business

As you watch the video during today's lesson, look out for and write down the answers to the following. Just the bear facts will do.

1. Can the Trading Standards Office act on it' s own initiative?

2. Can a company compare there own product with the product of a named competitor?

3. What is the ASA and what does it do?

4. What legal constraint's are imposed on the promotion (advertising) of cigarette's?

5. Who should the public complain to if their holiday accomodation does'nt match that advertised in the brochure?

Intermediate Business handout

Clearly the handout is an example of what happens when a teacher is not taking sufficient care to provide his or her learners with a good model of Communication Key Skills. The layout is easy on the eye because it has made use of a large font and careful spacing. To this extent, it demonstrates skill in IT. But what about the spelling? There are mistakes here that a spellcheck would have corrected – although there are others which would probably not be picked up electronically, being incorrect only in context. The punctuation leaves much to be desired. If you'd like to proofread and correct it – which is what the student teacher who produced it should have done – you'll find the corrected version at the end of this chapter.

A SUMMARY OF **KEY POINTS**

In this chapter we have:
> examined what it means to be a subject specialist in the Lifelong Learning sector;
> considered some of the implications of dual professional identity, as teacher and skilled vocational practitioner;
> encouraged you to identify strategies for updating your specialist skills and knowledge;
> explored strategies for developing your subject-specific teaching skills;
> considered how we can make the most of mentoring, both as mentee and as mentor;
> explored the importance of helping learners understand the social, economic and environmental context of your specialist subject;
> looked at ways to apply the Minimum Core to your subject.

Branching options

The paragraphs which follow are taken from the 2005 White Paper: *14–19 Education and Skills*. Read them carefully and then address one of the questions which follow.

2.6. The changes to our expectations of working life, too, have been profound. The modern world in the labour market and beyond makes greater demands on a young person's capacity to communicate, present themselves, work in teams and understand diversity. No longer is there an assumption that the sector in which a young person starts work is the one in which they will end their career. For most, movement between jobs is the norm; for many, movement between entirely different sectors of the economy a realistic prospect. Young people may also want to further their careers in other countries. We must expect that the ability to move successfully between jobs in this way will be a growing necessity for the young people of today over the course of their working lives.

2.7. In this context, the need to offer every young person the opportunity to become educated and skilled is not only an economic imperative, but a moral one. Young people who do not have a good grounding in the basics and the right skills and knowledge for employment will not have much prospect of making the most of themselves in life and at work. If young people leave full-time education without well-respected and recognised qualifications, then they are unlikely to be able to gain employment and then cope with the changing context of work through their lives. And the ongoing social and technological change that affects our world demands that more young people are prepared not only with transferable skills but also to adapt and learn throughout their lifetime. In simple financial terms, as Figure 2.2 shows, those who achieve higher levels of qualification will earn more.[1]

Figure 2.2: Education increases the productivity of the workforce, reflected in higher wages. Analysis of gross weekly earnings from the labour force survey show that earnings increase with qualification levels.

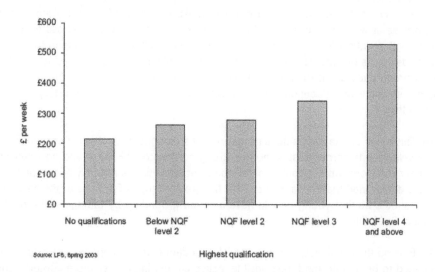

Source: LFS, Spring 2003

2.8. The wider economic need is significant too and the cost for all of us if we do not succeed, great. If we are to continue to attract the many of the high value-added industries to this country, and to compete effectively on the global stage, then we will need far more of our population to have high levels of education. A critical mass of highly-skilled people will continue to attract those employers to this country.

Figure 2.3. Correlation between offending behaviour and truancy

	Males		Females	
	12–16	17–30	12–16	17–30
	% offender	% offender	% offender	% offender
Truant at least once a month	47	21	30	9
Occasional truant	13	16	18	3
No truant	10	8	4	2

Source: YLS 1998/9 HO RS 209 – note 12–16 year olds were asked about truanting in the last year. Those aged 17+ were asked about truanting in their last year of school.

We also need to ensure that our population is not making choices based on stereotypes, but on the basis of clear advice and guidance. The benefits of more engaging work, higher living standards and prosperity will flow to all of us.

3.13. In this world of wider choice and broader opportunity for young people, we must ensure that every young person gets the preparation they need for later life, not just the opportunity to do what interests them. Above all, this means that we need every young person to achieve high standards in the **basics** of functional English and maths in particular. In the forthcoming Skills White Paper, we will set out how we will match this focus on functional skills for young people with a similar focus for adults who have been failed in the past.

3.14. Without these basics for modern life, no young person can consider themselves truly educated. Without these basics, no one can make the most of everyday life or better themselves at work. Without these basics, no one will be able to progress to learn as much as they otherwise could, whatever their other abilities. So, we intend to raise the bar, to ask more of schools, colleges and young people in this area so that no one thinks that a broad package of qualifications without these basics can suffice. No one who is capable should leave education or training without achieving functional mastery of English and maths.

3.15. This focus on the basics does not represent a diminution of creativity or other skills: no novelist can become great without a strong command of English and no scientist or engineer can work without control of number. But education is not only about the basics. We are determined that the launch pad for the greater range of options of the new 14–19 phase should be that young people have a sound grounding by the age of 14 in all the National Curriculum subjects.

3.17. Beyond these subjects, we need to be confident that everyone leaving education is equipped to be an informed, responsible, active citizen. In an ever more complex, interdependent world, where an engaged population is crucial to the health of our society, we continue to put citizenship at its heart too. And we need real confidence that our schools and colleges really do give young people the skills they need for employability for a young person who is not employable has few opportunities in life and for further learning.

If you're using this book to support your professional development leading to a teaching qualification or other formal CPD programme, you may find it useful to choose a question according to the level for which you are currently studying. These are indicated in brackets.

1. Reflection and self-evaluation (NQF level 5)

a) In what ways do the arguments of paragraphs 2.6 and 2.7 apply to learners in your own subject specialist area?
b) How does the argument about 'the basics' apply to your own specialist area?

In what ways might you draw on these two arguments to inform the planning of your next lesson?

2. Evaluation: theory and practice (NQF level 6)

a) What links can you identify between the claims put forward in paragraphs 2.6–2.7, and the argument set out in paragraphs 3.13–3.17?
b) What examples from your own subject area would you offer to illustrate what's being said here?

3. Engaging critically with the literature (NQF level 7: M level)

a) Critically analyse the meaning of the following words and phrases as they are used in the paragraphs quoted above, and consider how their usage here compares with the way they are used within your own specialist subject.

i)   career
ii) moral
iii) economic
iv) high standards in the basics
v)   low-skill
vi) education
vii) active
viii) employable.

b) How well do these paragraphs reflect the degree to which your own subject relates to the wider social, economic and environmental context?

REFERENCES AND FURTHER READING

Heller. J. (1961) *Catch 22*. New York: Vintage.
Spenceley, L. (2006) Smoke and Mirrors: an examination of the concept of professionalism within the FE sector. *Research in Post-Compulsory Education Volume 11, No 3*, pp. 289–303.
Wallace, S. and Gravells, J. (2007) *Professional Development in the Lifelong Learning Sector: Mentoring* (Second Edition), Exeter: Learning Matters.

And here, just for the record, are the corrections of the mistakes you will have noticed in the business studies handout at the beginning of the final task.

GNVQ Intermediate Business
As you watch the video during today's lesson, look out for and write down the answers to the following. Just the bare facts will do.

1. Can the Trading Standards Office act on its own initiative?
2. Can a company compare their own product with the product of a named competitor?

3. What is the ASA and what does it do?
4. What legal constraints are imposed on the promotion (advertising) of cigarettes?
5. Whom should the public complain to if their holiday accommodation doesn't match that advertised in the brochure?

7
Theories of learning

The objectives of this chapter

This chapter sets out a range of currently accepted theories of learning and relates them to familiar classroom and workshop situations. It goes on to explain how teachers themselves can set about theorising, based on their own professional experience. The material in this chapter links closely to the Standards for QTLS, particularly in helping you to:

- **draw on theories of learning to critically inform your own practice and to meet the needs of individual learners (BK2.1; AP4.1);**
- **draw on theories of learning in order to motivate and support learners (AK1.1; AP1.1);**
- **draw on theories of learning to establish and maintain a supportive and safe learning environment (BK1.1; BP1.1);**
- **understand the principles, frameworks and theories which underpin your practice (AK4.1; BK2.1).**

Introduction

What do we mean when we use the term *theory of learning*? Broadly speaking, we are talking about how people learn and what factors are most likely to help them learn best. From a teacher's point of view, the important thing about theories of learning is their practical application. In the classroom or the workshop a theory is only going to be useful if it works.

The relevance of theories of learning

In this chapter we'll look at a range of learning theory, and in each case you'll be encouraged to ask yourself:

- is this true in my experience?
- can I think of examples from my own experience which illustrate this theory in action?
- can I usefully apply this to my own professional practice?

So let's ask, first of all, what do we mean by *learning*? The simple, textbook answer to the first question would go something like this:

Learning is a permanent change in behaviour, attitude or understanding. This sounds okay on paper until we begin to apply it to our own experience. What about all those French verbs or chemical formulae we memorised for our exams in school? Still remember them? No? You may not have retained them *permanently*, but you would still probably want to claim that you did *learn* them. What we mean by *learning*, therefore, is not quite as straightforward as it might at first seem.

How would you yourself define learning? Write down your definition and put it to one side. When you've worked through the next few pages you'll be asked to return to your definition and re-appraise it.

The teacher-learner relationship

Let's approach our question about learning now from a different direction, and ask ourselves: what do we hope will result from the interaction between teacher and learner? Whatever the answer is, there is no reason why its effects should be confined to the learner. The equation that has the teacher as subject and the learner as object only encourages the idea of the active teacher and passive learner. This is what Freire (1972) refers to as the 'banking' concept of education, where the learner becomes the receptacle for knowledge skills or attitudes all mediated through the teacher who, apparently, remains unchanged by the process. In other words, the learner is the customer and the teacher is the ATM machine, dispensing 'learning'. Freire, however, would encourage us to see learning not as a transaction but as a developmental relationship through which both the educator and the educated (or *'educatee'*, as Freire terms it) are engaged in the process of learning.

Another way out of the mindset that sees the teacher as a glorified ATM is to make a semantic escape, as Rogers (1983) does when he discards the term 'teacher' and uses instead 'facilitator of learning'. Like Freire, he presents the learning process as one which is to the mutual benefit of learner and facilitator. Here is what he has to say about how learning is brought about. His use of exclusively male pronouns looks odd to us today, so these have been changed for the purposes of quoting this short passage:

> [T]he initiation of such learning rests not upon the teaching skills of the leader, not upon [their] scholarly knowledge of the field, not upon [their] curricular planning, not upon [their] use of audio visual aids, not upon the programmed learning [they] utilize, not upon [their] lectures and presentations. No, the facilitation of significant learning rests upon certain attitudinal qualities which exist in the personal relationship between the facilitator and the learner.
>
> (Rogers, 1983, p121)

There are two things that must strike us about this. Firstly, the list of teaching skills which he enumerates here could almost be seen as a paraphrase of the QTLS Standards; and secondly he is claiming that *none of them is more important to the learning process than the relationship* – of trust and respect – between the teacher and the learner. Now, of course, fashions come and go in education as in other areas of human affairs, and we shall map some of these paradigm changes as we progress through this chapter. The two ideas we've just considered – that relationship is central to the teaching-learning process, and that the teacher is also changed by this interaction just as the learner is – are at present less 'fashionable' than they were 20 or 30 years ago. We talk increasingly of the teacher 'delivering' the curriculum, as though they were handing out learning in an image reminiscent of Freire's 'banking' metaphor. It could certainly be argued that the rise of competence-based models of education and training has contributed to this change, arising as they do from the instrumental view of education as a process designed wholly, or at least largely, to meet the needs of employers and the economy. The emphasis in the Foster Report (2005) on FE's role as provider of skills training appears to support this instrumentalist view.

Let's focus in on some of the language we're using here.

- **How would you distinguish between 'learning' and 'development'?**

- **Do you see a difference between the terms 'teacher' and 'facilitator'? If so, what is it?**

- **Does the language we use about learning really matter? What about that word 'delivering' for example? Do *you* think it reflects on the teacher's role and status?**

Models of learning

The way we think about learning, and the theories we expound to explain our thinking, can be usefully expressed in diagrammatic form as models of learning or models of the curriculum. For example, we have just considered two very different ways of viewing the learning process. The 'delivery' or 'banking' model presents the curriculum content as central to the process. All decisions about how we plan the learning will be based on *what* we have to teach rather than on *whom* we have to teach. We could represent this idea as follows:

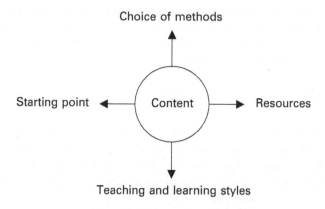

Fig 1: Delivery model of learning

What is important here is the body of knowledge, or the set of competences, which must be transferred to the learner. A 'successful' learner, therefore, is one for whom this transfer has been satisfactorily completed. This model can lead quite naturally to other assumptions, such as the idea that the learner who lacks this body of knowledge or skills, or fails to assimilate it successfully, is, as a consequence, in a state of deficiency. It can also encourage us to think about learning in terms of the active teacher and passive learner – in theory at least – as the teacher busily transfers knowledge or skill to the learner who waits, like a baby bird with its beak open for the next delivery of worms.

On the other hand we might believe, with Rogers, that it is the learner and the way the teacher relates to them which is the central focus in the learning process. Here the starting point is not *what* but *who*; not what is to be learnt, but the potential learner. It is the needs of the learner, therefore, which will govern our choice of methods, our starting point, and so on. And here we don't define 'needs' simply as lack of the required learning, but rather in terms of individual needs based on the learners' prior experiences and learning. We might represent this model like this:

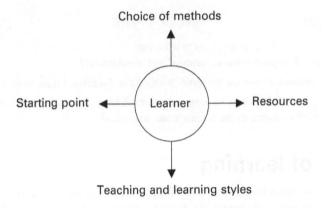

Fig 2: Learner-centred model of learning

Here it is the people – the teacher and the learner – who are important. What is gained from the learning process is thereby left more open-ended; and the measure of success less clear cut. It can represent, among other things, the idea of learning for its own sake, or for the purpose of fulfilling individual potential. In a climate of instrumentalism (where learning has to have some practical and pre-specified 'use' – for example as a means to an economic end), this model may be less in evidence.

CLOSE FOCUS CLOSE FOCUS **CLOSE FOCUS** CLOSE FOCUS **CLOSE FOCUS**

1. Where does your own planning start – with the curriculum content or with the characteristics and needs of the learners? Of course, it's likely to be a combination of the two. But it will be useful for you to reflect, as you plan your next lesson, how you weigh the demands of the curriculum against the needs of the learners and the manner in which you conduct your relationship with them. You may also find it useful to consider what pressures, within your organisation or outside it, may influence your choice of starting point.

2. Go back now to your definition of learning that you wrote down at the beginning of this chapter. Are you still happy with it, or do you want to revise it in the light of what you've read?

Learning theory

We've seen that there are different ways of thinking about learning in terms of the roles of teacher and learner. To some extent it has been a discussion about values, about whether it is the learner or the learning which is most important; whether learning is to be valued as a means to an end or as an end in itself; and whether it is the activity of the teacher or the learner, or the quality of the relationship between the two, which is of most value in the learning process. In this next section we shall keep these questions about value in mind as we go on to explore some key theories about what motivates us to learn and under what conditions we learn best.

The Behaviourists and Neo-Behaviourists

When people think of Behaviourists they tend to picture someone in a white coat teaching tricks to laboratory animals, or inducing neurosis in small children by frightening them with loud noises. Not only does this give the Behaviourist theories a bad press, it makes some teachers wonder how this work can possibly have any relevance for their own professional practice. The reality, however, is that the Behaviourist model can be a very useful one for understanding what motivates learners to comply, to cooperate and to learn.

Of the behaviourists, Pavlov (1849–1936) is perhaps the most widely recognised name. He is remembered for his salivating dogs which illustrate very usefully the central Behaviourist idea that all behaviour can be predicted, measured and controlled, and that learning is simply a matter of stimulus and response. When Pavlov's dogs were about to be fed, a bell was rung. They learned to associate the sound with being fed, and were eventually observed to be salivating at the sound of the bell, before the food appeared. The sound was the stimulus; salivation was their response. This Behaviourist mantra is sometimes repre-sented thus: S-R (**S**timulus-**R**esponse); and was applied not only to animal behaviour but was used, for example by Watson (1878–1958), to explain human behaviour, too. The idea that human psychology or motivation could be viewed as a series of behaviours based on stimulus and response may seem to us now a rather reductive and mechanistic view, and one which it would be difficult to apply to the practicalities of teaching and learning in any humane way. More relevant to our purposes is the work of the Neo-behaviourists, the best known of whom is perhaps Skinner (1904–1990).

The Neo-behaviourists, or New Behaviourists, built upon the work of Pavlov and Watson and introduced two new ideas into behaviourist theory. One was the suggestion that human behaviour is goal-oriented; that someone learning something will often have a sense of purpose in doing so. In other words, human consciousness is not confined to the present moment, because we can both remember past experiences (in a more conscious way than on a mechanistic S-R level), and we can imagine a future, even one which goes beyond our own lifespan. Skinner and the other Neo-behaviourists also emphasised the importance of *reinforcement* and *behaviour modification*. Put simply, reinforcement means rewarding a desired behaviour in order to encourage someone to behave in that way again; and beha-viour modification describes the process of doing this. We modify someone's behaviour by rewarding or reinforcing the desired behaviour. Conversely, we can use negative reinforce-ment to discourage undesired behaviour. For example, we might pay someone lots of attention when they're behaving in the way we want them to, but ignore them completely when they aren't. In this way we *modify* their behaviour into the sort of behaviour we want from them.

At its most straightforward this has been taken to mean that we can be motivated to learn by reward, and that by 'reward' we might mean something as basic as the avoidance of pain. In other words, the consequences of our actions or responses – rewarding or painful – can lead us to change, repeat or give up those actions or responses. For example, if you find you are praised for attempting to answer a question, even if you get it wrong, you'll be even more inclined to risk offering an answer next time too. If, however, your teacher's response to a wrong answer is withering sarcasm or a disapproving 'No!' you'll probably not feel like sticking your neck out the next time. In these circumstances, praise from the teacher would be called, in Neo-Behaviourist terms, *positive reinforcement*. Positive reinforcement can be any response that makes the recipient feel so good that they're likely to repeat the same behaviour next time the opportunity arises so that they will come in for that same reward. The teacher could have given sweets. They could even have given five-pound notes. But praise will work just as well and it's easier on the pocket.

It's important to remember, however, that the same dynamic can work in a less obvious and less positive way too. Imagine that, instead of putting up your hand to offer an answer (or shouting it out if you want to be less formal about it), you get up and wander about the classroom, distracting other learners and generally making a nuisance of yourself. This may very well get you lots of attention from the teacher, albeit of a disapproving kind. Nevertheless, you may well feel that disapproval is better than no attention at all. You may even feel that disapproval is the only kind of attention that you can ever realistically hope for, so you'll take it, thank you very much. In this situation the pay-off is having the teacher's attention at all. Being told repeatedly to sit down and be quiet is the positive reinforcement which perpetuates that very behaviour.

In other words, the Neo-Behaviourist model can be useful to draw upon when we reflect on how our responses as teachers to our learners' behaviour can affect that behaviour in the future. Although, of course, we must ensure that our responses are consistent.

TASK TASK **TASK** TASK **TASK** **TASK** TASK **TASK** TASK **TASK** **TASK** TASK

Applying Neo-behaviourist theory
Read through the following scenario and consider how we might draw on Neo-behaviourist theory to a) explain what is happening, and b) come up with some helpful advice for the teacher concerned. You might like to make some notes so that you can compare your answers with those suggested in the discussion that follows.

> Owen is having difficulty with getting his lessons started. Learners turn up late in ones and twos, and he has to keep starting over so they don't miss anything. He used to wait about 10 minutes after the official start time before he began, but even so, people came straggling in 20, 25, even 30 minutes late; and sometimes he had to recap so many times that he began to feel as though he was stuck in a time loop. Now he gives it 15 minutes before he makes a start, but things haven't improved. What's he going to do?

Discussion

a) What's happening here? Well, to put it simply, the learners' lack of punctuality is being reinforced because Owen is rewarding it by starting later and later and by providing a recap for late-comers so that they suffer no negative consequences for being late. In other words, Owen is in the process of modifying their behaviour in the wrong direction, while they have very successfully 'modified' his to their own advantage. They've succeeded in getting him regularly starting the lesson 15 minutes later than scheduled.

b) What helpful advice could you draw from Neo-behaviourist theory? Well, you'd probably advise him to take control of the situation by warning the learners that all lessons will start on time, and that if they're late with no good reason it will be their responsibility to catch up by borrowing other learners' notes, or visiting the library or college intranet, or whatever. Then he should consistently stick to that, and not reinforce latecomers' behaviour by giving them any special attention. He should, however, devise some system of rewarding punctuality in order to positively reinforce it. He could also consider introducing enjoyable starter activities which again would reward punctual learners for their punctual behaviour and positively reinforce it (that is, encourage them to repeat it). He could even introduce a penalty or sanction for lack of punctuality, such as making the consequence of lateness a shorter break. All of these strategies can be justified on Neo-behaviourist principles.

The Gestaltists

Gestalt is a German word meaning a perceptual pattern or configuration whose qualities can't be adequately described in terms of its separate parts. Gestalt psychology is quite incompatible with the ideas of the Neo-behaviourists which we have just been considering, and could even be said to be in direct contradiction of Behaviourist psychology. The names associated with this school of thought are generally less well known than those of the Behaviourists and Neo-behaviourists. A key figure was Koffka (1886–1941), who taught for most of his career in the USA. In his view the S-R (stimulus-response) model of human behaviour and learning was over-simplified and inadequate. Between the stimulus and the response, argued the Gestaltists, the human mind goes through a process of organising or reorganising its perceptions. Human subjects cannot therefore be said to simply respond to the stimuli around them; the interaction between subject and stimulus is far more compli- cated than that, and cannot be understood simply by breaking the process down into constituent stages. The teacher (and the psychologist) should view the learner's experience as a *gestalt*, a whole, in which the learner achieves understanding by a process of reorga- nising their thoughts. Often this will involve discovering how one fact might relate to another, or how a 'gap' in the pattern or structure should be filled. The idea of wholeness, then, is important in two ways: as a way of construing the learning process, and as a significant part of that process when learning leads to insight and we suddenly 'see the whole picture'.

The Gestaltists' view – that learning is a complex process which involves the learner in drawing on their previous experience and in constantly reorganising their data and ideas, and which will occasionally lead to wholly new ideas and insights – is an important one for us to keep in mind as teachers. It will remind us of the importance of encouraging learners to find their own solutions, and to make their own connections and discoveries. It will also prompt us to ensure that learners have *understood* how they have achieved their task or solved their problem. And, of course, it will serve to remind us of the limitations of unre- flective or rote learning.

The Cognitivists

In Chapter 10 of this book we talk about the three domains of learning: Cognitive, Affective and Psychomotor. Cognitive is to do with thinking; and so, as you might expect, the Cognitivists argue that *thinking* is central to the learning process. In other words, like the Gestaltists, they argue that learning is about much more than the modification of behaviour through positive or negative reinforcement. It is, claim the Cognitivists, about the learner gaining progressively more and newer knowledge, while at the same time adapting or discarding old knowledge which no longer fits their growing insight into the world. From the teacher's point of view this has important implications for the structuring and planning of lessons. The most important is that these should provide learning opportunities which will develop the learners' understanding and allow them to explore the relationships between ideas and concepts, rather than, for example, simply learning to recite the bare facts about them. Perhaps the two best recognised names among the Cognitivists are Dewey (1859– 1952) and Bruner (b. 1915). Dewey is most often associated with the idea of 'discovery learning' and the so-called progressive methods of classroom practice that began to fall into disrepute in the 1980s. His advocacy of a learner-centred approach where the curricu- lum is designed to meet the needs of the learner rather than devised according to established principles, traditions or socio-economic imperatives is recognisable in the lear- ner-centred model we looked at earlier in this chapter. Bruner also took a person-centred approach, arguing that the process of learning involves more than simply acquiring new skills or knowledge or understanding; it is central to the development of the individual as a whole. He saw knowledge not as thing or object to be dispensed or acquired, but as a process. The structuring and sequencing of learning is, according to Bruner, of key importance in the teaching-learning process.

The Humanists

We've already mentioned one of the key thinkers of the Humanist school earlier in this chapter. Carl Rogers (1902–87), you remember, argued that the relationship between learner and teacher (or, in Rogers' terms, *facilitator*) is the key to successful learning. Indeed, he went further than this, claiming that the facilitator/teacher should demonstrate an *'unconditional positive regard'* for the learner (Rogers, 1983). In other words, the teacher's attitude should be non-judgemental and accepting; and the learner should be made to feel valued and cared for. A tall order in some cases, you might think.

Abraham Maslow (1908–70) is another major figure of the Humanist school of learning theory. Like Rogers, he argued that learners need to feel safe and valued before they can fulfil their potential for learning. He used the term *'self-actualisation'* to express the notion of the individual's realisation of their full human potential. In order to reach the point where they are capable of achieving this, it is necessary for the individual's more basic needs to have been met. You may be familiar with Maslow's most widely recognised theory: the hierarchy of needs. Unless our basic needs for safety and comfort, a sense of belonging and a sense of self-worth are met, argued Maslow, we will be unable to self-actualise; that is, reach a state of readiness for real learning and development. In terms of our professional practice as teachers, this requires us to pay close attention to practical issues such as: Are our learners warm enough? Are they hungry or tired? Do they have anxieties which are creating a barrier to their learning? Do we scare them? Are we sufficiently approachable? Are they being bullied? Are they scared of looking stupid? According to Maslow's theory, any obstacle to a learner's well-being may also be an obstacle to their learning.

The Humanists are often regarded as being somehow in opposition to the Behaviourists. Indeed, their school of thought grew to some extent out of resistance to Behaviourist thinking, which was seen as mechanistic and dehumanising. For the Humanists the important issue is the essential dignity and self-worth of every individual, and the potential of every individual to achieve, in Maslow's term, *self-actualisation.*

However, to view the Behaviourist and Humanist theories as an either/or choice would be to throw away much that is useful. Taken together, they offer the teacher a range of possible strategies and responses to try out depending on the circumstances and the situation. Undeniably there are contradictions. Faced with a disruptive student, for example, a Behaviourist might caution: 'Ignore her. Any attention you give her will amount to *positive reinforcement*. She'll take it as a reward and keep on repeating the behaviour'. The Rogers-inspired Humanist, however, could well advise: 'Despite this learner's disruptive behaviour, she still deserves your *unconditional positive regard*. How can you possibly ignore her?' And the Humanist inspired by Maslow would probably say: 'This learner can't learn *until her basic needs are met*. Perhaps she is afraid. Perhaps she fears that if she actually sits down and tries to apply herself to the task you've set her, she won't be able to do it and will lose what little self-esteem she has'.

Which path to choose? You are the teacher. Part of what it means to be a professional is to take the responsibility to weigh up the situation, draw on your theoretical knowledge, and make a choice.

Applying theory

The different schools of theory, in the order in which we have considered them here, illustrate a movement from the mechanistic, instrumental model of teaching and learning, where the emphasis is on shaping the learner to accommodate the learning, to a more complex, person-centred model where the learning process is shaped to accommodate the needs of the learner. These, of course, are the two models we looked at in the early section of this chapter. To some extent, this is also a development over time, as you'll have seen from the dates of the lives of the major theorists. But this doesn't mean that earlier theories have become outmoded as alternative theories have developed. On the contrary, learning theory in its entirety provides a wealth of ideas from which the teacher can draw in order to understand both what is happening in a learning situation, and what strategies might be most effective in supporting and improving the learning experience.

TASK TASK **TASK** TASK **TASK** **TASK** TASK **TASK** TASK **TASK** **TASK** TASK

Putting theory into practice

Read through the following short scenarios and decide in each case what you would advise the teacher in question to do. Explain which learning theory or theories you would draw on to justify your advice. Make some notes as you proceed through the task, and then compare your own advice and arguments to the discussion that follows.

1. A Functional Skills Numeracy class is going badly. The teacher is moving on very quickly from question to question. As soon as someone gives a right answer, he's on to the next. A lot of the learners aren't clear about how the answers were arrived at. They've noted the answers down, but still haven't 'got it'. The teacher tells them not to worry. All they need is the answer. Pretty soon they're losing interest and talking among themselves. He's lost them.

2. In a level 2 childcare class there are two discrete groups of learners: the six loud ones and the five quiet ones. The quiet ones seem timid. They hardly ever speak up in class. If they do, the louder ones tend to laugh or make snide comments. The teacher expects the quiet group to do better in their assignment because they appear to be paying attention. However, it's the noisy group who get the best marks, even though they're the ones who make the most noise and behave in an antisocial and sometimes menacing way. The teacher is puzzled. What's going on here?

3. The motor vehicle lecturer doesn't let anyone get away with anything. If a learner gets anything wrong, he tells them they're useless. He rarely bothers with names. It's always, 'Oi, you!' or, 'Hey, cloth ears!' He has very high standards and means to keep it that way. And he can't understand why most of them do so badly in their assessments, even though he's covered all the competences and drilled them big time.

4. A trainee teacher is having some difficulties with one of her learners on an Access to HE course. It's a mature learner who's hoping to go on to study for a Sociology degree. The trouble is, she dominates all the group discussions, and the trainee teacher can't get her to shut up. She listens politely and agrees with her; but the woman just goes on and on. The other Access learners seem happy to let this happen, because it gets them out of having to say very much. But this means that the trainee teacher isn't able to form an idea of how much they are understanding or enjoying the sessions. In fact, she can't get to know much about them at all, because Ms Talkative just won't shut up.

Discussion

1. We know from Gestalt theory that 'having the right answer' isn't enough. Learners need to understand the process of getting there. They need to see the whole pattern, to fill in the gaps. Unless they have a conceptual grasp of the whole picture, their learning will be uncertain. In order to regain the learners' interest the teacher will have to go beyond the *what* of the answer and spend some time focusing on the *why*. When he receives a correct answer, he will need to ask, 'Yes, good; and how did you arrive at that?' Only in this way can he be sure that all the learners – those with the answers and those without – have securely understood the processes involved.

   This approach is also consistent with Cognitivist theory, as it encourages the learners to understand the process, and to make the connection between a series of ideas. They will learn more effectively by understanding the answer than by learning it off by heart.

2. It's likely that the problem here is that the quiet group of learners do not feel comfortable or even safe in the presence of the louder, aggressive group. We could express this in terms of Humanist theory by referring to Maslow's *Hierarchy of Needs* and pointing out that as long as these quiet students feel threatened, their need for safety and security is not being met and that therefore they are not able to feel any motivation towards fulfilling their higher needs, including learning and self-development. The teacher would be well advised to try addressing the problem of these learners' under-achievement by tackling the classroom management issue, devising strategies for tempering the behaviour of the noisy group and for encouraging the two groups to integrate.

3. It's pretty clear that what's missing here is a positive relationship between teacher and learners. The learners probably feel no sense of being liked or valued by their teacher. They're not really treated as individuals in their own right, as he doesn't even use their names. His interactions with them are brusque and critical. In terms of Humanist theory, what's missing here is some of that unconditional positive regard that Rogers talks about. If this teacher tried relating more positively to his learners he might well find that their standards of achievement improve.

4. At the moment, Ms Talkative is being rewarded for her behaviour by being given the teacher's almost undivided attention. As long as she keeps talking, none of the other learners are getting a look in. Using a Neo-behaviourist approach, this teacher could try modifying the learner's behaviour by withdrawing the reward. The reward in this case is her undivided attention. To do this she will need to withhold eye-contact, cut the learner off by directing her questioning to the others, and not nod or smile or praise Ms Talkative's contributions. If this sounds somewhat harsh, it is less so than the alternative which would be to impose a 'punishment' or sanction such as glaring at her or embarrassing her by telling her to be quiet – a step which would obviously take the teacher beyond what was professionally or ethically acceptable. (In answering this question, did you identify any appropriate sanctions the teacher *could* legitimately use?) At the same time the teacher could give enthusiastic praise to any other learner who spoke up. This reward would encourage them to repeat this behaviour, and draw them into taking a more active part in lessons.

Propositional knowledge

In working through these accounts of learning theory you will no doubt have been relating them in your mind's eye to your own experiences in the classroom, as teacher or learner or both. It's likely that some aspects of theory will ring truer for you than others. What is most important to remember is that, however famous a theory might be, if it doesn't work in practice then it's not much use to you. One of the many advantages of keeping a reflective journal is that you are able to review and analyse your own experience, and from this to build your own accumulation of knowledge – knowledge derived from trying out different ways of doing things, and seeing what works. In doing this you are inevitably coming up with your own theories about how and why people learn. You are theorising. Part of the mark of a true professional is that you will continue learning and theorising and adapting those theories in the light of your experience (do you spot the Cognitivist model there?) for as long as you call yourself a Teacher.

A SUMMARY OF **KEY POINTS**

In this chapter we have:

> discussed the relevance of theories of learning to teachers' professional practice;

> examined a range of theories and applied them to classroom practice;

> considered how professionals can use their own experience as a basis for theorising as well as for the critical analysis of existing theories;

> looked in particular at Neo-behaviourist, Gestaltist, Cognitivist and Humanist theory and their practical applications;

> related the theories to two opposing models of learning;

> considered the appropriateness of these key theories to a sector whose increasing focus, since the Foster report (2005), is on skills training.

Branching options

The following tasks are designed to allow you to apply or explore further some of the contents of this chapter. If you are using this book to support your professional development leading to a teaching qualification, or certification for CPD, you may find it useful to choose a task according to the level at which you are currently working. These are indicated in brackets.

1. Reflection and self-evaluation (NQF level 5)

Look carefully at your lesson plan for the next lesson you're scheduled to teach.

a) With reference to the theories of learning we've looked at in this chapter, what theoretical justification can you offer for i) the way you've sequenced lesson content; ii) the activities you've planned for the learners; iii) the timings you've allowed for each stage of the lesson; iv) the use of resources; v) the organisation of the learning environment?

b) In the light of the learning theories we have considered here, what changes, if any, would you wish to make to your lesson plan?

2. Evaluation: theory and practice (NQF level 6)

To what extent do you agree with Rogers' emphasis on the relationship between teacher and learner as the key to successful learning? What evidence, from your own experience and from your reading, can you offer to support your point of view?

3. Engaging critically with the literature (NQF level 7: M level)

Look again at the following sentences from Rogers which were quoted earlier in this chapter; and look also at the quote from Skinner which follows it.

> *[T]he initiation of such learning rests not upon the teaching skills of the leader, not upon [their] scholarly knowledge of the field, not upon [their] curricular planning, not upon [their] use of audio visual aids, not upon the programmed learning [they] utilize, not upon [their] lectures and presentations. No, the facilitation of significant learning rests upon certain attitudinal qualities which exist in the personal relationship between the facilitator and the learner.*
>
> (Rogers, 1983, p121)

> *Education is what survives when what has been learned has been forgotten.*
>
> (Skinner, 1964)

Given that Rogers was a leading Humanist and Skinner a pillar of the Neo-behaviourist school, how do you account for the apparent compatibility between the views expressed here? Are they indeed compatible? And, if so, can you identify a theory or philosophy underlying, and common to, the work of both theorists?

You may find it useful, in answering these questions, to explore some of the reading listed at the end of this chapter.

REFERENCES AND FURTHER READING

Freire, P. (1972) *Pedagogy of the Oppressed*. Harmondsworth: Penguin.

Hergenhahn, B.R. and Olson, M.H. (2005) *An Introduction to Theories of Learning*. N.J: Prentice Hall.

Maslow, A. (1987) *Motivation and Personality*. New York: Harper and Row.

Rogers, C. (1983) *Freedom to Learn for the 80s*. Columbus, OH: Merrill.

Smith, A. (2004) *The Brain's Behind It: New Knowledge about the Brain and Learning*. Stafford: Network Educational Press.

Wallace, S. (2007) *Managing Behaviour in the Lifelong Learning Sector*. Exeter: Learning Matters.

Wallace, S. (2007) *Getting the Buggers Motivated in FE*. London: Continuum.

Wheldall, K. (1987) *The Behaviourist in the Classroom*. London: Allen and Unwin.

Websites

www.infed.org/thinkers/bruner.htm for further information on Bruner.

http://webspace.ship.edu/cgboer/rogers.html for further information on Rogers.

8
Planning for learning 1: planning your lessons

The objectives of this chapter

This chapter is designed to help you in the practical planning of your lessons. To do this it addresses the areas of essential knowledge, skills and values relevant to planning for learning, as set out in the Professional Standards for QTLS. Specifically, these include helping you to:

- **plan programmes and individual sessions of teaching which meet curriculum requirements and are coherent, inclusive and flexible (DK1.1; DP1.1);**
- **plan teaching sessions which meet learner needs (DP1.2; DK1.2; DP2.2);**
- **include learners in the planning process (DS2; DK2.1; DP2.1; DK2.2);**
- **plan for the effective use of resources in supporting learning (DP1.2).**

Introduction: why plan?

When trainee teachers return after their first visit to a college, one or two of them always tell the same story. They have asked an experienced member of staff for tips on lesson planning or for permission to look at his or her plan for a particular lesson, only to be told: 'Oh, there's no time for that, not in the *real* world. You just keep it in here.' And the experienced teacher has tapped his or her head and smiled. And the trainee teacher, left holding forlornly on to their own carefully drawn A4 lesson plan, wonders whether their PGCE course is offering duff advice.

Not so. The process of constructing a visible lesson plan is not simply an instrumental exercise; it has an equally important developmental function. In other words, its purpose is not only to plot the course of the lesson. The very process of drawing up the plan encourages the teacher to reflect on how and why the content is chosen and sequenced and best presented. It also remains useful well beyond the end of the lesson. As a record of intention, it allows the teacher to review and reflect upon what went to plan, what did not and why. It provides the teacher with a record of teaching and learning strategies from which to identify which ones the learners respond to best and whether any are being over- or under-used. It allows the teacher to check whether assessment strategies have been incorporated to monitor the achievement of each planned outcome. And much, much more – as we shall see. A lesson plan that is formulated only in the head and remains there does not help facilitate any of these activities, all of which are central to good professional practice. The time saved in not committing a lesson plan to disk or to paper is a false economy. It's likely to result in time being spent later looking for assessment evidence or for gaps in the coverage of the course specifications; or time wasted on teaching and learning strategies to which learners have already shown themselves to be unresponsive. There is, of course, an instrumental argument, too, for producing lesson plans on paper (or at least on disk) in that they are needed to satisfy the requirements of Ofsted inspections and the college's own self-assessment programme. But these requirements simply reflect the key issue that documented planning is, in itself, both a function and a measure of reflective professional development.

To plan at all, however, we first need to know where we are going. We need a clearly articulated target; a target that is sufficiently clearly stated so that we will be in no doubt as to whether we have achieved it. In lesson planning we refer to our targets as learning outcomes or objectives. Sometimes these are stated for us in the course specifications or syllabus. If we are involved with the teaching, learning and assessment of learners or trainees working towards a competence-based award such as an NVQ, the targets will be stated for us in terms of the performance criteria the learners must meet. The learning outcomes for your lesson plan must be clear and they must be observable in some way in order for you to know whether learning has actually taken place.

TASK TASK **TASK** TASK **TASK** **TASK** TASK **TASK** TASK **TASK** **TASK** TASK

Consider the following topics which learners might be expected to learn, and decide how you would know, by the end of the lesson or series of lessons, whether the learning had been successful:

- tying a reef knot;

- knowing why Napoleon was exiled to St Helena;

- understanding the factors involved in social exclusion;

- the difference between a theme park and a tourist attraction;

- not to allow contamination between cooked and uncooked meats.

Tying a reef knot

The only way you'd know whether the learners had learnt this successfully would be to see them do it. Your target, or learning outcome, therefore, would be: 'By the end of the lesson the learners will be able to tie a reef knot.' And so within the planned lesson you would have to provide opportunities for them to practise this and to demonstrate their learning. How many times would you want to see a learner tie the knot correctly before you assessed him or her as having correctly achieved the outcome?

Knowing why Napoleon was exiled to St Helena

The big question here is, how will you know whether learners know this by the end of the lesson? You will know whether you've explained it to them, but it doesn't necessarily follow they've understood. You can't see whether they know it in the same way you can see whether they can tie a reef knot. 'Know' is not, therefore, a very useful word when constructing outcomes. So what would constitute reliable evidence that learners did know why Napoleon was exiled to St Helena? Well, they could list the reasons or they could explain the reasons. They might do this during questions and answers in class or as part of a written assignment, or both. Your outcome will then be: 'By the end of the lesson the learners will be able to explain [or list the reasons] why Napoleon was exiled to St Helena.' Only if they list or explain will you be able to ascertain reliably whether they *know*.

Understand the factors involved in social exclusion

This sounds like an outcome, but it's of very little use to you if you're looking for evidence that learning has taken place. Unless your learners live in a comic strip, there'll be no light bulb suddenly appearing above their heads to indicate they've understood. 'Understand' is no more observable than 'know'. They simply aren't useful terms when constructing learning outcomes. Here again, 'list' and 'explain' serve our purpose far better. They will provide observable evidence of whether or not learning has taken place. But remember, if you are to know whether by the end of the lesson the learners will be able to list the factors involved in social exclusion, you must include in your lesson plan some learner activity or activities that will enable you to assess whether they can in fact list these factors correctly.

The difference between a theme park and a tourist attraction

Again, 'know' and 'understand' won't help us with our planning but 'list' or 'explain the differences' will.

Not to allow contamination between cooked and uncooked meats

This is an interesting one because it is about good practice and is therefore an aspect of their learning learners should always be seen to demonstrate when the context demands it. It isn't enough they know it should be done and can explain why. They must be seen to do it. The outcome, therefore, needs to be very specific. The learner will avoid contamination between cooked and uncooked meats by always storing and displaying the two separately, and never handling them with the same implements. Compare this with the reef knot. How many times would you need to assess learners on this outcome before you were satisfied it had been achieved?

Having argued for documented lesson planning and for clearly stated, observable outcomes, the next questions are: what should be included in the plan, and what is the most useful format to use? To consider these, let's have a look at the two lesson plans below.

TASK TASK **TASK** TASK **TASK** TASK **TASK** TASK **TASK** TASK **TASK** TASK

Read through these two versions of a plan for the same lesson, in conjunction with the handout the teacher has prepared:

- **Which version of the lesson plan would be more useful to the teacher during the planning stage, and why?**

- **Which would be more useful to the teacher during the lesson itself, and why?**

- **Which would be more useful for the purposes of evaluation and reflection after the lesson, and why?**

LESSON PLAN

Date:
Subject/level: Business Advanced; Year 1; No. of learners: 15
Duration: 45 mins.
Topic: Preparing presentations.
Aims: To encourage the learners to think about the elements that go into
      making a good presentation.
        To make the topic enjoyable and interesting by 'auctioning' these
        elements, one by one, to the highest bidder.
<u>Outcomes</u>: Learners will be able to: 1) List the key elements that go into giving a good presentation; 2) identify those they consider most important; 3) explain and justify their choice; 4) draw up an appropriate plan of action, with rationale, in preparation for their next presentation.
<u>Content</u>:
1) Introduce topic (3 mins)
2) Learners brainstorm key elements; teacher lists them on board
3) Auction sheets. Each learner decides how much to bid for what
4) Hold auction
5) Whole group discussion about individual and group priorities
6) Individual work on action plans.
<u>Methods</u>: Brainstorming; game; whole-group discussion.
<u>Assessment</u>: Individual and group responses. Completed action plans and ratio-
nales.
<u>Resources</u>: Whiteboard, pens, auction sheet handouts.
<u>Key Skill opportunities</u>: Calculating sums to bid (A of N); group discussion and written plan (Communication).

Lesson plan version A

Time	Content	Outcomes	Method	Learner Activity	Assessment	Skills	Resources
10.30	Introduce topic		Exposition	Listen, ask questions		Listening (Com)	
10.33	Elements of a good presentation	List elements of a good presentation	Brainstorm	Learners brainstorm elements	Observe individual responses		Whiteboard and pens
10.38	Teacher explains auction		Exposition	Listen, ask questions, plan bids		Calculating bids	Auction sheets (handouts)
10.42	Hold auction	Identify elements they consider most important	Game/simulation	Bid for elements they've chosen	Observe and record bidding		
10.52	Discuss individual and group priorities	Explain and justify their choice	Whole group discussion	Listen and contribute to discussion	Observe individual responses	Discussion (Com)	
11.00	Individual action plans	Draw up an individual action plan for preparing and making a presentation	Individual practical work	Apply what they've learnt to drawing up their action plans	Assess action plans		

Aims: To encourage the learners to think about the elements that go into making a good presentation.
To make the topic enjoyable and interesting by 'auctioning' each element to the highest bidder.

Date: _____   Subject/level: Business Advanced Y1. Duration: 45 mins. No of learners: 15

Lesson plan version B

The Presentation Skills Auction

You have £2000 with which to bid for the skills and qualities you think would be most useful in making a clear and interesting presentation.

All the skills and qualities listed below will be auctioned to the highest bidder. Decide what you want to bid for, and write the figure for the highest bid you are prepared to make in the 'Amount I will bid' column. The total of this column should not come to more than £2000.

If you fail in a bid, you cannot use the sum you allocated to bid for anything else.

As the auction proceeds, write down in the right-hand column the winning bid against each item.

Useful skills and qualities for presentation	Amount I will bid	Winning bid
Careful planning		
Clear voice		
Well-produced visual aids		
Good sense of humour		
Ability to speak without notes		
Smartly dressed		
Logical sequencing of material		
Using a vocabulary the audience understands		
A pleasant, informal approach		
Leaving time for questions at the end		

Presentation skills auction: revised handout

There is something to be said for both these lesson plan formats. The first may seem more immediately accessible in terms of 'telling the story' of the lesson. There's less need for abbreviation and we may feel more comfortable with this familiar, discursive form. The second looks as though it may be more time-consuming to prepare and, if we haven't written it ourselves, we have to work harder initially to follow what's happening in the lesson. But if we look at our first question ('Which version of the lesson plan would be more useful to the teacher during the planning stage, and why?') the answer would almost certainly be version B, for the following reasons.

Its systematic layout, using rows and columns, makes it more difficult for the teacher to overlook any aspect necessary to the planning process. For example, following the rows against each objective/outcome, the teacher can see clearly whether the planned learner activity is designed to bring that outcome about and whether an appropriate and realistic assessment activity is in place to monitor whether the outcome has been achieved. And following the rows under 'Method' and 'Learner activity', the teacher can check at a glance whether the plan has allowed for the students to become actively engaged in their learning and whether it provides sufficient variety of activity to stimulate and maintain their interest. This format also allows the teacher to plot exactly where the activities of the lesson will create natural opportunities for the development of Key Skills. Version B is therefore a useful instrument in the planning and preparation of the lesson. It is helpful to the process and is, in this sense, developmental.

Our second question asked: which would be more useful to the teacher during the lesson itself, and why? Here again, version B has some clear advantages:

- the two left-hand columns ('Time' and 'Content') allow the teacher to see at a glance what should be happening now, and what happens next;
- the 'Assessment' column reminds the teacher what he or she should be looking for at each stage of the lesson in terms of evidence of achievement;
- it shows at a glance the exact points in the lesson where the learners should be reminded of the opportunities to develop and demonstrate Key Skills;
- the 'Learner activity' column summarises what the learners should be doing at any given time if they are on task.

Our third question was: which would be more useful for the purposes of evaluation and reflection after the lesson, and why? Again, it seems clear the format most accessible to analysis is version B. The questions the teacher is likely to reflect on after the lesson – such as why the outcomes were or were not achieved; how enthusiastically the learners engaged with their learning; whether the pacing of the various stages worked in practice; and so on – can be reviewed more easily from this version of the plan. This is because it charts clearly the relationship of outcomes to activities (and of both these to assessment), and it also clearly displays the sequence and duration of the various activities.

Perhaps the greatest advantage of version B is that it reveals at a glance whether the key formula for effective lesson planning is in place. That is, whether for each objective or outcome there is an opportunity for the learners to practise and demonstrate achievement of that outcome, and an assessment method or instrument to measure and record that achievement. The rows and columns of version B make it easier for the teacher to check this formula is in place than does the more discursive format of version A.

Time	Contents	Outcomes	Method	Learner activity	Assessment	Functional Skills	Resources
What happens next?		What learners will be able to do by the end of the lesson	How they will learn to do it	How you will see them doing it	How you will check whether they can do it	What Functional Skills they will be able to demonstrate in the process	What resources you will need to support this learning

Version B: rows and columns format

If you felt version A has clear advantages that aren't mentioned here, you may wish to debate this with your mentor or colleagues. It is also an ideal question to reflect on in your journal, having first tried putting each of the versions into practice.

Reflective planning

We have discussed some of the ways in which a clearly drawn-up lesson plan can be helpful during the process of reflection when the lesson is over; now we're going to explore that process a little further. Having seen the teacher's lesson plan, let's look at the teacher's own journal account of how that lesson worked out in practice.

TASK TASK **TASK** TASK **TASK** **TASK** TASK **TASK** TASK **TASK** **TASK** TASK

- **How would you distinguish between the purpose of the first and second paragraphs?**
- **What aspects of the planning does the teacher identify as needing some revision?**

---

22 October

Had the 1st year Advanced Business this morning. They've got to do their first assessed presentations in two weeks and they've been making a great fuss about it - about being too nervous and all the rest of it. The problem I have with this group is that they never seem very motivated to do anything. I don't think I've ever seen a flicker of enthusiasm from them about anything, and it seems a shame, because they're a bright lot on the whole, and a nice bunch. So I've been casting around for some ideas to make the sessions really interesting, to have a bit of fun and make sure they're all involved. And I hit on this idea of an auction, with me as the auctioneer and them all bidding against each other for the aspects of a good presentation they think are most important. E.g. Careful preparation, time for questions, clear visual aids, and so on. I drew up printed lists of these various aspects with a box against each for them to record how much they were going to allow themselves to bid for that item. They were to have £2000 each, and couldn't let their bids run over that total. So really it was a way of getting them to think and prioritise and (hopefully) realise that no single aspect will ensure a good presentation without the others. The least confident or more artistic ones might otherwise spend all their time producing beautiful overheads, for example, and not put effort into other aspects at all. The discussion following the auction was designed to bring all this out. And then, with all this fresh in their minds, they could begin their individual action plans for the presentations. I'd decided to give Gaz the choice of joining in or, if he didn't want to, to monitor the auction and keep a record of the highest amount bid for each aspect so that we could refer to this in our discussion afterwards. The novelty of the auction, and the fact that it involved everyone in a way that was potentially fun, was supposed to jolt them out of their lethargy and motivate them a bit more. That was the plan.

I think on the whole it worked, at least for some of them. The brainstorm at the outset was a bit of a damp squib because only the usual three or four joined in. So it took longer than I'd bargained for to get a reasonable list up on the board that included most of the aspects I'd got listed on the handout. When I gave out the handout, I found I had to explain several times the rules about allocating their £2000. They wanted to know whether, if their bid failed, they could carry the allocated sum over and add it to another bid. I hadn't thought that one out – hadn't seen it coming. I said no. But on reflection it might have been useful for their Numeracy to do a few sums! As it was, they took for ever to decide themselves what to bid for and to write it down, so that by the time we started the auction proper we were more than half way through the lesson. But the auction went very well. I got into role, encouraging bids, slamming the hammer down. Gaz monitored the bids. The students all got animated and, for the first time, really engaged with what they were learning. The whole-group discussion afterwards worked well, too. I think everyone had something to say, and some of them got quite heated about their own view of what was important in a good presentation. The trouble was, there was hardly any time left for the writing of action plans, and this is a worry because all that energy and enthusiasm may have dissipated by next week and we'll have lost some of the ground gained. I set the action plans as homework, but that's never ideal. It means I can't be monitoring them during the process and prompting them or asking questions. Another problem I see in retrospect is that it was unrealistic to assume I could carry out any useful assessment based on the group activities. If they don't all contribute and there's no clear assessment evidence, such 'snapshot', impressionistic assessment isn't very helpful to anybody. The real assessment evidence will be the action plans, which I'll now have to nag them for. All in all, though, it felt like a moderate success. I got them engaged with their learning and let them see that learning can be enjoyable. I should be able to build on that now.

Discussion

The two paragraphs in this journal account each serve a different purpose. The first offers a justification or rationale for the way in which the lesson was planned. The second offers an evaluation of how far that plan succeeded in practice. These two stages of analysis are both of great importance to reflective practice. They may be carried out and presented with varying degrees of formality. If you are on a full-time or part-time PGCE or Cert Ed programme, for example, you may be required to present a written rationale and evaluation with your lesson plan each time your teaching is observed and assessed. The same may be true if you are involved in appraisal or in some phases of your college's self-assessment. Or you may set out your rationale and evaluation less formally in your reflective journal. Whatever the degree of formality, the rationale for your planning should be transparent and clearly articulated even if, in the first instance, to yourself only.

So, let's look at our second question now: what aspects of the planning does the teacher identify as needing some revision? Since we've been allowed to read part of his journal, we must know him fairly well. So let's call him Jim. His two main areas of concern are timing and assessment. He has underestimated the length of time needed to elicit ideas from the students about what goes to make a good presentation; the time needed to explain clearly how the auction sheet was to be used; and the time the learners would take to decide and calculate their intended bids. Jim has also realised that assessment of individuals during group activities can be difficult and unreliable, and becomes quite impossible when some learners do not participate fully in the assessed activity. Now, if Jim has a parallel class to teach, or another class who need to prepare for presentations in the near future and might respond well to this approach, the lesson plan can be revised in the light of these reflections and used again, perhaps with even more success.

CLOSE FOCUS CLOSE FOCUS CLOSE FOCUS CLOSE FOCUS CLOSE FOCUS

What advice would you give to Jim about the way the lesson plan could be revised or changed in order to overcome the difficulties of timing and assessment?

The problem of timing is a tricky one. It's difficult to see, in so short a session, how the lesson may be trimmed without losing some essential step in the sequence of learning activities. The only area of flexibility seems to be in the list of qualities that make a good presentation. Perhaps Jim himself could do a little prioritising here and produce a shorter list for the auction. This would cut down on the time needed by the learners to decide how to allocate their money, and cut down on the time spent on the auction itself. More time would perhaps then be available to spend on the crucial activity of action planning. It would perhaps be unwise to cut down on time spent on the whole-group discussion, as this is central to the sharing and examination of ideas.

As for the issue of assessment, it may well be that the learners' individual action plans will themselves be sufficient assessment evidence that the lesson outcomes have been achieved. As additional evidence, however, the teacher may decide to collect the completed auction sheets, since a comparison between these and the action plans may show some movement of ideas and indicate what individual learners have learnt from the discussion.

Planning, preparation and the reflective cycle

The reflective cycle that is central to the keeping of a journal, applies equally, then, to the process of planning and preparation. It looks something like the following. It follows the model of action–reflection–revised action, which should be central to the teacher's professional practice.

Plan and prepare

Evaluate **Implement**

The reflective cycle

What questions should I ask myself in the initial process of planning?

Our reading of Jim's journal extract and lesson plan already provides a number of ideas as to the questions it is useful to ask ourselves. These may include some or all of the questions in the following checklist. There may be many more questions you'll want to add to this checklist from your own experience or from your reading of the following chapters. For the time being, let's take the last question and look at it in more detail.

✓ Do the outcomes as I have written them, accurately reflect the requirements of the syllabus or course specifications?

✓ Are the outcomes observable, assessable and realistic?

✓ How will each outcome be assessed?

✓ Are the methods and learner activities appropriate to these learners?

✓ Do the activities provide sufficient variety?

✓ Do the learners have the skills (e.g. note-taking) to make best use of the learning opportunities?

✓ Are the planned activities achievable within the time constraints?

✓ Is there sufficient planned material for the time available?

✓ Do the planned assessment methods allow for accurate assessment of individuals' achievement?

✓ What opportunities are there for the learners to develop and demonstrate Key Skills? Is it possible to create more of these opportunities in the lesson?

✓ Are the learning materials (in this case the handout) clear, accessible and useful?

✓ Do the learning materials encourage learners to engage with, and to take responsibility for, their learning?

✓ Is anything in the planned lesson likely to create barriers to inclusiveness? How can I ensure the lesson presents no such barriers?

Initial process of planning: checklist

Planning for inclusiveness

As we saw in Chapter 3, inclusiveness, just as much as reflective practice, is a core value underpinning the Standards.

A key consideration in the planning and preparation of any lesson, therefore, is that it should create learning activities which are accessible to all the learners and which do not make any learner feel excluded, directly or by implication. Close reading of the journal extract we have just been considering suggests that Jim has been keeping this in mind. Mention is made twice of Gaz – presumably a learner – and the plan to offer him an alternative to joining in the auction. The rationale for the lesson includes this:

> *'I'd decided to give Gaz the choice of joining in or, if he didn't want to, to monitor the auction and keep a record of the highest amount bid for each aspect so that we could refer to this in our discussion afterwards.'*

and the evaluation tells us: *'Gaz monitored the bids.'*

We aren't given any clue as to why the teacher decided it was best to give Gaz a choice. Presumably the teacher's concern was that Gaz could experience some genuine difficulty over participating in the auction exercise. Notice that Jim did not take it for granted Gaz would not participate, but that he offered him an alternative and equally relevant learning experience and an essential role in the group exercise.

This strategy does not show up, however, on the lesson plan. We only learn of it when we read the lesson rationale and evaluation in the journal. If Jim wanted to demonstrate his lesson planning was informed by the need for inclusiveness, he would not be able to do this by presenting this lesson plan alone. The evidence would be there in the actual lesson, observed perhaps by a mentor or tutor or appraiser; and it would be in Jim's reflective journal, too, or documented separately in a written rationale. There is a good argument, however, for including such strategies in the written lesson plan. An additional column headed 'inclusion and differentiation' would remind the teacher at the planning stage to think carefully about the issue of inclusiveness in relation to the learners for whom the learning experiences are being planned. And it would act as a reminder after the lesson to evaluate the success or otherwise of these alternative strategies, which might also have included different ways of assessing or recording an individual's achievement.

In some cases, however, it's more appropriate for a learner to have his or her own individual learning plan (ILP). Imagine, for example, you are timetabled to teach basic skills. You have a group of eight learners, all of whom are at different stages in their learning and have different needs in terms of your support and input. One might be working on her comprehension and written English by reading an application form and filling it in; while another learner might still be at the stage of needing help to read simple sentences. A lesson plan that imposed the same activities on all the learners would, in this context, be a nonsense. For each learner you will need to produce an individual learning plan, with individual targets or planned outcomes and individual activities. As you move from learner to learner, giving help, advice and encouragement, you will be able to monitor the activity, progress and achievement of each against his or her individual plan.

More will be said about inclusiveness and reflective practice in the chapters that follow because, as core values, they inform every aspect of our work.

Should I write a formal plan for every lesson?

Despite what some cynical old hands will tell you, the answer to this is 'yes'. Formal planning is not an empty exercise. It allows us to think things through carefully and to make adequate preparations. It directs our attention systematically to the needs of our learners and the requirements of their syllabus or course specifications. It encourages us to allocate time productively and sensibly. It acts as a 'prompt' or 'script' of sorts while the lesson is in progress. And it helps us to focus on key issues and concerns when we come to evaluate and reflect. The lesson plan is not just instrumental but developmental as well; and for that reason it is worth every gram of effort we put into it. If you are planning a programme of learning or a scheme of work, you will be producing, in essence, a series of linked lesson plans. And here other factors (such as the sequencing of topics, the pace and the assessment deadlines) become important factors – factors that cannot be easily addressed without careful, formalised planning. So, yes, ideally, plan out each lesson. Not only is it good professional practice but it will also make your life easier in the long run.

The contingency plan

Remember that it's always a good idea to have a backup or contingency plan. This doesn't mean a whole full-blown alternative lesson plan. It means having a strategy up your sleeve in case something doesn't go according to plan. If the learners get through the lesson more quickly than you had expected, do you have some additional relevant task or input for them? If there's been some slip-up in communications – and you're met by a chorus of 'We've done this already!' – have you got a strategy for adapting the lesson so it becomes an interesting revision session? If something is taking longer than you planned, do you have a short-cut to the end of the lesson without abandoning any of the objectives? In case the OHP or 'Smartboard' aren't working, have you got a whiteboard marker in your pocket? These are all versions of Plan B; and Plan B should be the only plan you keep entirely in your head!

A SUMMARY OF **KEY POINTS**

In this chapter we have:
> discussed why lesson plans are important;
> considered the link between planning and learning outcomes;
> evaluated two different formats for lesson planning;
> identified the ways in which the components of a lesson plan are structured to form a coherent whole;
> discussed the importance of reflective planning and looked at how this works in practice;
> identified ways in which lesson planning links with the reflective cycle;
> looked at ways of planning for inclusiveness, and at individual learning plans;
> considered the importance of having a contingency plan.

Branching options

The following tasks are designed to allow you to apply or explore further some of the contents of this chapter. If you are using this book to support your professional development leading to a teaching qualification, or to formal recognition of CPD, you may find it useful to choose a task according to the level at which you are currently working. These are indicated in brackets.

1. Reflection and self-evaluation (NQF level 5)

Look at your four most recent lesson plans and answer the following questions.

- How useful is the format you have used? Are there ways in which you could improve on this?
- Are the learning outcomes for the lesson reflected in the learner activities you have planned?
- Have you indicated how each learning outcome will be assessed?
- How flexible is your plan? What if some or all learners complete their tasks early? Do you have a plan B?

In what ways will this reflection and self-evaluation inform the planning of your next lesson?

2. Evaluation: theory and practice (NQF level 6)

Have a careful look at the lesson plan below, and imagine it is for a lesson in your own specialist subject.

- What are its strengths and weaknesses?
- How would you change its format it in order to make it more effective as a resource for the reflective teacher?

Advanced level. Week 2. Number of students: 13

Time	Activity	Resources	Comments
0900	Lecture	OHP	Went ok
0950	Test		Poor results
1015	Give work back		Noisy
1030	Lecture	OHP	Went ok
1050	Test		Not bad

3. Engaging critically with the literature (NQF level 7: M level)

The QTLS Standards suggest that you should include learners in the planning process.

- Why might a teacher wish to do this? What theoretical or philosophical base might support such an approach?
- Using the internet or library as a resource, find a) an explanation of, and b) a rationale for the term,

Negotiated Curriculum. Consider the implications of such an approach in terms of lesson planning. How practical would this model be for your own teaching?

- Is there anything about the way you plan for learning that you'd like to change, having worked through this chapter?

REFERENCES AND FURTHER READING REFERENCES AND FURTHER READING

Butcher, C., Davies, C. and Highton, M. (eds) (2006) *Designing Learning: From Module Outline to Effective Teaching.* Abingdon: Routledge.

Website

www.adprima.com/lesson.htm for tips on lesson planning.

9
Planning for learning 2: evaluation and resources

The objectives of this chapter

We go on now to explore the importance of evaluation and to look at the role resources play in improving the quality of learning. It is designed to help you address the following areas of essential knowledge, skills and values as set out in the Professional Standards for QTLS.

- **be aware of the impact your own planning and practice has on individuals and their learning, and of the range of ways you can gather evaluation and feedback (AK4.2; DP2.1; DK3.1; DP3.1);**
- **find ways to share with colleagues the knowledge of best practice gained through evaluation (AK4.3; AP4.3);**
- **examine the importance of gathering feedback and evaluation, and use it as a basis for improving your own practice (AP4.2; AK7.3; AP7.3; DS3);**
- **make effective use of resources to support and improve learning (BS5; BK5.1; BP5.1; DP1.2).**

Introduction

We saw in Chapter 1 how important it is to reflect on our teaching and to ask ourselves questions about what did or didn't work well, and why. In the first part of this chapter we're going to look at more formal ways of evaluating our teaching, based on feedback from colleagues or mentors who have observed our teaching, and on the gathering and scrutinising of data such as learner questionnaires or assessment results. It's important, however, that we distinguish clearly between *evaluation* and *assessment*. Many student teachers find it all too easy to confuse the two and get themselves in a semantic muddle. So let's be clear about our definitions at the outset.

- *Evaluation* focuses on our own performance. It is concerned with the effectiveness of teaching and learning. It is based on data about how well our lesson plan worked in practice; whether the timings and sequencing were appropriate; whether the learners found the activities engaging; whether we used differentiation effectively to meet the needs of different learners; and so on. We can gather some of this data simply by careful observation, and more formally by eliciting specific evaluative feedback from learners or from lesson observations carried out by others.
- *Assessment* focuses on the learners' performance. It is about measuring achievement, both ongoing (formative) and at the end of the programme (summative). Although we can use assessment outcomes as part of our evaluation data, we need to analyse its implications carefully, as we'll see below.

We're going to look in this chapter at how we can elicit and use *evaluation* data, not only as a basis for improving our own teaching, but also to pass on to others who might be able to use it to improve their own. And, we're going to explore ways in which we can improve the effectiveness of our teaching through our use of resources.

Using assessment outcomes as a means of evaluation

The results of assessment can tell you more than simply how well each learner has achieved. They can also be used as an indicator of the quality of learning. A potential problem arises, however, if we take such data and assume uncritically that it is an accurate indicator of the quality of teaching.

CLOSE FOCUS CLOSE FOCUS **CLOSE FOCUS** CLOSE FOCUS **CLOSE FOCUS**

For the purposes of performance indicators, achievement figures are often assumed to be a measure of the quality of teaching. Why should this apparently obvious link be treated with some caution?

Discussion

If all the learners have met the pre-specified objectives, for example, we will probably feel satisfied that the teaching and learning have been effective. But this need not necessarily be so. We could as easily assume that these learners were a particularly able and well-motivated group who learned despite – rather than because of – the standard of teaching. Or we could even entertain the possibility that the entire group of learners already possessed this knowledge or skill. On the other hand, if you have a group of learners who are struggling with the level of work and whom you suspect should probably have been recruited to a different programme to better meet their current needs, you will be unnecessarily disheartened if you take their modest results as an indicator of inadequacies in your teaching. In this situation you would be quite justified in patting yourself on the back that they have achieved what they have, given their starting point. Indeed, those modest results may well have exceeded their and your own expectations. It is with this note of caution, then, that we approach the idea of using summative assessment as a means of evaluating our teaching. Even as a means of evaluation of the learning that has taken place, it is not always reliable, unless we are clear about learners' individual starting points and distance travelled in terms of the skills or understanding.

Ongoing assessment – the sort of feedback you obtain by observing the way learners are responding to the lesson, their body language, their answers to informal questioning, and the questions they themselves ask – may well provide you with a more reliable and timely measure of how well your lessons are succeeding.

Imagine, for example, you give a demonstration to your learners of a technique or procedure which they then, as individuals or in pairs, must practise for themselves while you observe them and provide guidance and advice. Having given what you believed to be a clear demonstration, you find that learner after learner is getting it wrong, missing out some essential step or neglecting a required safety procedure. Now imagine a slightly different scenario. Here you give the demonstration and, afterwards, find that only two of your 15 learners have not grasped how to do it. In both cases you have assessed learners as not achieving the learning outcomes you had planned. But the use you will want to make of this assessment decision is quite different in each case. In the first, where all learners are failing to meet the required objective, it is difficult to avoid the conclusion that something was amiss with the overall planning or the teaching of the lesson, or both. In the second, where the majority of learners have achieved the objective, you will need to focus on the needs of the two who didn't. The answer may be as simple as that these two were at the back and couldn't see the demonstration clearly or that they were paying insufficient attention. But the assessment you make of their performance must still be taken into account when planning the next lesson with this group.

Here is how one art and design teacher describes in his journal this process of using assessment information to inform subsequent planning.

---

3 April

Foundation Photography course, and we were floating the images off polaroid photos and distorting them to achieve effects like mirage or high winds. It's a delicate procedure – needs lots of patience and then a steady hand so the image doesn't disintegrate. I got them all gathered round, made sure they could all see. Got the old patter going so they didn't get too bored while we waited for it to soak. I was working on polaroids of some of their faces, so there was lots of laughing when I tweaked them about a bit to get the distortions. Managed to skim off three quite good ones on to white card. Then it was their turn, working in twos. Not very successful. Only about half the pairs got a result. The others seemed to get too impatient, or were too clumsy coaxing the image off the card. And then, of course, when they failed they got discouraged.

I've got to think of a different way to do this. They could all see what I was doing in the demo. And I took my time, and I talked them through it. I think the problem must've been that I made it look too easy. I didn't stress enough the care that's needed, the steady hand. And I didn't emphasise how patient you have to be, how long you may have to wait before it'll float off in one piece. When I do it again I'll make sure I'm bearing that in mind. But I'm not sure whether to get this lot to repeat it or whether the ones who didn't succeed will just feel too discouraged about it now. Perhaps I just ought to move on?

CLOSE FOCUS CLOSE FOCUS **CLOSE FOCUS** CLOSE FOCUS **CLOSE FOCUS**

Do you agree with this teacher? Should he just 'move on'? What would you do in his place?

Your own evaluation of your teaching and planning

In order to form a detailed judgement of how well your planned lesson has succeeded in supporting learner learning, it is useful to ask yourself some structured questions. These are a natural progression on the sort of questions we looked at in Chapter 1 when first exploring the idea of reflective practice. They will probably include some or all of the following:

1. How effective was the learning?
2. How were individual learners' needs met?
3. How might the lesson plan be modified/revised for future use?
4. How appropriate and effective were the teaching and learning materials and resources used?
5. How did you ensure you had feedback in order to help measure the quality of the teaching and learning?
6. How was it ensured that learners understood the purpose and nature of the assessment process'?

7. How was assessment information used to judge how the learning objectives had been achieved?
8. How was assessment information used in evaluating your own performance as a teacher?
9. Based on assessment information gathered in the lesson, how might the teaching be improved?

Using lesson observations as a means of evaluation

If you're currently working towards your QTLS qualification you'll not only be busy reflecting on your teaching, but will also be receiving regular observation reports from your mentor, your tutor, and perhaps others. Even if you already have QTLS you'll still have the benefit, from time to time, of formal feedback on your teaching, through the process of peer observation, inspection, mentoring and so on. So, how do we make best use of this sort of feedback?

First of all we must be receptive to it. We may not agree with everything that's been said, but where we do not, we should at least use it as a starting point for reflection. Having an observer's view of our professional practice can be very helpful indeed. We are often caught up in the demands of the lesson, and may not notice the learner who is looking puzzled, or the pair who are helping each other, or the fact that our OHP slides are difficult to read, or our voice difficult to hear from the back of the room. Observation feedback can provide valuable pointers for our ongoing professional action plan. And, if the feedback is done properly, it will highlight our strengths, too, and motivate us by confirming what we do well. In Chapter 15 we shall look at the rather worrying feedback received by one particular teacher, and discuss ways in which it might be used to inform his subsequent planning.

Obtaining and responding to learners' feedback

Structured comments like this from a tutor, mentor or appraiser are not the only source of feedback we can draw upon when we want to evaluate the effectiveness and quality of our teaching. We may be fortunate enough to be involved in team-teaching, a strategy which provides an opportunity to discuss and debate with a colleague various practical issues about our classroom style and practice. We may receive feedback on the effectiveness of our programmes from employers, from funding bodies or from inspection reports. However, one of the most important sources of feedback is from the learners themselves. Eliciting, reflecting upon and responding to learner feedback should be a necessary and integral part of our professional practice. It helps us to evaluate how effectively we are managing the learning process and can provide us with specific information about, for example, what aspects of their learning the learners are most enjoying, or how they are responding to the learning materials and other resources we are using.

One of the best ways to obtain clear and structured feedback from learners is to design a simple questionnaire and to ask the learners to complete it in class so you avoid the problem of chasing up those that haven't been returned. You should formulate your questions clearly and in such a way that the responses will be useful for purposes of evaluation. For example, the question 'What did you think of today's lesson?' is likely to prompt answers such as 'Good' or 'All right' or 'Rubbish' – which aren't enormously helpful. On the other hand, questions such as 'Indicate which one of the following activities you found most useful in today's lesson: small group discussion; role play; lecture'; and 'Explain in one sentence why you found that most useful' are more likely to provide the sort of information that will be helpful to you in future planning.

TASK TASK **TASK** TASK **TASK** **TASK** TASK **TASK** TASK **TASK** **TASK** TASK

Look carefully at these two examples of learner evaluation forms and consider the extent to which they would be effective in eliciting feedback that is useful to the teacher.

Learner Evaluation

Please answer each of the statements with a "Yes" or a "No"

1. The introduction to the lesson gained and held my attention.

2. The introduction told me clearly what the lesson was going to be about.

3. The introduction told me what would be expected of me in the lesson.

4. I felt comfortable about taking an active part in the lesson.

5. The teacher asked questions in a way that made me feel comfortable about answering.

6. I found the lesson interesting.

7. The lesson provided sufficient information for me to begin my assignment.

Thank you for completing this questionnaire.

Learner evaluation form (a)

Learner Evaluation Sheet

Please take time to answer the following questions as honestly as possible.
You do not have to give your name.

1. Did you enjoy the group work after the lecture?

   Yes ☐   No ☐

   If yes, why? If no, why not?

   _____

   _____

2. Did you enjoy the discussion which followed the group work?

   Yes ☐   No ☐

   If yes, why? If no, why not?

   _____

   _____

3. Do you feel you learnt anything useful from the group work and the discussion?

   Yes ☐   No ☐

   If yes, what do you think you learnt? If not, why not?

   _____

   _____

Thank you.

Learner evaluation form (b)

Both these questionnaires, though different in approach and layout, are going to provide the teacher with useful information. The first (a) is very simple. The advantage of this is that it shouldn't present a barrier to learners. The unelaborated, 'yes' or 'no' answers will provide only limited information, however. For example, the teacher won't know *why* the learner might have felt uncomfortable or found the lesson uninteresting. This presents a problem when using the evaluation to inform future planning.

The second (b) overcomes this difficulty by providing a space for the learners to elaborate on their answers. It is, sensibly, a very limited space, so the learner doesn't feel daunted by the prospect of making a response. This questionnaire also promises anonymity so the learners will feel they can answer the questions honestly. It seems to be designed to give the teacher a better idea of the learners' preferred styles of learning, whereas the first questionnaire would be more likely to help evaluate the learners' responses to the teacher's style of teaching.

TASK TASK **TASK** TASK **TASK TASK** TASK **TASK** TASK **TASK TASK** TASK

Let's see now how we would handle this in practice. Imagine you have asked learners to fill out an evaluation questionnaire. It requires their response to three questions. These are:

1. Did you enjoy today's lesson? YES/NO
2. What's the main thing you've learnt from today's lesson?
    . . . .
3. If you could change one thing about today's lesson, what would it be?
    . . . .

You're aware that this isn't a particularly inspiring or well-designed questionnaire, but you were short of time and you just want to get some evaluative feedback to discover why this class is generally so unresponsive.

When you take the completed questionnaires in, you're quite upset to find that the responses are not very encouraging. There were 15 learners present. Their responses are as follows.

1. Did you enjoy today's lesson? YES (1); NO (14).
2. What's the main thing you've learnt from today's lesson?
    Nothing (9) Not much (2) Something about reports (1) Don't know (3)
3. If you could change one thing about today's lesson, what would it be?

Only eight learners responded to this one. Their answers include: don't have it (1); go slower (1); not so much teacher talk (1); give us some notes (1); explain it clearer (1); don't switch projector off so quick (1); give us time to write it down (1); explain it again (1).

As a reflective teacher with your learners' best interests at heart, you are determined to overcome your dismay and turn this into a useful learning experience for yourself. You decide that part of the solution lies in re-thinking your use of resources for teaching and supporting learning. So what sort of resources might you introduce into your next lesson plan, and why?

Discussion
Four main issues emerge here.

1. The learners aren't enjoying their learning experience.
2. The learners aren't clear about what they are supposed to have learnt.

3. The lesson was paced too quickly for them to follow.
4. The means by which information was presented wasn't appropriate to their learning needs.

So let's consider what role our use of resources might play in addressing these.

Enjoyment: One option is to go for more impact and variety. Another would be to get the learners involved more in their learning. The best option would be to combine both of these. So what could we do? Perhaps we could construct a PowerPoint presentation that uses engaging images and a series of questions which can remain on the screen, one at a time, to be replaced by the answer only when learners have had time to consider, discuss and reply – a sort of 'test yourself', but with pictures. Data projection presentations must be thought through carefully, however. They aren't a replacement for the teacher; they are a resource to support learning. A long data presentation, however flashy, won't necessarily hit the spot. It still requires us to think carefully about our learners' needs. In this case the learners need to feel more involved and enjoy themselves; so a projection-based presentation/quiz could be a good idea. Or perhaps they would enjoy getting out of the classroom or workshop altogether. Let's not forget that we can use a computer room (if we can get access to one) or the library, or any of the accessible places in the wide world outside that will provide a useful context or example for their learning. You could organise a visit to the local High Street, for example; or a motor vehicle workshop. And if that sounds too high risk to contemplate, you could always invite in an 'expert' from an area of work appropriate to their studies: a retail manager, for example, or an experienced nanny. These are all potential 'resources' which might well re-engage the learners' interest and enjoyment.

Clarity: If the learners aren't clear about the purpose of the lesson, it would probably be a good idea to explain the objectives at the outset – displayed on a flip chart or whiteboard, or on the OHP screen. That way you can return to them periodically during the lesson, reminding the learners of what they are about; and at the end you can recap, pointing to the objectives again and getting the learners to help you check that they've been met. This is always a useful procedure. We could summarise it as:

- **tell them what we're going to do;**
- **keep telling them what we're doing;**
- **tell them what we've done.**

Board, flipchart and OHP are such standard bits of kit that we can sometimes almost forget they are there. But they provide a whole range of ways to clarify information. With this group you'll no doubt resolve from now on to write up clearly all new or unfamiliar words, all important learning points, all helpful contributions made by the learners themselves, and all key instructions. And while you're turning away from the class to write or to read what you've written, don't forget that anything you say may be difficult to hear, and therefore unclear. So don't let your use of these resources form any sort of barrier to communication. That would be quite the opposite of what they're meant to do. Always face the learners if you want to be clearly heard. And, of course, this face-to-face is particularly important if any of your learners has a hearing impairment.

Pace: The feedback indicates quite clearly that the learners find the pace of delivery too hurried for them to follow. They ask that the teacher 'go slower' and 'give us time to write it down' and 'explain it again'. As we've said before, many learners find note-taking difficult.

Add this to the fact that the teacher's sprinting through the lesson as though it was a warm-up for the Olympics, and the learners stand little chance of keeping up. What's needed here in the planning stage is to dispense with the hurry and allow plenty of time for questions, plenty of time for recap, and introduce some well-designed handouts with all the key points on (we'll say more about those in the next section). We often feel the pressure to gallop through the scheme of work so that everything's covered. But common sense will tell us that it's better for the learners to cover most of it and understand it well, than all of it and understand it very little.

Presentation: Presentation is all about the way we plan for the necessary knowledge or skills to be communicated to our learners. It appears from this feedback that, in this case, learning has been more about teacher input than about learner activity. This issue is closely related to *pace*, because we all know that, when there's a lot of material to cover, the quickest way to do it is 'from the front'. Quickest, yes; but, as we've just agreed, not necessarily most effective. Your response here will probably be to break up the lengthy periods of teacher input with some learner activity; and to look for more interesting ways of presenting the necessary skills and/or understanding which the syllabus or course spec requires. This brings us back to the range of possible resources we might use. As well as data projectors, internet access, OHPs, Smartboards, DVDs, visiting speakers, places to be visited and so on, we mustn't forget the learners themselves. They can often be our most useful resource, with their varying backgrounds of experience and their individual funds of tacit knowledge. And it's all there for us to use, with just a little skilful questioning.

Using resources effectively to support learning

In the evaluation task we've just completed, we saw from learner feedback that, sadly, three important things were missing from their learning experience. These were:

1. something to capture their interest;
2. something to provide variety;
3. an appropriate means of communicating knowledge or skills.

We're going to look now at how we can use resources – and in particular learning materials – to provide all three of these.

There are three key words here: interest, variety and appropriate. They are all equally important when talking about the design of learning materials. Let's take the handout printed on a sheet of A4 as our example. This is probably the most common learning resource teachers produce, although by no means the only one possible.

The handout has to be interesting if you want the students to 1) read it; 2) make sense of it; and 3) be able to recall some or all the content. I draw a distinction here between reading it and making sense of it because we've all had the experience of 'reading' something – perhaps when we're tired – and realising that, although our eyes have moved over it and we've perhaps turned several pages, we haven't taken a word of it in. If we want to read and digest something, we have to give it our full attention. The more interesting it is, in terms of layout, style and subject matter, the more likely it will be to seize our attention, even if we are tired. To take a very simple and obvious example, a single-spaced page of dense text is less likely to seize and hold the learners' interest than a page of well-spaced bullet points, however useful to the learners' academic needs you conceive that single-spaced sheet to be. Even if you sit up all night word-processing all the information they will need to pass their module test and put it all on a closely printed A4 handout, its usefulness is not necessarily something that will persuade the learners to read it. Sad but true.

Variety is important because, if you always present the information on your handouts in exactly the same way, the learners' interest may wane. As is true in many aspects of life, you are more likely to get their attention if you surprise them. Surprise is a good way to wake a class up and doesn't have to be any more dramatic than an unusually formatted handout. (So put that water-pistol away. Now.) And a handout must be appropriate – to the situation, to the subject matter and to the learners' abilities. A well set-out handout that employs a vocabulary beyond the grasp of most of the learners is going to serve little purpose except to discourage and demotivate.

Key Skills level 3

Apostrophes

Apostrophes are used to denote possession or to indicate where a letter or letters are missing. To denote possession they attach to the end of the word that signifies the possessor, so that if we are writing about the papers belonging to the solicitor we express it as the solicitor's papers. If the papers belong to more than one solicitor, the possessor is signified by the plural and so we express it as the solicitors' papers. If the word signifying the possessor terminates in a letter s, we of course place the apostrophe after the s, but may then added a further s or not as we choose. Thus, Moses' leadership or Moses's leadership. Where the plural of the noun is constructed without a final s – as in children, for example, the apostrophe is employed in the usual way to indicate possession. Possessive pronouns do not take apostrophes. When used as an indicator that a letter or letters are missing, the apostrophe is positioned in the place of those letters, or, more properly where those letters would be if they had not been omitted. So we would write isn't for is not; and o'clock for of the clock; and so on.

Place apostrophes where appropriate in the following phrases:

The sheeps head; the soldiers gun; the judges wig; the womens movement.

Abbreviate the following, using apostrophes:

You are silly; he is not; she would not have; all is well; I did not know.

Handout 1

Nails and screws

Round wire nail – general purpose	Round-head screw – iron to timber
Oval wire nail – short-grain wood	Raised-head screw (brass) – easy removal
Lost head nail – invisible work	Star-head screw- reduces slippage
Cut nail – reduced risk of splitting	Countersunk – general purpose
Cut floor brad – floorboards	Zinc-coated screw – rust-resistant
Clout nail (galvanised) – roofing, fencing	Panel pin – thin wood or ply
Dome-head screw – hides head (e.g. for mirrors)	
Hardboard pin – hardboard	

Handout 2

So, what changes would you want to make? The first handout, I would suggest, makes a relatively simple subject sound unnecessarily complicated by its use of a rather dry and formal vocabulary. It just doesn't communicate very clearly, and this is unfortunate, given it is designed to help learners with their Communication Key Skills. The apostrophe is one aspect of English punctuation that follows clear and simple rules, and it's a pity, therefore, the handout presents a potential barrier to learning. Its other drawbacks are that it presents the information in small, densely packed script, and that at least one of the examples it asks learners to work on is quite ambiguous. Did you spot it?

The second handout is very simple and straightforward. The text is spaced out and broken up into clear individual points. But it could have been made so much more interesting – and useful – if it had provided an illustration of each screw or nail as well as the name and purpose. The learners' grasp of the nail's name and purpose has an extremely limited usefulness if they don't know what it looks like and can't distinguish it by sight from other types. This illustrates one of the important points to bear in mind when preparing handouts and other learning materials: the learners can write down names and definitions from the board or the screen if necessary, but drawings, charts and diagrams are not so easy to copy. This is where handouts come into their own. Another way handout 2 could have been designed is as a *gapped handout*. The teacher could have produced a list of the nails' and screws' purposes, together with illustrations, but have left the name of each blank, providing just a dotted line on which the learners could fill in the correct name. This would encourage the learners to listen carefully to what the teacher is saying, and would also help to make the information stick in their minds, as information tends to do when we have to listen for it and write it down. Of course, this type of gapped handout requires the teacher checks carefully to see all learners are taking away accurate information. But it is one of the most constructive ways in which handouts can be used and is certainly worth trying.

TASK TASK **TASK** TASK **TASK** **TASK** TASK **TASK** TASK **TASK** **TASK** TASK

Now read through this redrafted version of the apostrophe handout we have just looked at. Are there any further improvements you could suggest?

Communication Key Skills Level 3

Apostrophes

The rules for using apostrophes are very simple. They are as follows:

1. Using the apostrophe to show that something belongs to somebody
The apostrophe always attaches to the end of the owner or owners.
So, if the bowl belongs to the dog, it is the dog's bowl.
If the hat belongs to the man, it is the man's hat.
If the bowl belongs to several dogs who have to share it, it is the dogs' bowl.
We don't put another 's' on the end of dogs' simply because it would become too much of a mouthful to say. It would sound something like, 'the dogzizz bowl'.
If several men had to share one hat (an unlikely situation, certainly), we would have to call it the men's hat.
So that is the rule. The apostrophe attaches to the end of whoever is the owner or owners. Now you try.
 The beard of the man becomes . . . .
 The glare of the sun becomes . . . .
 The end of the year becomes . . . .
 The games of the children become . . . .
 The wool of the one sheep becomes . . . .
 The wool of several sheep becomes . . . .

2. Using the apostrophe to show that something is missing.

It is easy to remember this rule if you think of the apostrophe as a sort of wedge holding open the gap where one letter or more is missing.

So, for example, when we abbreviate I am to I'm, the apostrophe shows us where a letter (in this case the 'a' from 'am') is missing.

When we abbreviate is not to isn't, the apostrophe shows us where the 'o' used to be.

When we abbreviate it is to it's, the apostrophe shows us where the 'i' used to be. And do remember, it's always and only means 'it is' or 'it has'.

It's that simple. There is never any reason to get it wrong.

NB The apostrophe in o'clock is there because the full phrase was originally of the clock. The apostrophe marks the place where the 'f ' and the 'the' used to be.

So now try using apostrophes to abbreviate the following:

You are	He is
I am not	What is going on?
Where is it gone?	How is Dad?
It is a nice day, is it not? [literally: is not it?]	

What about some of the stray apostrophes we encounter here and there?

You may have seen market stalls advertising GRANNY SMITH'S 1.20/kilo. This is a rogue apostrophe. Whoever wrote the notice has got it wrong. Go and ask them, 'Granny Smith's what?'

You may have seen, even in respectable literature, references to NVQ's. This apostrophe is not strictly wrong; but it is quite unnecessary. No letters are missing; no ownership is being indicated; but there is a tradition in English for using apostrophes when making a plural of numbers (e.g. 1880's) or initial letters. However, this can confuse the issue, and NVQs is a perfectly correct usage in the 2000s.

CLOSE FOCUS CLOSE FOCUS CLOSE FOCUS CLOSE FOCUS CLOSE FOCUS

Is that an improvement, do you think? Is there anything you would still like to change? Does the handout encourage independent learning, for example? Do the exercises give enough practice and cover a sufficient range? What about the length? Do you think the material should be divided between two handouts, perhaps, rather than given out all as one? If so, what would your argument be for this?

TASK TASK TASK TASK TASK TASK TASK TASK TASK TASK TASK

If your own grasp of apostrophes is shaky, have a go at the exercises on the handout. They will give you an indication of whether you are meeting this aspect of the Level 3 Key Skills requirement in Communication. The correct answers can be found at the end of this chapter.

A SUMMARY OF **KEY POINTS**

In this chapter we have:
> examined the distinction between *evaluation* and *assessment*;
> explored strategies for evaluating our professional practice;
> considered the importance of using lesson observations as part of our own evaluation process;

> explored some of the issues around using assessment outcomes as a means of evaluating the effectiveness of our teaching;
> considered ways in which resources can be used effectively to support learning.

In the branching options which follow, we shall focus on ways in which we can share and disseminate the reflections about best practice which result from our evaluation of our own teaching.

Branching options

1. Reflection and self-evaluation (NQF level 5)

a) What sources of evaluation and feedback can you identify from the most recent five days of your teaching? These might include:
   - lesson observations by your mentor/tutor/colleague;
   - your own reflections in your log or journal;
   - results of learner assessments or assignments;
   - the response or behaviour of your learners;
   - your own reflections in coursework for your QTLS;
   - written feedback from learners (e.g. evaluative questionnaire);
   - spoken feedback from learners;
   - the appropriateness or otherwise of timings or activities in your lesson plans.
b) Decide what these sources tell you about your strengths and about areas where you need to rethink your practice. Draw up two points for development and incorporate these into your professional action plan.
c) Look again at your own strengths which this evaluation exercise helped you to identify. Are there strategies or resources or ideas here which colleagues might benefit from knowing? Discuss with your mentor the most appropriate way of sharing these.

2. Evaluation: theory and practice (NQF level 6)

Read through the following list of ways to disseminate good practice. Using the internet, library, or discussion with your mentor or colleagues, add to this list if you wish, and then decide which would be the most suitable way for you to share the ideas, strategies or resources which your own evaluation has shown to be examples of successful practice.

- Team teaching.
- VLP (virtual learning portal).
- Conference presentation.
- Team meeting.
- Presentation at staff development day.
- Paper for publication in-house.
- Contribution to professional development programme.
- Mentoring or coaching.
- Paper for publication nationally.
- Other.

When you have chosen what you consider to be the most appropriate means of dissemination, describe in your professional action plan the rational for your choice and how you will implement it.

3. Engaging critically with the literature (NQF level 7: M level)

a) Using electronic or library resources, search the academic journals – one of the most formal means of disseminating good practice – to find a paper which addresses, or is relevant to, one of the following themes:
   - **self-evaluation and/or reflective practice;**
   - **the effective use of resources to support learning;**
   - **strategies for disseminating good practice.**

You might find it useful to start your search with these journals:
   Research in Post-Compulsory Education, Journal of Vocational Education and *Journal of Further and Higher Education*.

a) How would you summarise the argument of your chosen paper?
b) What critique would you offer of the paper's argument, based on your own experience and wider reading?
c) From your evaluation of your own teaching, what idea, strategy or resource do you think would be of benefit to other teachers? Now sketch out how you would plan a paper of your own to disseminate this, using headings only, aimed at the journal you have chosen.

REFERENCES AND FURTHER READING

Forsyth, I. (1999) *Evaluating a Course: Practical Strategies for Teachers, Lecturers and Trainers*. London: Kogan Page.

And if you had a go at the apostrophes handout yourself, here are the correct answers to check against your own!

The beard of the man becomes: The man's beard.
The glare of the sun becomes: The sun's glare.
The end of the year becomes: The year's end.
The games of the children become: The children's games.
The wool of the one sheep becomes: One sheep's wool.
The wool of several sheep becomes: Several sheep's wool (because the plural of sheep is still sheep).
You are = you're.
He is = he's.
I am not = I'm not.
What is going on? = What's going on?
Where is it gone? = Where's it gone?
How is Dad? = How's Dad?
It is a nice day, is it not? = It's a nice day, isn't it?

10
Learning and teaching 1: methods and styles of teaching

The objectives of this chapter

This chapter suggests a range of teaching and learning methods designed to encourage learners to engage actively with their learning and to help you to plan a variety of learning experiences which will maintain the interest of the learners and meet their different individual needs. It addresses the advantages and disadvantages of learner- and teacher-centred methods and suggests some useful strategies for setting up and managing group work. It also looks at learning gained through experience and ways in which the teacher can facilitate or draw on this. In particular it will help you to:

- **implement effective learning activities which meet learner needs and curriculum requirements (BK2.1; BP2.1; BP2.3);**
- **take into account learners' preferred styles of learning (BK2.3; BP2.3);**
- **structure and present information and ideas in a way that is accessible to the learners (BK3.1; BP3.1).**

Introduction: strategies, methods and domains

It will be useful if, at the outset of this chapter, we take some time to define the terms we shall be using. First of all, for the sake of clarity, let's draw a distinction between strategy and method. Sometimes, in reading about teaching, you'll find these terms used interchangeably but it is helpful if we assign them an accurate and specific meaning. Let's agree for now that, when you divide learners into groups, you are using a strategy: group work. The activity you and they will engage in while they are in those groups is the teaching and learning method. For example, you may divide learners into small groups (strategy) in order for them to engage in a small-group discussion (method), a simulation (method) or a game (method). Or you may plan to have them working as one large group (strategy) in order to engage in the same methods of learning: discussion, simulation, game. This is an important distinction to make because dividing learners into small groups does not in itself constitute a method. It is simply a strategy by which one or another method may be implemented.

Similarly, we must be careful to distinguish between a method and a resource. If we plan for learners to watch a video, this is not a method any more than taking material from a textbook is a method. The method will be the briefing that precedes the video (exposition) or the question-and-answer session or discussion that follows it. The video itself is a resource and, like the strategy of dividing learners into small working groups, it is simply a means to enliven, facilitate or inform the learning method you have chosen to use.

In some of the discussion that follows, we shall be looking at how our choice of teaching methods will depend, amongst other things, upon our planned learning outcomes. That is, we shall be looking for the method which will best help the learners to learn whatever it is we have planned for them to learn in that lesson. When you read textbooks on education, you will often find that learning is divided into three categories or domains: the cognitive, the psychomotor and the affective. The cognitive domain covers the learning of knowledge, facts and understanding. The psychomotor domain is the learning of practical, physical skills. The affective domain is the area of learning that relates to feelings and attitudes. These are quite useful general categories to use when thinking about our choice of teaching and learning methods. They present, however, a rather simplified typology and should not necessarily be accepted uncritically when reflecting in any depth upon your teaching. For example, where would discovery or aesthetic response be accommodated within those three domains? And how would you frame observable outcomes in the affective domain? These are issues you can explore through the further reading listed at the end of the chapter. For the purposes of this chapter, however, we can use these commonly accepted domains as a rule of thumb when planning our methods.

Learners' preferred learning styles

Have a look at this excerpt from Nicola's journal. Nicola has been teaching part time for several years but has recently been appointed to a full-time post. She is now working towards QTLS.

---

29 September

Had the first year foundation degree group again today. They're all mature learners – all over 21 – and some of them a lot more mature than that! Because they're also my tutor group I'm getting to know them quite well. And I was thinking to myself the other night how well I was getting on with them and feeling really pleased with myself for putting a lot effort into planning the sessions I do with them – making it really interesting, getting them actively involved. And I had the impression they were all really enjoying it. Then today I came up against a bit of a problem with Kev and it's shaken my confidence a bit – not just because it's made me question what I'm doing but also because I just didn't see this coming.

What happened was this. I wanted to get them doing a bit of background reading for themselves so I decided a good way to get this in motion was to get them to prepare for a debate. We'd include questions from the floor so that would mean they'd all have to read around the subject, not just the proposers and seconders, but everybody. This seemed like a really good way to explore some of the ideas we'd been talking about and at the same time motivate them to get reading so they could participate. I thought a debate would help as well to illustrate the difference I was talking about between fact and opinion. Anyway, I was explaining all this to them, explaining what we were going to do, and asking for volunteers to propose and oppose and act as chair. And then Kev, who'd been frowning all this time, starts shaking his head. And I say to him: 'What's up Kev?' And he says something like: 'Have you got a lot of time to fill up or something?' He didn't say it aggressively but I got that feeling you get when you're being challenged – sort of cold and a bit panicky. But I just smiled and said: 'No. But something's bothering you about this, Kev. What's the matter?' And then it all came out.

He said, quite nicely – he was smiling all the time – that he felt they were being a bit patronised. He didn't see why they were expected to do all these activities when what they'd come here for was to learn a body of knowledge. What was the point, he said, in being long-winded about it? Surely it was much simpler and more sensible for me to tell them this information and sum up the arguments

---

than for them to all trail off to the library, all scrabble for the same books, all read the same stuff, come back and debate the issues and end up with a possibly more diluted and less accurate version of the arguments, but having spent four times as long on it.

The awful thing was that, when he said it, it sounded so obvious. And I suddenly felt really silly, as though I'd got it all wrong. While I was spluttering around, trying to answer him, he said that what he expected on a degree course were well delivered lectures – that all these other activities were what you did in primary school and that intelligent people just needed a good lecture. Anything else for him was a waste of time. He was still smiling. He wasn't trying to be nasty, I don't think. But all the others looked so embarrassed, it was really difficult to judge how many of them agreed with him. And I began to wonder whether I'd been completely deluding myself in thinking they liked my teaching and were enjoying the course.

Let's stop there for a moment. Up to this point, Nicola's journal entry is largely descriptive but we'd best not make a judgement about that until we've read the rest of the entry, which we will do in a moment. First, we need to consider what exactly is happening in this situation Nicola describes. Some of the questions we might ask are as follows.

- **Is Kev justified in his views?**
- **How well has Nicola handled the situation so far?**
- **What should she do about it?**
- **Should she concede to Kev, scrap the debate and stick to lectures from now on?**
- **Should she ask the rest of the class what they think?**
- **Should she politely acknowledge what Kev has said but get on with the lesson as planned?**
- **Should she justify her approach, explaining to the learners why she plans her lessons as she does?**
- **How would she justify her approach? What arguments could she use?**
- **Is she right to view Kev's comments as a challenge?**
- **Should she have ignored Kev's head-shaking and so avoided this challenge blowing up in the first place?**

Before going on to read the next part of Nicola's journal, you will find it useful to consider the above questions carefully. You may like to make a few notes in response to each one.

Anyway, in the end what I did was to sit down, with my chair in front of my desk so there wasn't a barrier between me and them (although I'd really have liked one at that moment!), and I said: 'OK, well, let's talk about this.' And I talked to them a bit about learning styles and how some people like to get actively involved with their learning and some just like to have it all set out for them; and how some people like lectures and are great at taking notes and others lose concentration and aren't sure what to take notes about and what not. And I was getting smiles and nods from quite a few of them so I guessed they could relate to what I was saying, and I also guessed they were probably quite relieved I was taking charge of the situation and turning it into an opportunity for us all to learn. Because, on reflection, I think that was what I was doing. And what I learnt from it was that I ought to have raised this right at the very beginning of the course – I ought to have seen it as an issue and built it into the induction programme. And that's what I'll do next time. I'll probably use that old Learning Styles Questionnaire that pops up at every staff development session you ever go to. The learners may not have come across it before and would probably find it quite interesting. I told this lot about it, anyway, and promised to bring a copy in for them to do next time. Then I asked them whether they wanted to go ahead with the debate, and almost all of them said yes. Thank goodness. But which still left me the problem of Kev. So I asked him whether he'd mind chairing the debate because we'd need someone who was good at taking notes. He seemed quite happy to accept and I think this also helped show him I didn't bear him any ill-will for what he'd said. The real challenge is going to be how to accommodate him and his preferred way of learning in future lessons – because I always plan for lots of learner activity. I avoid giving lectures. That's not my style.

Nicola is now reflecting on what happened as well as describing what came next. Her reflection follows the basic model for reflection on practice we encountered in Chapter 1.

- **What problem was there?** *The problem of Kev and his preferred way of learning.*
- **Why did it arise?** *I ought to have raised this right at the very beginning of the course – I ought to have seen it as an issue and built it into the induction programme.*
- **How can I avoid it happening again?** *And that's what I'll do next time. I'll probably use that old Learning Styles Questionnaire.*

Nicola isn't very complimentary about the Learning Styles Questionnaire (Honey and Mumford 1986) – perhaps because it does tend to be rather over-used these days and has come in for some criticism, as you'll discover in the branching options at the end of this chapter. It isn't the only way she could have found out a little more about the way her learners prefer to learn, however. She could (and arguably should) at the outset of the course have helped them to draw up individual learning plans or contracts which would identify their individual needs, preferred modes of learning and targets for achievement. Nevertheless, she's broached the subject now and seems largely to have rescued the situation.

She does, however, raise a very interesting question for us to consider because she's telling us not only about her learners' preferred styles of learning but also about her preferred style of teaching. She is more comfortable with using methods that centre on learner activity rather than those, like the lecture, where all the focus is on the teacher. We will all, as teachers, feel more comfortable and confident about using some methods rather than others. Some teachers find the idea of giving a lecture rather intimidating – having to speak fluently for an extended length of time with all those pairs of eyes on you. Others thoroughly enjoy delivering a lecture. They enjoy the opportunity to perform, to coax a reaction, such as laughter, from their audience. They may also feel safer when they are giving a lecture. After all, they have total control over the planning, timing and delivery and, in this sense, find it a far less risky business than using a method such as role play or a game where learners are given free rein and it is hard to estimate the time needed and impossible to control the outcome. It is likely that you, yourself, will have a repertoire of methods you feel fairly confident about using. If you are at the very beginning of your teaching career, this repertoire will perhaps exist only in your head. If you have been teaching for a little while, full time, part time or on teaching practice, you will be able to make a list of the methods you have used and would use again. A very useful exercise is to list these in the back of your journal and date the list. Each time you add another method to this list, date it. Your aim should be to extend this repertoire as far as possible so that you become confident about using a wide range of methods. The wider the range of methods you use, the more likely it is you will be matching the preferred learning styles of all your learners. This flexibility will also allow you to use the method best suited to achieving the outcomes as set out in the syllabus or course specifications and will bring variety and interest to your lessons. Later in the chapter we shall see what can be learnt from the experiences of one teacher who is struggling to do this. In the mean time, let's return to Nicola and her account of how she responded to Kev's challenge.

What is your view of the way Nicola handled the situation? Is this how you would have done it? And what about the strategy she uses with Kev?

On the whole, she seems to have dealt with the immediate situation very well. These learners are adults, after all and, in discussing the issue openly and honestly with them and introducing some level of compromise and negotiation, she is acknowledging this. It may also be a gentle but effective way of challenging Kev's accusation that the learners are being 'patronised'. Should her approach have been different if this was a group of 16-year-olds, do you think?

The strategy with Kev also appears to be a useful solution to the immediate problem. It ensures he will still be actively involved in the lesson she has planned, despite his reservations; and it also recognises and utilises one of his strengths – note-taking – and allows the group to benefit from it. However, Nicola still needs to find a way to accommodate Kev's preferred learning style in the longer term.

But now I'm beginning to wonder whether saying it's not my style is just an excuse. The purpose of teaching has to be that the learners learn. The purpose isn't that the teachers do what they feel comfortable with. So maybe I ought to get myself organised into giving a lecture now and again. It might have some real advantages. For one thing, it'll get us through bits of the course material quite quickly. For another it'll give the learners a good incentive to improve their note-taking skills – and I'll maybe save enough time, by using a lecture or two, to build in a session on note-taking for those who need it.

Actually, I'm feeling quite enthusiastic about this now. I remember a lecturer we had once or twice at university who used to build a lot of question and answer into her lectures. It was probably to keep us awake – but it worked and it was quite fun. And I also remember she used to use OHTs with the key points on so that we were never in doubt about what we ought to make notes about – we just copied these down. I reckon I could start off with a sort of quiz, like 10 or 15 questions which they have to write down the answers to if they know them, and then I could do the lecture as a way of giving the correct answers to these questions, and elaborating on them. I think that would be quite fun. And if I build some lectures into my lesson plans, Kev (and any of the others who felt the same but didn't say so) may feel better about engaging with the less formal methods, just knowing that isn't all there is.

And I think another thing I'm going to have to start doing is asking the learners to evaluate the lessons, perhaps at the end of each week or fortnight. Find out what methods they've responded to best. Find out if they feel they're missing something. In future I'm going to make sure I see this sort of thing coming.

Nicola is right, of course, when she identifies the purpose of teaching as being that learners should learn. It sounds obvious but in fact it is possible sometimes temporarily to lose sight of it. Using it as a touchstone, it will always help us to get our bearings when there are decisions to be made. In this case it helps Nicola to realise she may have to abandon comfort and take some risks if she is to achieve this purpose for all her learners.

Taken together, the three extracts provide a model of how best use can be made of a reflective journal for the purposes of professional development. The problem is described and reflected upon and then a solution, or series of possible solutions, emerges. In future journal entries Nicola will no doubt reflect upon the success (or otherwise) of her venture into lecturing, and work out where to go from there. The model of a lecture she proposes is an interesting one. We tend to think of such formal methods as demanding that the learner 'audience' be passive recipients of learning. But, of course, lectures can be made interactive in all sorts of ways, and this will often add to rather than detract from their impact. Developing and trying out such ideas is one of the more creative aspects of teaching.

You may not have agreed with all that Nicola writes in this third extract. You may question, for example, whether she should trouble herself so much over the idiosyncrasies of one learner and revise her methods just to meet his needs. The point here, I think, is that although Kev is the one who spoke up, there may well have been others in the class who were feeling the same – who were finding themselves not able to respond very positively to the methods Nicola was using. But whether that is the case or not, what Kev has helped Nicola to realise is that she was choosing teaching and learning methods according to the criterion of which ones she felt comfortable and confident with, rather than according to her perception of learner needs. This is an easy trap to fall into. And so, in effect, when she decides to extend her repertoire of methods to include lectures, Nicola is not simply responding to Kev's wishes but rather is using the incident as a catalyst to move her forward in her professional development.

Learning in groups

Dividing students into groups to learn is a useful strategy, and so let's discuss here some of the reasons why this is so before we go on to look at the sorts of methods group work will allow you to introduce.

TASK TASK **TASK** TASK **TASK** TASK **TASK** TASK **TASK** TASK **TASK** TASK

1. List what you consider to be the advantages of having learners work in small groups.
2. List any disadvantages you can think of.

You may be able to draw upon your own teaching experience for this or, if you are at the very beginning of your teaching career, you may draw instead upon your experiences as a learner. Remember that these personal experiences of learning will always be an important source of ideas and information to you as a teacher.

Some of the advantages and disadvantages of group work you may have identified might be as follows.

Advantages

✓ Quiet or reticent learners may find it easier to contribute to discussion in a small rather than a large group.

✓ Lazy learners find it harder to 'hide' in a smaller group.

✓ Small groups make it easier for learners to offer one another peer support.

✓ Learners feel less exposed when offering an answer to, or on behalf of, a small group than they would if answering as individuals.

✓ Working in groups helps learners to develop skills of cooperation and compromise.

✓ Working in small groups helps to develop learners' social skills.

✓ Undertaking a task as part of team helps prepare learners for the world of work.

Disadvantages

✗ It can be difficult to assess individual attainment when work is produced by a group (see Chapter 13).

✗ Powerful personalities can dominate a group.

✗ Some learners may contribute little or nothing and simply become 'passengers' within the group.

✗ While the teacher is observing or helping one group, other groups may stray from the task.

✗ Group work usually involves methods that take up much more time than whole-class, teacher-focused learning.

✗ Learners may get bored with always working alongside the same small group of individuals.

✗ Learners, if left to their own devices, will tend to form groups with their friends, thus restricting the scope for interaction within the class.

✗ When learners have been working in small groups it can be difficult for the teacher to get them to stop what they're doing and regain their attention as a whole group.

There is one further point to be made which is neither an advantage nor a disadvantage and that is that group work will suit the preferred learning styles of some, but not of others, as we saw from Nicola's journal. This means we should avoid making this our only strategy, however firmly we believe in its benefits.

There are so many real advantages to small group work – not least that it is an excellent way to get students to take responsibility for, and actively engage with, their learning – that it is worth having a look at our list of disadvantages to see if we can offer some ways to address them.

Some solutions to the difficulties of assessing work generated by a group are addressed in Chapter 13, so let's go straight on to how we might avoid the danger of one learner dominating a small group. This is only a problem if it's to the detriment of the others' learning experience. If this is the case, you might consider appointing an observer to every group and making sure the observer or observers you appoint are those whom you fear might otherwise disrupt the learning. The task of the observer is to feed back to you, and through you to the group, their factual observations of how the group went about their task and who contributed what to the group effort. This serves a dual purpose. First, the dominant learner is still actively involved in the lesson but unable to disrupt the group work; and, secondly, the learners begin to gain an awareness of how their group is functioning and their role within it. Another way to ensure the dominant learner does not present an obstacle to the learning of others is to intervene directly in order to manage what is happening in the group.

Appointing an observer who will feed back information about who's contributed what may also serve to encourage those tempted to be passengers to contribute more to the group. Alternatively, the learner who is reluctant to participate, or who finds participation difficult, could be chosen to be the observer in order to ensure he or she had an active role in the learning. Knowing that one of their number will observe and give feedback on the dynamics and the progress of the group often gives learners an added incentive to remain on task, even when the teacher's attention is directed elsewhere.

In order to avoid learners always working in the same groups, there are a number of strategies you can use to ensure the working groups are not always friendship or clique groups and not simply groups of convenience where learners end up working with whoever they happen to be sitting next to. There are several reasons why you might want to manage the formation and composition of groups. You may wish to separate learners who, together, are potentially disruptive or lazy. You may wish to ensure that an isolated learner is not habitually left out. Or you may wish to place learners who are having difficulties in a group with learners who can help them. You can, therefore, draw up before the lesson the list of names of learners whom you want to be in each group. You can read this out or you could use some other approach (such as writing on assessed work you are handing back each individual's designated group for the next activity). However you choose to do it, the important thing to keep in mind is that this strategy of learners learning in groups is something you, as teacher, should actively manage. The success of the learning experience may depend very much on how the groups are constituted and so, if you leave this to chance, you should have a good reason for doing so.

If you simply want to be sure the learners are working with a variety of others rather than always getting into the same groups, you might try dividing them into groups by the 'numbering off' method. If you want to divide the class, for example, into four groups, you count around the class, giving each learner a number (one, two, three, four; one, two, three, four) until they've each got a number, one to four. Then you tell all the ones to get together, all the twos to get together, and so on. This gives you four fairly random groups and is a useful approach if you need to separate certain individuals to help students improve their learning.

Breaking the ice

For learners to work well in groups they need to feel reasonably comfortable with one another. It is sensible, therefore, to make sure right at the beginning of the course or programme of learning that you incorporate into your lesson plan an activity or activities which will:

- **familiarise the learners with one another;**
- **familiarise them with the idea of working in groups;**
- **establish the model of active learning, where learners are active participants rather than passive recipients.**

These sorts of introductory activities are sometimes called 'ice-breakers'. They are quite straightforward to devise but here are some you might like to try, if you have not done so already.

To help learners remember each other's names (and to help you, too), make sure they are seated in such a way that they can all make eye contact with each other, and ask each one to introduce him or herself to the rest by putting an alliterative adjective before his or her name: Confrontational Kev or Happy Helen, for example. It is remarkable how much easier this makes it for everyone to remember a name. A variation on this is to ask learners to say their names, followed by four words about themselves. For example: 'I'm Kev. I paint my nails.' Or: 'I'm Helen. I like Star Trek.' Whatever variation on this you use, when all the learners have had their turn, go round again, getting them to repeat their line but also to introduce the person on their right by repeating theirs. For example: 'I'm Confrontational Kev and this is Happy Helen.' And then: 'I'm Happy Helen and this is Shopaholic Shona.' And so on. Another variation is to follow this sort of exercise by asking the learners to find someone else in the group who reads the same newspaper, takes the same-sized shoe or has the same favourite TV programme as he or she does. This gets them moving around and talking with one another and allows you more easily to introduce collaborative and co-operative learning strategies from the outset of the programme.

Choosing the method

We have already talked about the desirability of being able to draw upon and feel comfortable with a wide repertoire of methods for teaching and learning. We've mentioned, too, some of the criteria you will use for selecting a method. These can be summarised as follows:

- the nature of the topic to be taught and learnt;
- the preferred learning styles of the students;
- the proposed learning outcomes;
- the preferred teaching style of the teacher;
- the requirements for assessment;
- the level of the learners' motivation and interest;
- whether or not learners have the required skills (e.g. note-taking for lectures or guided research);
- the constraints upon, and availability of, resources.

If you have followed the suggestion made earlier in the chapter, you will already have made a list in your journal of the methods you have tried and feel reasonably familiar with. But what other methods might you try?

TASK TASK **TASK** TASK **TASK** TASK **TASK** TASK **TASK** TASK **TASK** TASK

Write down as many teaching and learning methods as you can think of, whether you've tried them or not. If you quickly run out of ideas, you may like to ask your mentor or a colleague. If you keep this list somewhere safe – on disk, for example – you can turn to it for ideas when planning your lessons.

Now read through the following journal entry, written by a trainee teacher on a full-time PGCE PCET course, and think about what advice you would want to give him.

21 February

Half-term, thank goodness. I'm supposed to be using this block of teaching practice to demonstrate I can use a range of methods. I've got my tutor saying to me: 'Be adventurous. Make the lessons a bit more exciting.' And then I've got my mentor at college saying: 'There isn't time. You just have to do it my way. That's the way they're used to.'

The trouble is, although he's a nice guy, his way is so monotonous. He just more or less dictates notes to them or makes them copy formulae off the OHP. He's got this theory that dictation is an excellent form of classroom control. He says to them something like: 'You're going to need this for your exam. Take it down carefully. I'm only going to say it once.' And then he says it slow and steady or he puts it up for a minute on the OHP, and they scribble it down, and the slow ones try to peer over to see what the others have written for the bits they've missed – and there isn't a peep out of them. But I don't want to do it like that. For a start, I think the learners need to be more actively learning, instead of just writing down everything he says so they can churn it all out again in the exam. What's all that about, anyway? They sigh and look miserable and you can see they're not enjoying it. But he's really resistant to me trying anything else. And because that's all I see him do, I've no idea how another approach might go down with that class. He wants me to do a session after half-term on Probability. And I can think of an excellent way to do that – bring in some dice, get them all shaking a number of throws and recording them, and calculating the probability, and checking each other's scores. No dictation. No talking at them while they scribble away in silence. So I'm going to plan the lesson and write a really clear rationale for it, and see if I can persuade him to change his mind.

The trainee teacher's idea is interesting but as yet it is only half formed. He's not quite clear yet about his strategy: will the learners be engaged in this activity individually, in pairs or in small groups? He'll need to decide this in order to plan his resources – the dice, the shakers, the sheets on which to write their scores, perhaps. Presumably he'll have to brief them before the activity and explain something about probability, then elicit and discuss their results afterwards and reiterate the explanation so it is reinforced for them in the light of their learning. Therefore, although he won't be talking at them while they scribble away in silence, he will be incorporating some exposition into his lesson plan, as well as some use of the question and answer method.

Let's imagine, then, he uses the strategy of dividing the learners into groups of three for this exercise of throwing the dice and writing down the score. Bearing in mind the activity will take four to five minutes and that these learners have been completely unaccustomed to active learning – in this lesson at least – what do you think would be the best means of getting them into groups? And what would you call the method of teaching and learning which is being used in this throwing and recording of dice?

Since he cannot know how the learners will respond to group work and since this activity will be relatively brief, it would probably not be worthwhile asking the learners to get up and walk around and reseat themselves when they might more easily work in threes with the two people seated nearest to them. I wonder, however, how the trainee teacher will move among the groups to observe and manage this learning experience? From what he writes in his journal, we could be forgiven for assuming the seating arrangement for the learners is along formal lines – probably a series of rows – which doesn't easily facilitate collaborative work or whole-group discussion of the outcomes. Since he is responsible for managing the learning experience of the learners during this class, it might be sensible for the student teacher to rearrange the classroom furniture to a more appropriate configuration, if possible, before the lesson begins.

What should he call his proposed method? We could call it a practical experiment, which it certainly is. But, perhaps more importantly, we should recognise it as an activity that involves learning through experience. Instead of copying down a theorem, a formula or a law from the board or the OHP, the learners are testing it in practice; they are learning about probability through their own experience of throwing the dice and watching others throw. There are several methods that encourage or allow learners to learn through experience. As well as practical experiments, these include simulation, role-play, demonstration and practice, discovery learning, games (particularly communication games) and presentations. You may be able to think of others. What is common to all these methods is the need for the teacher to structure, manage and reinforce the learning experience carefully, and to give the learner accurate and constructive feedback.

CLOSE FOCUS CLOSE FOCUS **CLOSE FOCUS** CLOSE FOCUS **CLOSE FOCUS**

The opportunity for the trainee teacher to put his plan into action depends upon how successful he is in persuading his mentor that a departure from the usual strategies and methods might be useful at this point. You may find it useful to draft out for him the rationale he plans to write in order to explain why he is planning to teach this lesson in this particular way. You don't need to be a maths or numeracy specialist to do this. You simply need to have reflected, as he has, on the real purposes of teaching and learning and on the relationship between motivation and method.

In the next chapter we shall be aiming to extend your repertoire by looking at ways to implement a range of more innovative or 'high risk' methods.

A SUMMARY OF **KEY POINTS**

In this chapter we have:
> **defined our key terms:** *strategies, methods* and *domains*;
> **considered the importance of taking into account learners' preferred styles of learning;**
> **discussed the advantages and disadvantages of having learners working in small groups;**
> **looked at some examples of 'ice-breakers';**
> **explored how we go about choosing an appropriate method for supporting our learners' or trainees' learning;**
> **looked at the possibilities and advantages of innovative approaches.**

Branching options

The following tasks are designed to allow you to apply or explore further some of the contents of this chapter. If you are using this book to support your professional development leading to a teaching qualification, or as part of formal CPD, you may find it useful to choose a task according to the level at which you are currently working. These are indicated in brackets.

1. Reflection and self-evaluation (NQF level 5)

Go back to the list of teaching and learning methods you compiled for the task earlier in this chapter.

a) Decide on one of the methods you have listed which you haven't tried before but which you think will be appropriate to the curriculum and learning needs of one of your current groups of learners.
b) Draw up an appropriate lesson plan incorporating this method and put it into action as soon as you have the opportunity.
c) In evaluating the effectiveness of your chosen method, what criteria will you use?

2. Evaluation: theory and practice (NQF level 6)

We have discussed in some detail the idea that learners have their preferred ways or styles of learning. We must also assume that teachers have their preferred styles of teaching, too; and this, of course, will influence their choice of methods and strategies.

a) On reflection, what is your own preferred style of teaching? Do you prefer to be a facilitator, or would you rather remain centre stage? Or is your preferred style something in between? To what extent do you allow this to limit your choice of methods?
b) What other considerations govern your choice of methods? For example:
   • Your specialist subject?
   • Your learners' current level of attainment?
What other factors might influence your choice?
c) Drawing on the theories of learning we discussed in Chapter 7, and on your wider reading, what theoretical rationale would you offer for your current range of teaching and learning methods?

3. Engaging critically with the literature (NQF level 7: M level)

Reference was made earlier in this chapter to the 'Learning Styles' questionnaire. We can take this to be the questionnaire designed by Honey and Mumford (1986), which for several years has been widely used in the sector. It has recently, however, been seriously criticised, particularly in terms of the uncritical use made of it by many teachers.

a) Using the internet, research the current state of the debate over 'learning styles'. What are the main criticisms being advanced?
b) What is your own position in this debate? What evidence would you offer to support your view?

REFERENCES AND FURTHER READING REFERENCES AND FURTHER READING

Cannon, R. and Newble, D. (2000) *A Handbook for Teachers in Universities and Colleges: A Guide to Improving Teaching Methods.* London: Kogan Page.

11
Learning and teaching 2: extending your range

The objectives of this chapter

This chapter explores some of the methods of teaching and supporting learning with which you may be less familiar, either because they appear more daunting to organise and facilitate or because they could potentially be difficult to control. It also looks at some of the skills involved in using ICT and in e-tutoring, an area of practice with which not every teacher may yet be familiar. In the process, the chapter addresses the relevant areas of essential knowledge, skills and values relevant to your professional development as a teacher and subject specialist, as set out in the Professional Standards for QTLS. These include helping you to:

- **choose teaching methods and learning activities which are appropriate for your subject area and meet your learners' needs (CP2; BP2.2; BP2.3; BP2.4);**
- **introduce flexibility by using ICT and e-learning where appropriate (BK2.4; CK3.5; CP3.5).**

Introduction

This chapter is designed to encourage you to move out of your comfort zone and try some approaches to learning and teaching which may feel less familiar or less 'safe'.

High risk strategies and methods 1: games

Most experienced teachers will tell you that there are two very different reasons why we would categorise games as a 'high risk' method of teaching and learning. We can summarise these reasons as issues about *focus* and *control*. But once these are addressed and overcome, games can be a very valuable addition to your repertoire as a teacher. So let's have a closer look at those two issues.

- *Focus.* A potential problem with games is that learners may have a *thoroughly enjoyable time* but remain unclear about what it is they have actually learnt or achieved.
- *Control.* Learners who are having a *thoroughly enjoyable time* are likely to exhibit behaviour that is more noisy, boisterous, and generally uncontrolled than usual. And, yes, for some classes, this is really saying something. It can also be difficult to predict the timing for games, which presents problems for those who like to have a water-tight lesson plan. And, of course, the very nature of games makes it difficult to predict their outcome.

So why is it worth it? Well, we've already seen the answer to that – twice. Games can provide learners with a *thoroughly enjoyable time*. And, in doing so, they:

- provide motivation;
- remind learners that learning can be fun;
- engage learners' attention;

- harness their competitive spirit;
- provide opportunities for achievement;
- challenge learners' preconceptions that lessons are boring;
- have the potential to draw in disengaged learners;
- have the potential to develop life skills such as communication, cooperation and teamwork.

TASK TASK TASK TASK TASK **TASK** TASK TASK TASK TASK **TASK** TASK

Advantages and pitfalls of games

Here are some teachers talking about their experience of incorporating games into their lesson planning. Read the accounts carefully, making a note for yourself of:

a) the ways in which games can be used to advantage in order to support learning, and how this might be applied in your own subject;

b) rules of thumb which should be borne in mind when using games as a method.

1. I decided to use a quiz format for the revision session. As well as using it for my own evaluation purposes, my aim was to help the learners identify the gaps in their own knowledge and give them an opportunity to fill those gaps by listening to their classmates' answers. I put them in two teams. This worked well because it injected some competition and teamwork into the activity. I kept score as well as adjudicating – so I was able to settle any disputes. But I let each team devise some of the questions to ask the other. That way they had more ownership over the whole thing. And we had clear rules. We negotiated those first of all. So they had ownership over those, too; and they pretty much abided by them. It all worked really well.

2. It was a communication game. This class tends to divide into cliques: noisy ones, quiet ones, interested ones . . . I wanted to draw them all together as well as get them thinking about how they listen and communicate. So I set them to solve a crime. They each had one clue. If they all shared their clues they'd have the answer. It all had to be done verbally. It got them talking. But it took them a long time. First off, the quiet ones didn't get a word in, so none of their clues went into the equation. When they finally got drawn into it and contributed their bit it was all solved and the class was really pleased with itself. But I don't think they'd have really understood what it was they'd learnt if I hadn't taken quite a long time afterwards to go over it with them. They saw the objective as, 'Solve the Crime'; and I saw the objectives as, 'Identify and implement the communication skills necessary for working cooperatively as a group.' That debrief session was all about moving their focus from the first to the second. And I did it by asking them things like *How might you have solved it more quickly?* and *What have you learnt from this about your own strengths or weaknesses as a communicator?* I had to help them clarify and consolidate what it was that they'd actually learnt. And, believe me, they'd learnt a lot.

3. I thought it would help them memorise the names of some of the tools if we played that game where you set objects out and remove one at a time and the players have to say which one has disappeared. I set it up using the OHP and a transparency with removable overlays. I showed it for a few minutes while we named all the tools together. Then I switched it off, removed one, and switched it on again. They had to name the one that was missing. We did this several times. It was difficult to stop them shouting the answers, but I wanted everyone to get involved, not just the quicker ones, so I appointed a couple of the more vocal learners to keep score. That gave the others a chance. Finally we played it one last time and they all had to write the answers down individually. That way they had to think about how to spell it as well!

Discussion

a) You've probably identified some or all of the following ways of using games to support learning.

- **The competition inherent in most games can act as a powerful motivator.**
- **Games are an effective way of developing skills of teamwork.**
- **Using a game as a learning method is also a way of uniting a fragmented or cliquish group of learners.**
- **Games provide an opportunity for everyone to get involved.**
- **They also provide opportunities for you to allocate important but less active roles to learners who might otherwise dominate or disrupt.**
- **Games are useful for evaluation purposes and as a means of formative assessment.**
- **They provide a non-threatening way for learners to identify the gaps in their own knowledge, skills or understanding.**
- **They provide opportunities for peer learning.**

b) You will have identified several pointers for successful practice from these teachers' accounts. They include the following rules of thumb:

- **learners are more likely to join in willingly if they feel a sense of ownership through, for example, devising questions;**
- **rules should be made clear at the outset;**
- **learners are more likely to abide by these rules if they involve some element of negotiation;**
- **the learning objectives must be clearly explained, before and afterwards;**
- **a debrief session is important in helping learners clarify and consolidate what it is that they've learnt.**

CLOSE FOCUS CLOSE FOCUS **CLOSE FOCUS** CLOSE FOCUS **CLOSE FOCUS**

Having read and reflected on this, to what extent do you think you could usefully employ games for teaching and supporting learning in your own subject area? If you think you could, you could make a note for yourself on your professional development action plan to try out this method, bearing in mind the rules of thumb we've just identified.

High risk strategies and methods 2: role-play

Role play can be a very useful method if we want learners to understand how it feels to be someone else. It's invaluable for letting them feel what it's like – just for a moment – to be in someone else's shoes. In other words, role-play is a method we'd be most likely to turn to if we are supporting learning which falls within the affective domain, because it helps learners to gain some insight into the feelings and attitudes of others. A good example of its use in the world of work is in the training of foster parents. They may be asked to role-play a situation in which there is an interaction between the social worker, the child, and the natural parents, and where they take on the role of any one of those three. The objective is that they gain some deeper understanding of how it might feel to be that person in that situation and, as a consequence, are better able to empathise with the others involved, and to interact with them with a greater degree of insight and sensitivity.

So why do we class role-play as a high risk method? The answer is simple: its purpose is to engage learners on an emotional level, and, once you have done so, it may prove difficult to get them to disengage. We can see an example of this in the scene that follows, where Mo is talking to his mentor about a recent crisis in one of his lessons.

Mentor: *I'm sorry I wasn't able to observe you teaching this morning. Tell me how it went.*

Mo: *Not very well, actually. In fact I go hot and cold every time I think about it.*

Mentor: *You don't look too good. So what happened? It was the level 2 Retail group, wasn't it?*

Mo: *Yes. And I wanted to find a way to explain the social skills they need when they're dealing with customers face-to-face – and particularly about how to handle complaints. So I decided to use role-play.*

Mentor: *Why role-play?*

Mo: *Well, I thought it would be fun for them – a more interesting way for me to present it. And I thought it would, you know, bring it to life. Well, it brought it to life alright. It certainly did that. At one point I thought I was going to have to call security.*

Mentor: *What happened?*

Mo: *It was ok at first. I thought they might be too self-conscious to participate properly, but once I'd got someone to be the assistant manager, I had plenty of volunteers to be customers. The trouble was, once it got started they all turned out to have cast themselves in the role of complaining customers. The first 'assistant manager' got upset and went and sat down, and another learner immediately volunteered to take her place. I suppose, with hindsight, I shouldn't have let him. He's got a bit of an aggressive manner at the best of times. And as soon as the next 'customer' makes a complaint, this lad more or less tells him to eff off; and then suddenly they're shouting; and then there's some shoving and spitting; and...*

Mentor: *So how did you calm it all down?*

Mo: *Not very well. I was saved by the bell – literally. The buzzer went for end of class and everyone piled out, including those two, still slinging abuse at each other. I think I'll stick to OHP slides and small group discussion in future.*

Mentor: *That'd be a shame. I think it was a really good idea to extend your repertoire of teaching methods, and quite brave to step outside your comfort zone like that. The thing is, role-play is very useful, but it has to be handled with care. The first question I'd want to ask you is: why didn't you use a simulation exercise instead?*

Mo: *What's the difference?*

Mentor: *In a simulation the players are still themselves. It's only the situation that's simulated. On the other hand, in a role-play the players are being asked to assume another identity – to assume the role of someone who isn't them.*

Mo: *Can you just explain that again?*

Mentor: *Well, you'd use a simulation exercise to allow learners to practise a skill – in this case, having polite interactions with customers – as themselves, but in a pretend situation. You'd use role-play if you wanted learners to understand how it might feel to be that customer, or to be that assistant manager, if you were working with them on the level of feelings and attitudes. The trouble is, when you give someone permission to be someone else, that can act as a great dis-inhibiter and release all sorts of behaviour they'd normally keep the lid on. It sounds to me as though you might have tried to get them to run before they could walk. You threw them into a confrontational role play before they'd had a chance to develop, through simulation, the skills necessary to handle it.*

Mo: *Yeah. That makes a lot of sense. So how would I have set it up differently if I'd run it as a simulation?*

Mentor: *For a start, you'd have stood in as the customer yourself – complaining or otherwise. That gives you much more control over the situation. You can stress the fact that you're still you, but that this is now a shop, not a classroom, and one of the learners is going to pretend it's the very shop he or she does their work experience in. And then you run through whatever interaction you're going to have, and then you all discuss how it went. All nice and controlled. And nobody gets the idea they have permission to act out their inner psycho.*

Mo: *And if, after that, I want to move on to role-play, it'd be to help the learners understand the customer's point of view?*

Mentor: *Exactly. But with a volatile group like that, you'd make sure it was very tightly structured. You'd give the players role cards telling them exactly who they are and what point they want to get across; and you'd keep the drama to a minimum. And, if you were wise, you'd probably keep the role of assistant manager for yourself so that the situation couldn't escalate into trouble even if the learners wanted it to.*

Mo: *I wish I'd talked to you before.*

Mentor: *But it was a valuable experience.*

Mo: *Maybe. But what would I have done if that buzzer hadn't sounded?*

Mentor: *Ah, well, that's another key thing to remember about role-play. People often get right into character – because in a way you've given them permission to access all sorts of emotions that they keep the lid on when they're being themselves – and the only way you calm it down is by easing them back out again. So you need to remind them it was just a role. This may sound corny, but the classic way to do this is to get them to repeat their real name, their real identity, a couple of times. And then maybe shake hands with anyone they've been aggressive towards. But really, even better is to structure the whole thing so that this doesn't become an issue. Role cards are the key. And a thorough debrief, involving the whole group. Actually, from my point of view, the main drawback of role-play is that it's difficult to get everyone involved. I think a really good idea is to devise a set of tasks or questions for the non-players – the rest of the group – so that they have an active role as observers, rather than just a passive one.*

Mo: *You know what? It was my lucky day when they made you my mentor.*

Mentor: *Yeah yeah.*

So what can we learn from this? Let's summarise the mentor's guidance and what Mo has learned here.

- **We need to ask ourselves whether role-play really is the most appropriate method. Are our learning objectives in the affective domain? Do we want learners to understand how it might feel to *be in someone else's shoes*? Are we wanting to address their attitudes, values, or feelings? If so, let's go ahead with the role-play. But first...**
- **Let's remember to handle it with care.**
- **All learners who don't have a role to play should be given a clear task or set of questions which will help them to structure their observation of the role-play.**
- **It might be advisable to keep a major role for ourselves (e.g. the customer with a complaint) in order to maintain control over the scenario.**

- The role-play should be tightly structured. This means giving learners clear instructions and guidelines.
- It's useful to give the role players clear details of their role and their point of view. This can be done by using role cards.
- When the role-play is over, the whole group should be involved in a thorough debrief in order to clarify all the learning points which the activity highlighted.
- Role players themselves should be eased out of their roles, encouraged to repeat their real identity if necessary, and also encouraged to make peace with any player with whom they might have been in conflict while in role.

CLOSE FOCUS CLOSE FOCUS **CLOSE FOCUS** CLOSE FOCUS **CLOSE FOCUS**

How appropriate would role-play be for teaching and supporting learning in your own subject area? If you judge that it might be useful to do, you could make a note for yourself on your professional development action plan to try out this method, bearing in mind the guidelines we've summarised from Mo's experience.

High risk strategies and methods 3: simulation

Mo's mentor suggested that a simulation might have been easier to handle but that it was designed to serve an entirely different purpose. Let's explore briefly what she meant by this. She tells Mo that:

'you'd use a simulation exercise to allow learners to practise a skill.'

You can probably think of several examples of learning through simulation which can be found in most general PCET colleges. There is the training restaurant used by Hospitality and Catering, and the office environment used in Business Studies. There are the salons used by Hairdressing and Beauty Therapy. There's the motor vehicle workshop used by Mechanical Engineering, and the building site run by Trowel Trades. In all of these learning environments learners are trying out their newly acquired skills in surroundings which simulate the real work place. They aren't pretending to be someone else. They are being themselves, but practising what they have learnt as though it was for real. This is what we mean by simulation.

But simulations don't have to be confined to purpose-built learning environments like the kitchens in Hospitality and Catering. With a little imagination and creativity, simulations can be used in any classroom. In a Media class you can set up a simulation of a newsroom; in a Leisure and Tourism class you can run a simulation of a travel agent's office. So why are simulations included here with 'high risk' and non-standard methods? The answer is because, in setting up a simulation exercise, we are to some extent relinquishing the tight control we would have over the lesson if we were to use – say – the lecture or the small group discussion. The moment we step into, or create, a replica of the real world of work, we invite in the unpredictable. Look at what Mo writes in his reflective journal after taking on board his mentor's advice:

So when I taught the other level 2 group I decided to do the 'Responding to the Customer' bit as a simulation instead. It worked much better. But I still had a real problem with timing. I tried to give as many learners as possible the opportunity to deal with 'a customer' (me!), and I built in some debrief time after each simulation so that we could discuss how the situation had been handled. But some of the learners took so long either to get up and join in when it was their turn, or to settle down and behave like an assistant manager when they did join in, that we began to run out of time and I had to cut the interactions and debriefs shorter and shorter. I think next time I'll run this over two sessions. And it worked well having me as the customer. It meant I could at least keep control over the tone of the interactions and not let them degenerate into arguments. And it also meant I could vary the demands I was making so they were appropriate to the different learners' current levels of achievement.

We see from Mo's comments here that he's identified two main difficulties that can confront the teacher when trying to implement a simulation.

- **Learners may be reluctant to join in.**
- **Timings may be difficult to control.**

But he's also discovered some rules of thumb for getting the most learning opportunities out of a simulation, and helping it to run smoothly.

- **Ensure as many learners as possible 'have a go'; preferably all of them.**
- **Ensure there is adequate time for a debriefing where the learners are encouraged to evaluate their own and each others' performance of the task.**
- **Take an active part yourself so that you can prompt learners, keep up the pace, maintain appropriate behaviour, and provide differentiation in line with learners' needs.**

CLOSE FOCUS CLOSE FOCUS **CLOSE FOCUS** CLOSE FOCUS **CLOSE FOCUS**

Perhaps simulations would be appropriate for teaching and supporting learning in your own subject area. If you think that they might, but have never used them before, you could make a note for yourself on your professional development action plan to try out this method, bearing in mind the guidelines we've summarised from Mo's experience. If, in your view, they would be inappropriate for the teaching of your specialist subject, you may find it useful to discuss your reasons for this with your mentor or critical friend.

Developing new skills: e-learning

So far in this chapter we've looked at three very effective methods of teaching and supporting learning which may be less familiar to us than, say, group work and discussion, because they are what we term 'high risk'. We're going to turn now to another method which lies outside the comfort zone of many teachers, but for a very different reason. E-learning and e-tutoring is unfamiliar ground to many because it is relatively new. It is a way of learning which most teachers will not have experienced when they themselves were learners. In fact, it would probably be true to say that, in the face of rapid ILT (Information Learning Technology) developments, many teachers find themselves firmly in the role of learner.

The skills and strategies necessary for effective e-tutoring are not all the same as those required for face-to-face teaching, although there are significant areas of overlap. We'll look at some of these points of divergence in a moment. But first, let's acquaint ourselves with some of the terminology which will make it easier for us to describe the processes of e-learning.

- *Distributed learning.* In our traditional learning mode – the one we're all familiar with – the learners are all together in one place: the classroom, the workshop, the studio. With e-learning the learners are usually *not* in one place. They are *distributed* over a geographical area. This may be a campus, a city, a county, or the whole country. Your learners might even be distributed worldwide. Distributed learning makes impossible many of the methods we normally use to teach and support learning. We may still have a group of learners, but the way we manage their learning will necessarily be quite different from the way we would manage it if they were all in the same room with us, able to see us and see each other as a group.
- *Asynchronous learning.* In the mode of teaching and learning we are most familiar with, we will be interacting with all the learners in our class at the same time. This may be 9am until 11am on Wednesdays, or 6pm until 9pm on Thursdays, or whatever. The point is, all the learners will be learning at the same time, and we too will be there at the same time, supporting them. This is what we term synchronous learning. It's synchronised. It's happening at the same time. E-learning, on the other hand, normally allows individual learners to access their learning at any time. Their learning is therefore *asynchronous*. It's not synchronised. They're not all accessing it at the same time. This has enormous implications for the way you teach them and support their learning.
- *Asynchronous distributed learning.* In many cases, a cohort of e-learners can be accessing their learning at different times *and* from different places. And so we describe this as asynchronous distributed learning – not a phrase you'd want to use with a mouthful of crackers.

TASK TASK TASK TASK TASK TASK TASK TASK TASK TASK TASK

So how can this be managed? Take some time to think through the implications, for both the teacher and the learner, of asynchronous distributed learning. Make some notes under the following headings.

1. What specific barriers to learning might arise for the learner using this mode of study?
2. How might the teacher overcome them?
3. In what ways will the management of learning differ if you are supporting learners online?
4. What skills will you need to add to your repertoire as teacher in order to manage this effectively?

You might find it useful to discuss these issues and arrive at answers as part of a group, or with a colleague who specialises in e-learning.

Discussion

1. An obvious potential barrier to learning arises from the fact that most e-learning is text-based. E-learners will need, therefore, a level of literacy and communication skills appropriate to the programme. This is really an issue about access and recruitment. This aside, the main barrier to learning identified by most e-learners and e-tutors is the lack of face-to-face contact between teacher and learners and between the learners themselves. We often take this social aspect of learning for granted. This is because it underpins our traditional model of what learning is about. Relationships are an important part of this model; and, as we saw in Chapter 7, they are even considered by Humanist theorists such as Rogers (1983) to be absolutely central to the learning process.
2. So how do we, as teachers, overcome this? One way is to ensure we give the effective one-to-one support which e-learning makes possible. This involves, for example, being responsive to the messages and questions which learners post online. Another way we

can compensate for the loss of the social dimension is by facilitating online contact with other learners through designing cooperative online tasks and facilitating online discussions.

3. In what ways will the management of learning differ? Well, perhaps it's easier to begin our answer by identifying those aspects of the management of learning that will remain the same.

   - **We still need to set clear objectives and make sure learners are aware of them.**
   - **We still need to brief learners clearly for each task.**
   - **We still need to organise plenaries to review and consolidate learning at the end of each topic.**
   - **We still need to look for the best ways to motivate the learners and keep them motivated (particularly in the face of (1) above).**
   - **We still need to create interesting and engaging activities which will remind learners that learning can be enjoyable.**
   - **We still need to pay due attention to issues of differentiation and inclusion.**
   - **We still need to provide timely, clear and constructive feedback.**

You can probably carry on adding to this list yourself. But what is different about the way that e-learning is managed? Some professionals with extensive experience of e-learning (for example, Salmon 2002) suggest that the roles of teacher and learner are sufficiently different in an e-learning context to justify the use of a different terminology. Thus we get the term *'participant'* for the e-learner, and *'e-moderator'* for the teacher. The latter term shouldn't be confused with our everyday understanding of the moderator's role in the context of vocational qualifications. It is used in e-learning to emphasise the fact that the tutor designs and mediates the learning process, rather than being the source of the subject knowledge. In e-learning the source of the subject knowledge is the on-screen texts and the shared knowledge and understanding of the participants.

CLOSE FOCUS CLOSE FOCUS CLOSE FOCUS CLOSE FOCUS CLOSE FOCUS

We've explored the use of the term, 'e-moderator'; so now let's think about that other term: 'participant'. What does it imply about the role of the e-learner and the process of e-learning?

So, in the context of e-learning, how would we conduct, for example, a group discussion? Well, we have a term for this, too. It is known as a *threaded discussion.* It doesn't happen in 'real time', because participants will access the discussion at different points and make their contributions or state their point of view. The teacher's role in this is to mediate the discussion, keep it focused, pose the appropriate questions to draw out learners' tacit knowledge or help them to develop their ideas further. The threads are the individual learners' contributions, which they can access and review. The discussion may take place over a day, a week, a month. It will be up to the teachers to draw it to a close, perhaps with a plenary, and summarise the learning points. The contributions of individual participants – and their progress as the discussion develops – may form a valuable source of formative assessment. In some ways this is not so very different from managing a 'real time' live discussion; but in others it's very different indeed – not least in the fact that the timescale allows for substantial reflection and development of ideas.

Salmon (2002) presents a model of online learning which presents learning as a series of five steps. As learners proceed through the steps, the teacher's role changes and the amount of online interaction necessary to support them is reduced. Adapted to illustrate the management of learning, we can summarise her model like this.

- **Step 1: Teacher addresses access issues and motivational needs.**
- **Step 2: Teacher facilitates familiarisation and socialisation between participants online.**
- **Step 3: Teacher facilitates tasks and use of learning materials to support acquisition of subject knowledge.**
- **Step 4: Teacher facilitates construction of new knowledge, skills, understanding.**
- **Step 5: Teacher is responsive and supportive as participants reflect on their learning and work towards individual goals.**

(Adapted from Salmon (2002) p.11)

In this model the teacher/tutor/e-moderator moves from being proactive and directive (Step 1) to being responsive and supportive (Step 5), while the learner moves in the opposite direction, from being dependent and/or reactive (Step 1), to being independent and proactive (Step 5).

CLOSE FOCUS CLOSE FOCUS CLOSE FOCUS CLOSE FOCUS CLOSE FOCUS

How well do you think this model of learning would also describe traditional, face-to-face teaching and learning?

4. You'll have realised, from the list we compiled under management of learning, that you already possess, as a teacher, many of the skills essential for effectively supporting e-learning. So what do you need to add to this list? You've probably come up with some of the following.
   - **Confidence and competence in ILT (Information Learning Technology) skills.**
   - **A different way of managing your time. Teaching via e-learning will involve changing your working patterns. Your contact with learners won't be 'timetabled' in the traditional way.**
   - **A different way of thinking about your role. The learning 'content' will probably be mostly text-based, and so the purpose of your role will be to facilitate and support, rather than to 'deliver' your specialist subject. The skills of facilitation, will, however, be extremely useful in the traditional classroom, too.**

A SUMMARY OF **KEY POINTS**

In this chapter we have:
> considered ways in which we can extend our repertoire of teaching methods;
> explored some methods which are sometimes regarded as 'high risk';
> considered the advantages of using games, role-play and simulation as methods for supporting learning;
> identified some rules of thumb for the effective application of these methods;
> explored some of the terminology surrounding e-learning;
> identified appropriate strategies for teaching online.

Branching options

If you're using this book to support your professional development leading to a teaching qualification or other CPD accreditation, you may find it useful to choose a question according to the level for which you are currently studying. These are indicated in brackets.

Alternatively, you may like to work through all three questions.

1. Reflection and self-evaluation (NQF level 5)

a) Look back over your scheme of work or lesson plans for this year so far, and identify and make a list of the methods and learner activities you have used.

b) Reflect for a moment on your list by considering the following questions.
- **To what extent is the range of methods I use restricted by my specialist subject?**
- **To what extent is the range restricted by my own unwillingness to move beyond my comfort zone?**
- **To what extent is the range restricted by the environment, resources, or accommodation?**

c) Identify the opportunities for, and the possible advantages of, introducing a less familiar method and/or an element of e-learning into your planned teaching.

2. Evaluation: theory and practice (NQF level 6)

a) In this chapter we've identified some of the advantages of utilising less familiar or more 'high risk' teaching methods. To what extent can those advantages be explained by reference to theories of learning?

b) What do you consider to be the advantages and disadvantages of e-learning, and how would you use learning theory to support your answer?

(To address these questions you might find it useful to look again at the discussions about theories of learning in Chapter 7.)

3. Engaging critically with the literature (NQF level 7: M level)

Gilly Salmon (2002) suggests that, in an e-learning context, the role of the teacher *is one of process designer and promoter and mediator of the learning, rather than content expert.* (p4)

a) To what extent do you think this would be true in your own subject specialist area, and why?

b) What models of teaching and learning would support our applying this definition to traditional teaching contexts as well as to e-learning?

REFERENCES AND FURTHER READING

Gibbs, G. and Habeshaw, T. (1992) *253 Ideas For Your Teaching.* Bristol: Technical and Educational Services.

Rogers, C. (1983) *Freedom to Learn for the 80s.* Columbus, OH: Merrill.

Salmon, G. (2000) *E-moderating: The Key to Teaching and Learning Online.* London: Kogan Page.

Salmon, G. (2002) *E-tivities: the Key to Active Online Learning.* London: Kogan Page.

Saunders, D. (ed.) (1996) *The Simulation and Gaming Yearbook vol. 4: Games and Simulations to Enhance Quality Learning.* London: Kogan Page.

Weller, M. (2002) *Delivering Learning on the Net.* London: Kogan Page.

12

Assessment for learning 1: assessing needs; supporting access and progression

The objectives of this chapter

This chapter focuses on the importance of making an initial assessment of your learners' needs and previous experiences of learning. It looks at ways in which you can use this information to make judgements about learners' individual needs for support and how you can best meet these. It also explores the teacher's role in relation to access and progression. It will help you to:

- **design and use assessment as a tool for learning and progression, including initial and formative assessment (ES1; EK1.1; EP1.1);**
- **monitor learner progress (ES4; ES5);**
- **apply theories and principles of assessment (EK1.1; EK2.3);**
- **devise assessment for individual learners (*Differentiation*), taking account of issues of diversity and equality (EK2.1; EP2.1; EK2.4; EP2.4);**
- **encourage self assessment and peer assessment (EK1.3; EP1.3);**
- **recognise the importance of giving clear and accurate guidance to learners about employment and learning opportunities and how they might use their transferable skills in your specialist area (CK4.2; CP4.2; FK3.1; FP3.1);**
- **recognise the importance of encouraging learners to seek further learning opportunities and opportunities for progression, and to use appropriate available services (FK1.1; FP1.1; FS1; FS4).**

Introduction: why is initial assessment necessary?

Your first meeting with a group of learners who are embarking on what is, for them, a new programme of learning, represents the convergence of three key components in the learning process: the teacher, the learners and the syllabus or specifications of the course which has brought them together. Two of these components you are already familiar with (or at least it's to be hoped you are!). You have a thorough knowledge and secure understanding of what it is the learners are required to learn and, through the keeping of a reflective journal, you are coming to know yourself as a teacher fairly well – both in terms of your preferred teaching styles and of how securely your subject knowledge fits the demands of the syllabus. The third component, however, you probably know very little about at this stage. Or rather, you will have information but it will not necessarily be the information you most need to help the learners learn. You'll have their names, their ages, their current qualifications. But, nevertheless, these learners, in terms of their individual strengths and weaknesses, their individual learning needs, will at this stage represent the unknown component in the equation.

The class known for convenience sake as HNC Computing, or Year 2 Sport and Leisure, or Functional Numeracy Level 2, is unlikely to be an homogeneous group – a collection of people with identical past experiences of learning and identical current learning needs. The 'class' is a group of disparate individuals, each with their own needs and expectations. The following is a list of some of the things you probably won't know about them.

- **Why they are doing this current course.**
- **How their previous experience has made them feel about education and training.**
- **Their level of confidence.**
- **How much the previous knowledge they have gained through experience or learning will be of relevance to their current course or programme.**
- **Whether they have personal circumstances or undeclared learning difficulties that are likely to affect their commitment or concentration in the short or long term.**
- **How they relate with other members of the group.**
- **Whether they will seek attention or be reluctant to speak up.**
- **What activities best suit their individual learning styles.**
- **Their expectations of the course or programme.**
- **Their level of motivation.**

This is not an exclusive list. You may be able to suggest many more unknown factors we could add to it. What it makes quite clear, however, is that when a new group of learners embarks upon a programme of learning it is we, the teachers, who first of all have some essential and very rapid learning to do.

You will sometimes hear teachers talking about the assessment of entry behaviour. This can be confusing for a new or student teacher because it doesn't really refer to behaviour at all but rather to the learner's level of knowledge and skills on entering the course or programme of learning. Ascertaining the entry behaviour of a learner is important for two reasons. It helps to identify whether he or she will need ongoing additional support in coping with the demands of the programme or initial help to 'bridge' the gap between his or her current skills and knowledge and those required to begin his or her current programme. And, secondly, it can help to identify relevant areas of skills and knowledge the learner already possesses, either through prior experience or prior learning – in which case he or she can be advised to apply for accreditation through the process referred to as APEL or APL – Accreditation of Prior Experience and/or Learning. Entry behaviour, though, is only a part of what we need to know about the learner, as the list we have just seen makes clear. So how do we go about discovering some of the other information we need about learners if we are to be as effective as possible in helping them to learn?

Meeting a new group of learners

Let's have a look first at what one teacher, Jodie, has to say about the first meeting with a new group of learners. The learners are newly enrolled on an Access course designed to prepare them for entry to higher education, where they hope to apply for degree courses in the area of social sciences. The module Jodie is to teach contains elements of sociology and law.

TASK TASK **TASK** TASK **TASK** **TASK** TASK **TASK** TASK **TASK** **TASK** TASK

As you read the extract below from Jodie's journal, consider the following questions:

- **What assumptions had Jodie made in planning the lesson?**
- **What might Jodie have usefully learnt in the course of the lesson about individual learners' needs or prior experiences?**
- **Can you identify any specific points at which Jodie made an unwise or ill-informed decision?**
- **What advice would you give to Jodie about how to plan the next session with this group?**
- **How might Jodie have made this journal entry more useful in terms of professional development and the planning of future practice?**

---

12 September

The new Access group. There were nine of them. I wanted to start out the way I mean to carry on – lots of discussion, lots of learner involvement. Get things buzzing right from the start. They need to know the course isn't a doddle and that you don't just get into HE by wanting to. And they also need to feel they're getting value for money, and that they're not wasting time and that they go away having learnt something. It was timetabled for room 42 which was a bit of luck because it's a nice room, all set up for PowerPoint and video, and plenty of space to move the furniture about. So I got in there half an hour early at 8.30 and put the tables into rows so they'd know there was going to be some serious learning going on, but well spaced out so they could sit where they felt most comfortable. What I'd decided to do was jump straight in with something that was interesting and that they could probably relate to – and that was the role of the lay magistrate. And I thought we'd have a look at a fictional case and they could get in small groups and decide on the sentence and then we'd see how much agreement there was between the groups. This would get them thinking about issues like subjectivity and arbitrariness and hopefully raise some strong opinions so I could get a whole-group discussion going. I chose an offence they'd all be likely to have an opinion about as well – ABH [actual bodily harm] – a bloke up for hitting his wife.

I'd done a bit on PowerPoint about the role of the lay magistrate and about the bloke's past form and present circumstances which would inform the decision about the sentence. I was still trying to set this up and check it at 8.50 when the first learner arrived. She could see I was busy but she came straight over and started bending my ear – telling me her life history and everything else. She was quite a lot older than me and I didn't want to seem rude, but I ended up not being able to take in anything she said and not being able to get the PowerPoint presentation sorted either. The rest of the learners started to arrive. When I looked up again there were three women who looked to be in their twenties and seemed to know each other, and they'd gone straight to the back and were laughing. They kept looking over at me and then away again, and I wondered whether p'raps they were laughing at me. It made me feel a bit uncomfortable. The first woman, Tina, was still talking away at me. A bloke came in – white hair, in his fifties maybe – and sat down right at the front; and then a young bloke, who looked a bit lost and asked Tina if it was the right room – obviously thought she was the teacher. And then two other youngish women, separately, who sat down in the middle well away from each other and from the young lad. That was eight. One missing, but it was time to start. I was just going to suggest to Tina that she might like to go and sit down, when she suddenly ups and says to the three at the back: 'Come on, ladies. Don't sit right back there. Come and join the rest of us.' They just stare at her for a bit, and then one of them says: 'Do we have to?' And I realise <u>they</u> think she's the teacher as well.

So I decide to establish a bit of order. I clap my hands and say: 'Right, folks, let's make a start. Tina, would you go and sit down, please.' And then I introduce the lesson. I say a few words about the Access course as a whole, and the standard of work that'll be required. And then I get straight on to the topic of the lesson. Having failed to get the PowerPoint to play nicely I have to just talk at them but I think to myself that's no bad thing because they'll have to get use to this if they're going on to HE. I would've used the whiteboard but because I was planning to use PowerPoint I haven't brought any markers. So I just talk. I keep expecting Tina to interrupt, but she doesn't say anything. In fact she doesn't even make eye contact. So that's a relief. The three at the back just stare at me. They don't seem to be taking any notes. The white-haired bloke, though, he's writing away. Every time I pause for breath I can hear his pencil scrabbling along trying to catch me up. The younger bloke is still going through his bag and pockets for a pen when I'm already half-way through what I've got to say. Needs to learn to be more organised, obviously.

When I get to the specific details of the case we're going to look at, one of the women sitting on her own says: 'They ought to hang him.' I pretend I haven't heard. The white-haired bloke looks round to see who's spoken, and there's a bit of sniggering from the back. Soon after this the last learner arrives, 25 minutes late but not particularly apologetic. He sits down on the end of the middle row nearest the door, but for some reason keeps his jacket and gloves on. He's probably somewhere in his thirties.

When I finish giving them the background to the task, I tell them to get into groups of three to decide on the sentence. Nobody makes a move, except the three at the back who get their heads together and start working on it. So I tell the rest of them they've only got 10 minutes so they'd better get on with it. Tina turns her chair around so she can work with the quiet woman on the middle row and the learner who's just come in; which leaves the white-haired bloke, the young lad and the woman who said 'Hang him' – and they're all sitting in different parts of the room so I have to sort them out and get them to move their chairs, and finally they're all working – except the latecomer who, of course, has missed most of the background and the briefing. So I think to myself: well, Tina'll fill him in. She'll like doing that. So I go over and ask her and she more or less says: 'I'd have thought that was your job.' The trouble is, she's got this really loud penetrating voice, so everybody heard her say it. Anyway, I sat in with that group so I could bring the late bloke up to speed. Tina for some reason had gone from having too much to say to the other extreme and just wasn't joining in at all. It ended up as a discussion between the quiet woman and the late man – and hardly a discussion, really. He insisted that all of the sentencing options were too severe and that the police shouldn't get involved in 'domestic matters'; and even though she argued quite well that the culprit should at least do some community service, the bloke just laughed. Before I could weigh in, there was a sudden raising of voices in the group with the two blokes in it. It's a horrible feeling when you hear something like that – a feeling like it's all going to go out of control. I got over to them as quickly as I could and found the white-haired man and the Hang-him woman in the middle of a biff, and the young lad bright red and looking as though he was going to die with embarrassment. I couldn't really get to the bottom of it, but it seemed what had happened was that Hang-him had accused the men of wanting to give a lenient sentence because all men sympathised with wife-beaters. Something like that. I tried to joke them out of it, but then she started on this heated argument with me. She was so angry she was almost in tears. So I decided I'd better cut my losses, call time and bring the whole class back together again.

I said to them all: 'So, if you had had the task of lay magistrate, what sentence would you have decided was appropriate? Let's start with you three.' And I pointed to the three women at the back, because they seemed at least to have been getting on with it. They'd decided on probation, with the argument that therefore if he did it again he'd go to prison. So I asked Tina's group whether they agreed. Tina said she had no idea because she hadn't been able to hear a word they said. The late bloke just folded his arms and grinned and shook his head as though in disbelief. When I asked him for his response he said something to the effect that if you started putting everybody who hit their wife in jail there'd be no room for the real criminals. So then Hang-him just went ballistic, shouting at him and pointing, and he just sat there with his arms folded, laughing, and the three women at the back, watching it like a tennis match, mouths open. So I threw up my hands and said: 'Okay, okay. Let's have break. Back here in 15 minutes.' It felt like a nightmare and I was desperate to get out, just for a few minutes and have a think about what to do. But although most of them went off for a break, the white-haired bloke stayed behind to tell me that the young bloke had difficulty taking notes and wanted to tape-record my input but was too embarrassed to ask. So I said to tell him that was fine. And then the white-haired bloke – Tim, it was – started telling me all about how he works for the parole board at the prison, and about the sort of decisions they have to make – quite interesting, but I hadn't really got time to listen. Then the quiet woman, the one who'd been in the group with Tina and the late bloke, came up and asked whether I'd be able to supply her with copies of any overheads or board work because she was partially sighted and even if she sat at the front she couldn't always read easily from the screen or board. So I said that was fine, too. All this left me about five minutes to rescue the lesson. But then I remembered the video on young offenders, which was fairly relevant to what we'd just done. So I raced off and fetched it. It filled the second half of the lesson, thank goodness, although with bright sunshine through the windows and no blinds the picture was a bit indistinct.

Tina and the Hang-him woman didn't come back after the break. I don't know whether to be concerned or relieved. I assume it means they've decided the course isn't for them. You do tend to get a high drop-out rate on these sorts of programmes.

What assumptions had Jodie made in planning the lesson?

It becomes evident, as we read the journal extract, that Jodie's planning, teaching and classroom management are based on assumptions about the learners and the course which, even after the events described, the journal never really explores or questions. These are some of the assumptions you may have identified.

> *'I wanted to start out the way I mean to carry on – lots of discussion, lots of learner involvement. Get things buzzing right from the start. They need to know the course isn't a doddle and that you don't just get into HE by wanting to.'*

Here Jodie makes several assumptions. One is that the first lesson with a new group should launch straight in to the course content or syllabus, before knowing anything about the experiences, skills and attitudes within that group which might facilitate or impede the process of learning. Another is that a new group – new to each other and new to the teacher – can comfortably cope with 'lots of discussion'. Yet another is that the first session with a group should set the tone and style for the rest, allowing no lead-in time for introductions. When we first meet someone new, in whatever context, we would normally spend some time getting to know a little about him or her in order to pick up clues about how to conduct our interaction. This applies equally to the meeting between a teacher and a new class. It also applies to the learners, who are meeting each other for the first time. Jodie seems to be assuming here that the teacher need play no part in ensuring learners who will be working together have adequate time initially to get to know one another.

Also implicit within this passage is Jodie's assumption that the learners are likely to see access to HE as something easily achieved. This is an assumption about their assumptions! And the chances are it is a quite mistaken one. Adults returning to education are often underconfident rather than overconfident about their abilities. The necessity of impressing upon them that this course will not be 'a doddle' may be less appropriate at this stage than the need to reassure the learners and help them to build their confidence.

> *'So I got in there half an hour early at 8.30 and put the tables into rows so that they'd know there was going to be some serious learning going on, but well spaced out so they could sit where they felt most comfortable.'*

There's an interesting assumption here that learners will equate desks set out formally in rows with the idea of 'serious learning', and that such a classroom layout will signal this to them as they enter the classroom. It is equally possible that rows of desks will remind them of school, or of formal examinations; and Jodie has no idea – and appears uninterested in – whether this will have positive or negative associations for individuals in the group, which might affect levels of motivation.

> *'[There] were three women who looked to be in their twenties and seemed to know each other The first woman, Tina, was still talking away at me. A bloke came in – white hair, in his fifties maybe – and sat down right at the front; and then a young bloke, who looked a bit lost... And then two other youngish women, separately...'*

Jodie gives us descriptive information about the learners – their approximate age, their manner, where they sit – but there seems to be an underlying assumption that this is the only information about them of any relevance. There is not even any effort made to identify each individual against his or her name on the class list or register. They are seen in terms of their gender, age and position in the classroom, as though only these factors differentiate them and that their learning needs can all be assumed to be identical. Jodie's assumption is, for example, that they are all able to take notes as appropriate and that they are all able to see the board or screen clearly. These assumptions can be represented like this:

learner = learner = learner = learner

In the context of learner needs and experiences, this equation can never be correct.

> *'I would've used the whiteboard but because I was planning to use PowerPoint I haven't brought any markers. So I just talk.'*

Poor Jodie. But there's a moral here. Technology can sometimes let us down. Just as in lesson planning, where it is always important to have a 'Plan B', so with resources. Just in case the OHP doesn't work, or isn't there, and just in case the PowerPoint can't be coaxed to work, always carry a whiteboard pen. And just in case the whiteboard pen dries up, always carry another one! Jodie assumed the technology would work. This is never an entirely safe assumption.

What might Jodie have usefully learnt in the course of the lesson about individual learners' needs and prior experiences?

> *'She could see I was busy but she came straight over and started bending my ear – telling me her life history and everything else... I was just going to suggest to Tina*

that she might like to go and sit down, when she suddenly ups and says to the three at the back: "Come on, ladies. Don't sit right back there. Come and join the rest of us."'

How are we to interpret Tina's behaviour? Jodie sees her first of all as a bit of a nuisance, a cause of distraction from the job of setting up the PowerPoint presentation. The assumption being made here is that she is pushy and overconfident; and this seems to be reinforced by her appearing to usurp the teacher's role. But look at what happens when Jodie decides (almost literally) to put her in her place:

'Right, folks, let's make a start. Tina, would you go and sit down, please.'

From this moment on, Tina avoids making eye contact, contributes nothing to the lesson and does not return after the break. What are we to make of this? Jodie blithely assumes she has found the work too difficult and, in any case, seems relieved not to have her back. But we could put an entirely different interpretation upon Tina's behaviour from the moment she enters the classroom. Perhaps, like many adult learners, she is underconfident rather than overconfident. Jodie doesn't listen with any close attention to the 'life history' Tina is telling; and this is a pity because that 'history' may well relate to her current needs and aspirations as a learner. Perhaps Tina is saying it's been a long time since she was in a classroom; perhaps she is seeking reassurance. And perhaps – just perhaps – her intervention in encouraging the women at the back to move forward was intended to be helpful, to establish solidarity with the teacher rather than to threaten the teacher's position. When Jodie tells her to 'go and sit down please', Tina may interpret this as being treated like a child just when she is trying to negotiate her status as an adult learner. Her own apprehensiveness at returning to learning may well make it impossible for her to see that Jodie's response arises out of insecurity. Jodie is the teacher; and it may be Tina's belief – although we know better – that teachers never feel insecure. From our position as detached observers we are able to see that Tina's behaviour offers valuable clues about her learning needs. This is something that Jodie, even after writing up the journal, has not even begun to consider.

What else have we learnt? We have learnt that the quiet young man lacks note-taking skills and – just as important – we have learnt he is reticent about approaching the teacher to seek help. This means we cannot assume everything is well with him just because he remains quiet. We have also learnt that Tim has experience that may be valuable and is certainly relevant to the course. We have learnt, too, that the younger man has confided in him and that Tim is prepared to adopt an avuncular or protective role towards him. Another useful thing we have learnt is that Tina (and this may possibly apply to others in the class, too) would like the teacher to repeat responses made by other learners in order to make sure they are clear and audible to the rest of the class. And we have learnt the quiet young woman is partially sighted and may be unable to see clearly what is on the screen or board.

All these are very useful pieces of information for the teacher. Jodie happens upon them quite by accident when in fact this first lesson should have been designed with a view to discovering these learning needs and all the other information the teacher will need to be most effective in facilitating learning.

There are other things Jodie might usefully have learnt from this lesson, although the journal extract suggests they have not really been taken into account. One is that the learner whom Jodie refers to as the 'latecomer' seems to enjoy provoking controversy. We cannot be sure whether he actually holds the views he expresses, but the simple fact he enjoys expressing them means he is a potential cause of offence to others. The learner whom Jodie refers to as 'Hang-him' also expresses strong views with which she exhibits some emotional involvement. Factors such as these are important for the teacher to bear in mind when planning learning activities and choosing topics for discussion.

CLOSE FOCUS CLOSE FOCUS CLOSE FOCUS CLOSE FOCUS CLOSE FOCUS

What evidence is there from the journal extract that Jodie took any of these factors into account as the lesson progressed? What use could Jodie make of this information when planning future lessons for these students?

Can you identify any specific points at which Jodie made an unwise or ill-informed decision?

We have covered some of these indirectly already. Jodie's rather brusque treatment of Tina could be considered unwise and ill-informed since it seems to result in alienating and driving away a previously well-motivated and potentially valuable member of the group, as well as causing a learner unnecessary distress. The formal arrangement of the desks into rows was probably not a good decision, particularly on the first occasion the group met. It did not encourage any sense of group cohesion nor facilitate group discussion. The learners were not only not able to make eye contact with one another but some would see no more of their fellow learners than the backs of their heads. It was not an arrangement likely to make the learners feel sufficiently at ease to talk with confidence about themselves, their experiences, their needs and concerns. A boardroom or horseshoe arrangement of tables would have been more appropriate in this instance.

At various points during the lesson, Jodie makes the decision to discount or ignore certain signals that some of the class may be experiencing difficulties or even distress. There is the decision to ignore the fact that Tina has gone quiet – it's seen as a relief rather than a sign something has been mishandled – and the decision to ignore the young man's search for a pen, which is seen as a sign of disorganisation. If Jodie had paused at this point and offered a pen it might have provided the learner with an opportunity to ask whether he can tape-record the session instead. Ideally, of course, the teacher should have ascertained at the outset the learners' level of confidence about note-taking and offered help and advice as appropriate, particularly if this is a programme of learning for which such a skill is essential.

There is also the question of Jodie ignoring the woman's comment of 'Hang him':

> 'When I get to the specific details of the case we're going to look at, one of the women sitting on her own says: "They ought to hang him." I pretend I haven't heard. The white-haired bloke looks round to see who's spoken, and there's a bit of sniggering from the back.'

Of course, we don't know why Jodie decided to ignore this, although we might make an informed guess. Perhaps it's out of a wish not to encourage a potential trouble-maker. Perhaps it seems, as it did with Tina, that the teacher's authority is being challenged. The learners, however, do not ignore it. They are probably curious to hear the justification for this rather extreme statement. Some of you may agree with Jodie's decision to let it pass on the grounds that the voicing of extreme views should not be encouraged by providing a platform. In some circumstances this may well be the appropriate decision to make. Here, however, one cannot help feeling that if Jodie had picked up on the comment at this stage and chaired the ensuing discussion, the issue would have been less likely to have exploded into an acrimonious exchange when the teacher was occupied elsewhere. Whatever view we take on the initial decision to ignore the comment, we would probably agree that when anger exploded over in the small group Jodie was unwise to try 'to joke them out of it', since to that group at least it was clearly no joking matter. Jodie's next decision, however, seems staggeringly ill-judged, given what has already emerged about the views and attitudes of at least two of the learners. Nevertheless, Jodie attempts to orchestrate a whole-group discussion, apparently oblivious to the fact this will place 'Hang-him' and the 'latecomer' – two complete strangers meeting for the first time – in a position which encourages the one to goad and the other to grow even more angry and distressed. We might go further than this and decide it was ill-judged in the first place to introduce an emotive issue such as this to a group of strangers about whom even the teacher as yet knows very little.

There are other examples of poor decision-making, too, which you may have identified. How about the division of learners into small groups? Would it not have been better to allocate learners to the three groups rather than leaving it to the learners themselves? This would have provided an opportunity for the three women at the back to get to know some of the others, and would have avoided the awkwardness some of these strangers might have felt about whether a group would include or exclude them. Then there's the decision to run a video for the second half of the lesson – a decision taken after Jodie has learnt one of the learners can't see the screen clearly. An alternative plan would have been to get the learners to introduce themselves, to invite Tim to say something about his role or even to have a post-mortem about the group discussion. If we were to ask Jodie what were the relevant intended learning outcomes from showing the video, I wonder what the answer would be? There is certainly a suspicion that the decision to show the video was based on the immediate needs of the teacher rather than those of the learners.

What advice would you give to Jodie about how to plan the next session with this group?

The essential task Jodie has to undertake in the next lesson with this group is to establish the learning needs of the individuals in order to devise ways in which they can be provided with the support they need. This is what should have been done during the first session with these learners so that in subsequent lessons (and possibly tutorials) learner progress and the effectiveness of the support strategies can be carefully monitored.

Let's look on the bright side, however, and say this first lesson was not entirely wasted. Jodie did discover (albeit accidentally) some of the needs and prior experiences of these learners which will prove useful for planning how best to help them learn. Even though we fear the lesson may have done more harm than good, particularly in terms of learner motivation, we now have an opportunity to suggest to Jodie a better way of doing things. Let's go through the sequence of events and pinpoint the changes we would make, bearing in mind all the time that our aim, as set out at the beginning of this section, is to establish the learning needs of the individual learners in order to devise ways in which they can be provided with the support they need.

1. If Jodie is going to get there early to set out the furniture, the best layout will be one in which all the learners can make eye contact with one another and with the teacher.

2. Setting up the PowerPoint really isn't an essential in this first session. The aim should be to find out as much as possible about the learners. The emphasis should not be

upon the teacher's 'performance' but upon his or her ability to draw the learners out, to listen and to assess. The priority at this stage would be to listen to what a learner (like Tina) has to say, rather than to fiddle with equipment.

3. Rather than launching straight into the course, Jodie should plan some 'ice-breaking' activities designed to help the class feel more at ease, to get to know one another a little and to learn one another's names. This sort of activity can be very helpful in allowing the teacher to identify learners who may need specific support or who may have experiences and knowledge which can be drawn upon as a resource.

4. This informal activity should be followed by activities that will allow a more formal assessment of learner needs and experience – an assessment that can be documented in order to plan strategies for learner support. All kinds of classroom activities would suit this purpose – it doesn't demand a test or exam. But the discussion Jodie set up wasn't particularly helpful in this respect. Sometimes the learner will have indicated on their enrolment form if they require support in a particular area of their learning. This is the sort of information that it is important for the teacher to possess when planning for learners' learning.

5. If the course or programme of learning is likely to require that the learners possess the skills to make clear and relevant notes during the lessons or as part of their reading and research, it might be useful to build a session on note-taking into this first lesson – as a refresher for those already competent and a chance for others to learn or improve. This would also be a means for the teacher to identify anyone needing particular support in this respect.

6. There may be much more specific advice you would offer to Jodie.

   - **How would you suggest the teacher handles the latecomer who seems to enjoy provoking an argument?**
   - **How can Tina be reassured and her enthusiasm usefully employed within the group?**
   - **How can the sensibilities of the angry learner be accommodated in future lesson planning – and should they be?**
   - **How can Tim's experience be validated and utilised within the group?**
   - **Should Jodie make any reference to the unfortunate first lesson when next the class meets?**
   - **Should it be used as a point for discussion or should it be forgotten as quickly as possible?**

CLOSE FOCUS CLOSE FOCUS CLOSE FOCUS CLOSE FOCUS CLOSE FOCUS

In what ways was the discussion Jodie had planned unsuitable or unreliable for the purpose of assessing learner needs?

You may find it useful practice to draw up a formal lesson plan for the next session with this group, following the advice and guidelines in Chapter 8. If you decide to include subject-specific rather than general introductory material, plan it as though this was an Access class relevant to your own subject area.

How might Jodie have made this journal entry more useful in terms of professional development and the planning of future practice?

If you have read Chapter 1, you will have seen at once that Jodie's journal entry does not follow the reflective pattern. It describes what has happened in great detail but doesn't reach the second step of asking: what have I learnt from this? Nor the third: what would I do differently next time? There is no attempt in this extract from Jodie's journal to use the experience for the purpose of professional development. It provides us with no evidence Jodie is a reflective practitioner. This is at its clearest when Jodie offers an interpretation of learners' behaviour. For example:

> *'Tina and the Hang-him woman didn't come back after the break. I don't know whether to be concerned or relieved. I assume it means they've decided the course isn't for them. You do tend to get a high drop-out rate on these sorts of programmes.'*

Torn between feeling concern or relief, Jodie decides to feel relieved. This avoids the necessity for reflection and turns a blind eye to the possibility that such an outcome may be directly attributable to something the teacher has said or not said, done or not done. If Jodie doesn't begin to reflect, it is likely the same mistakes will be repeated.

A final question: did you visualise Jodie as a man or as a woman?

Access and progression

So far in this chapter we have looked at the importance of assessing our learners' needs so that we can design our lesson planning and our assessment strategies in the best possible way to meet these. But we have other responsibilities, too, when it comes to meeting our learners' needs, and these are to do with supporting the learners' journey through their post-compulsory education or training. We need to ensure that they are able to *access* the organisational support and services which are appropriate to their individual needs; and that they are able to identify an appropriate route of *progression*, whether this is directly to employment, or on to further education and training. In order to do this effectively there are several areas of knowledge with which you yourself will need to be currently familiar. These include, as a minimum:

- **the learner support services offered by your college or organisation. These might include, for example, additional support for learners with dyslexia; the provision of an amenuensis for learners unable physically, through injury for example, to write; the provision of a signer for learners with a hearing impairment; and so on;**
- **the counselling services available for learners;**
- **the legal services available, possibly through the Students' Union;**
- **the careers guidance available;**
- **the current developments and employment opportunities locally and nationally in your own specialist area;**
- **the current progression routes for learners wishing to go on to further qualifications in your specialist area, and where and how these can be accessed.**

TASK TASK **TASK** TASK **TASK** **TASK** TASK **TASK** TASK **TASK** **TASK** TASK

Test your own current ability to support the access and progression of your learners by attempting to answer the following questions. They will help you to identify any gaps in your knowledge and understanding. Make a note of these, if there are any, and set yourself the further task of researching the appropriate answers.

1. A learner has been turned out of the family home and is experiencing substantial emotional and financial difficulties. Where, within your organisation, do you refer them on to, and how?

2. A learner has broken their wrist in a football game. They can't now take notes or use their keyboard to produce their assignment. Where, within your organisation, do you refer them on to, and how?

3. A learner asks you where they will be able to look for employment locally in your specialist subject. Are you able to give them this information?

4. A learner asks you how they can improve their qualifications. Are you able to advise them on the next appropriate step, and where they can access it?

5. A learner has ambitions to work in quite a specialised field within your subject. Are you able to advise them precisely what qualifications they need and what their next step should be?

6. One of your learners has a hearing impairment. Do you know a) where he can access the necessary support, and b) how to adapt your teaching and communication strategies so as to ensure he is not disadvantaged?

7. One of your learners has dyslexia. a) What support is available for her within the organisation, and b) what measures does your organisational policy require you to take in order to ensure that she is not disadvantaged in formal assessments?

Discussion

If you were unable to answer any one of these questions, incorporate the discovery of an accurate answer into your current action plan.

A SUMMARY OF **KEY POINTS**

In this chapter we have:
> **examined the importance and purposes of initial assessment;**
> **looked at how to plan for initial assessment;**
> **considered ways in which you can take account of individual learners' needs and prior experiences;**
> **discussed ways to use initial assessment as a basis for future planning;**
> **explored how the choice of learner activity can facilitate or hinder the assessment process.**

Branching options

The following tasks are designed to allow you to apply or explore further some of the contents of this chapter. If you are using this book to support your professional development, either for CPD or leading to a teaching qualification, you may find it useful to choose a task according to the level at which you are currently working. These are indicated in brackets.

1. Reflection and self-evaluation (NQF level 5)

Choose one of the groups of learners you have recently taught. Then reflect on the following questions, making notes, where appropriate, in your professional journal or for discussion with your mentor, tutor or a colleague.

a) What information did you have about these learners before your first session with them?

b) How did this influence your planning of that initial session?

c) What strategies for initial assessment did you incorporate into your lesson plan for that first session?
d) To what extent did that first session yield sufficient information for you to evaluate the learning needs of a) the group, and b) individual learners?
e) What, on reflection, might you do differently next time, if anything?

2. Evaluation: theory and practice (NQF level 6)

Much of our practical consideration of assessment, particularly in vocational areas, is based on the concept of *outcomes*. So, for example, at the stage of initial assessment, we are making a judgement about whether a learner can or can't perform some task; does or does not know some body of factual knowledge. Kolb (1984) would argue that this is at best only a partial view of learning. His model of 'experiential learning' is presented as a continuing process of creating knowledge out of experience; whilst on the other hand a definition of knowledge based simply on outcomes could, he argues, have a negative impact on the learner's ability to modify and adapt and make sense of their experience.

Consider how we might usefully apply Kolb's model to the initial assessment of learners, and discuss your ideas with your mentor, tutor or a colleague.

3. Engaging critically with the literature (NQF level 7: M level)

Using electronic or library resources, search the academic journals to find a paper on initial assessment in the Lifelong Learning sector. You might like to start your search with these journals: *Research in Post-Compulsory Education*, *Journal of Vocational Education* and *Journal of Further and Higher Education*.

a) How would you summarise the argument of your chosen paper?
b) What critique would you offer of the paper's argument, based on your own experience and wider reading?

REFERENCES AND FURTHER READING

DfES (2006) *FE Reform: Raising Skills, Improving Life Chances.* Norwich: TSO.

Foster, A. *et al.* (2005) *Realising the Potential: A Review of the Future Role of Further Education Colleges.* Annesley: DfES.

Gardner, J. (ed.) (2006) *Assessment and Learning.* London: Sage.

Kolb, D. (1984) *Experiential Learning: Experience as the Source of Learning and Development.* London: Prentice-Hall.

13
Assessment for learning 2: assessing learner achievement

The objectives of this chapter

This chapter examines some of the questions most commonly raised by teachers in the PCET sector about the practicalities of assessment. It gives advice on the clear formulation of outcomes and the subsequent selection and implementation of appropriate assessment strategies. It provides examples of the preparation, implementation and recording of assessment. In particular it gives some advice on how to assess the achievement of individuals involved in a group task; and how to present feedback to learners in a positive and constructive way. It is intended to help you to:

- **design and use formative and summative assessment as a tool for learning and progression (ES1; EK1.1; EP1.1);**
- **monitor learner progress (ES5; ES4);**
- **apply theories and principles of assessment (EK1.1; EK2.3);**
- **devise assessment for individual learners (*Differentiation*), taking account of issues of diversity and equality (EK2.1; EP2.1; EK2.4; EP2.4);**
- **encourage self assessment and peer assessment (EK1.3; EP1.3);**
- **give clear and constructive feedback (EK4.1; EP4.1);**
- **apply concepts of validity, reliability and sufficiency (EK2.2; EP2.2);**
- **monitor and record assessment decisions (EP5.1; EK5.2; EP5.2; EK5.3; EP5.3).**

Introduction: why assess?

This may sound like a silly question. Of course teachers assess. That's an essential part of what we do. But it's worth establishing the answer to this question before we proceed with the rest of the chapter so we can use it as a signpost or a compass to make sure we stay on the right track.

Imagine a lesson which has been so enjoyable the learners are still talking about it down in the refectory, and the teacher is walking down the corridor to his or her next class feeling a glow of pride, and even elation, that his or her teaching went so well and the learners so obviously had a good time and responded with enthusiasm. Everyone is feeling good about the lesson. But what if – and this is quite possible – in terms of the required learning outcomes, no learning has taken place at all? The learners may have learnt other things – that this teacher's classes are enjoyable, for example, or that college can be fun – and these are certainly worthwhile outcomes in themselves. But if the learners are not achieving the outcomes required by their course or qualification, the lesson is not achieving its primary purpose.

To put it another way, the teacher's primary objective is to facilitate learning. A very good way to do this is to ensure the process of learning is enjoyable. But this should not be confused with the erroneous idea that, as long as the learners have enjoyed themselves and responded warmly to the teacher, or as long as they have sat quietly and appeared to listen, the lesson has been successful. The lesson has been successful if the learners have achieved, or been set on the way to achieving, the learning outcomes – although admittedly this is more likely to happen if the learning experience the teacher has planned for them has been enjoyable and if they have listened to what the teacher had to say.

For a student teacher, or a teacher at the beginning of his or her career, it is usually (and understandably) the case that the focus of his or her anxieties, and therefore his or her planning, is upon the performance of teaching rather than upon the achievement of learning. I use the word 'performance' here advisedly, because the inexperienced or student teacher tends to envisage a lesson as a time to be filled by his or her own activity. They have to be 'teaching' all the time – which can mistakenly be taken to mean doing all the talking, making themselves the constant focus of the class, having to fill any potential silence with words. This, ironically, may mean the learners have less opportunity to learn and that the teacher has no time to focus on whether they are doing so. If we remember, however, that the primary objective is about learning and that this, after all, is what all the teaching is *for*, we can begin to adjust our focus and to recognise that the careful planning, implementation and recording of assessment are central to what the lesson is about. It's not just about teaching; it's about learning. The teaching is only a means to that end.

If we turn back to the lesson plan we worked on in Chapter 8, we can see clearly that the framework upon which the rest of the lesson hangs is as follows:

Objective/outcome	Activity	Assessment
What the learner should be able to explain or do at the end of the lesson	What the learner will do during the lesson in order to learn and then demonstrate this	How evidence of learner achievement will be gathered and recorded

Lesson plan: framework

The teacher's activity is built around this framework to support and facilitate it. The teacher's activity is never the starting point for planning. Implicit in the framework are the following questions:

1. What should the learners be able to do by the end of the lesson?
2. What do they have to do to:
    *   **achieve that;**
    *   **demonstrate they've achieved it?**
3. Can they do it?

If the answer to 3 is 'yes', then (unless you've been teaching them something they already knew) the planned learning has taken place. If the answer, for a substantial number of learners, is 'no', that's an indication that, for those learners, the planned learning has not taken place, however good the teacher's 'performance' has been, and however much the learners have enjoyed the lesson.

Planning assessment

To look in more detail at how we plan assessment, let's go back to Jim, whom we met in Chapter 8. Jim, whose subject is business studies, had planned, taught and evaluated a lesson on planning presentations. This lesson is a useful one for us to focus on because learner presentations are a requirement common to many PCET curriculum areas and are themselves commonly used as a method of assessment. Presentations are a learning outcome requirement for Jim's group at Level 3, as are group discussions – an area Jim identified as problematic in terms of assessment. What we are going to do, therefore, is to put ourselves in Jim's shoes and plan the assessment component of a lesson for the same group later the same term.

We will take our planned learning outcomes from the Key Skills specifications for Communication (www.qcda.gov.uk). This is intended to be helpful to you in two ways:

1. Implicit in the Standards' Minimum Core is the assumption that teachers' own communication skills will meet at least Level 3. This exercise will help you to assess yourself against this standard.
2. This assumption about PCET teachers' communication skills arises from the fact that most or all teachers in post-compulsory education and training will, directly or by the example they set to learners, be involved in the learners' development of communications as a Functional Skill.

The Functional Skills learning outcomes we shall plan for are these:

- *'Take part in a group discussion';*
- *'Make a formal presentation of at least eight minutes, using an image or other support material'.*

Following his original lesson, Jim reflected in his journal that he had underestimated the difficulty of assessing individual learners during a group activity, such as discussion. Now that some time has passed and the learners are ready to give their presentations, Jim needs to revisit these objectives to ensure that, this time, he is able to assess each learner's ability to contribute to a discussion. He has two double sessions of an hour and a half set aside for the presentations, and 15 learners to assess. He plans to have eight presentations during the first double lesson and seven during the second on the following day. He will use the same lesson plan for each of these two sessions.

TASK TASK **TASK** TASK **TASK** TASK TASK **TASK** TASK **TASK** TASK

Decide how an opportunity can be built into the lesson plan to allow the learners to contribute to a group discussion. You can assume for this purpose that the topic of the presentations is a complex one.

For presentation and discussion, plan the 'Outcomes', 'Learner activity' and 'Assessment' columns for the lesson plan. Now, focusing on the 'Assessment' column, decide how you will track and record each learner's achievement against each of these outcomes.

Outcome	Learner activity	Assessment
Make a formal presentation of at least 8 minutes, using an image or other support material	What will the learners do?	How will you assess them?
Take part in a group discussion	What will the learners do?	How will you assess them?

Your assessment planning has probably produced one of the following two sequences.

Either

The seven or eight learners each make their presentations of about seven minutes which, allowing for setting up, changing over, and so on, will take up about an hour. The remainder of the lesson – about thirty minutes – will be spent in a whole-group discussion around the topic or the qualities of the presentations themselves.

Or

After each of the learners makes his or her presentation, three or four minutes is spent in group discussion, either about the qualities of that presentation or about the topic.

Whichever model you decided upon, the 'Assessment' column would show the teacher (and perhaps the learners, too) observing the presentations and recording each learner's achievement against the agreed criteria. For example:

- **speak clearly and adapt your style of presentation to suit your purpose, subject, audience and situation.**

Similarly, for the group discussion, however it is scheduled, the learners will be observed and their achievement monitored and recorded against the criteria including making:

- **clear and relevant contributions in a way that suits your purpose and situation.**

It is likely the teacher alone will undertake the monitoring and recording of achievement in the discussion as it would be difficult for the learners simultaneously to be fully involved and to observe accurately. The assessment framework of your lesson plan, therefore, will look something like the following.

Outcome	Learner activity	Assessment method
1	Make an 8-minute presentation	Teacher observes and records against Key Skills criteria C3.1b
2	Whole-group discussion about presentation topic	Teacher observes and records against Key Skills criteria C3.1a

Assessment framework

CLOSE FOCUS CLOSE FOCUS **CLOSE FOCUS** CLOSE FOCUS **CLOSE FOCUS**

Now we have a clear plan of what we are assessing and how, we need to ensure we have the appropriate means to monitor and record that assessment. Focusing on the 'Assessment method' column, consider what sort of documentation you, the teacher, would need to have with you in the lesson in order to monitor and record the assessment.

This could be done in several ways and the form in which the assessment is documented may depend upon the requirements of, for example, the institution and the awarding body. The teacher may create a separate record for each learner, listing the relevant Key Skills criteria, with room against each for a comment about the learner's achievement or progress. It would look something like the following:

Functional Skills *Communication* Demonstrated during a presentation to the whole group on . . .	Learner's name [A. Learner]	Assessed by [J. Teacher]
Take part in a group discussion	3.1a1 make clear and relevant contributions in a way that suits your purpose and situation;	
Make a formal presentation	3.1b1 speak clearly and adapt style of presentation to suit purpose, subject, audience and situation;	
Signed: [A. Learner]	**Signed**: [J. Teacher]	**Date**:

Monitoring and recording assessment

The right-hand column may then be used to indicate whether, or to what extent, the learner has met each criterion. A comment here is far more useful to you and to the learner than a tick or a cross.

An alternative format for monitoring and recording would be to record the progress of everyone in the class on one sheet. In this case the students' names would be listed down the left-hand side and the criteria across the top. This would give a grid on which to record achievement.

	C3.1a.i	C3.1b.i
Learner **A**		
Learner **B**		

Monitoring and recording all the learners' assessments

The disadvantage of this format, of course, is that it is little more than a tick-list and therefore cannot be of much use in feeding back helpful developmental advice to the learners. Teachers do not always have a choice in the design of the documentation they use for assessment. They always, however, have a choice about how assessment information is fed back to the learner, and there is more to say about that important process later in this chapter.

Reliability, validity and sufficiency

These three are the key to accurate assessment. The assessment planning we have just undertaken was relatively straightforward. We had clearly written, externally set criteria against which to judge the learners' performance. The criteria were written in the form of outcomes that were observable so that the teacher would have little trouble interpreting them in practice. Nevertheless, even these relatively clear criteria may raise some questions in the teacher's mind. For example, in a presentation the learner should use a range of techniques to engage the audience. We are told this should include an image or other support material. But what support material should we expect the learner to use? What constitutes support material? This matters because, if we decide it means one thing and one of our colleagues teaching a parallel class or a teacher in another college somewhere decides it means something else, learners whom we judged as having failed to meet the criteria may have been judged successful if they had been assessed by one of these teachers instead. This is what we mean when we speak of assessment lacking reliability. An assessment is reliable if different teachers carrying out the assessment come up with the same result. The clearer the criteria, the more reliable the assessment will be. And, as we have seen, the slightest room for ambiguity in the interpretation of criteria puts the reliability of assessment at risk. In some subjects, such as English literature or the fine arts, criteria for assessment are far harder to formulate without losing in the process some essential component, such as critical sensibility, which is difficult to articulate accurately in terms of observable outcomes. This means that, generally speaking, reliable assessment of an A2 essay on *Othello* is more problematic than reliable assessment of a Functional Skill or of an element of a competence-based qualification, such as an NVQ because there's more room for assessor subjectivity. An essential role of the external verifier or moderator is to check that assessment decisions are reliable.

Another important issue for the teacher engaged in assessment is the sufficiency of the assessment evidence. To illustrate what's meant by this, let's look again at those Functional Skills we've been working with. One of the criteria for taking part in a discussion is that the learner should encourage others to contribute when appropriate. But how many times must the learner be observed to do this before he or she is considered to have met that particular criterion? If they are observed to create such opportunities once or twice, is that sufficient evidence upon which to assume they could and would do it again? What constitutes sufficient evidence is often left, in the first place, to the professional judgement of the teacher; but it is also part of the external verifier's or moderator's role to give advice and to make judgements about sufficiency.

It is when we turn to the method of assessment that we encounter the question of validity. A method of assessment is valid if it is capable of assessing accurately what it sets out to assess. If, for example, you decided to assess learners' group discussion skills by setting them an essay entitled 'Describe how you would take part in a group discussion', the assessment would not be valid. The assessment evidence you would end up with would tell you something about the learners' essay-writing skills and perhaps about their theoretical grasp of how they should conduct themselves in a discussion. But it would still not tell you whether the learners were capable of contributing appropriately to a group discussion in practice. The only valid way to assess that is to organise a group discussion and to observe how the learners contribute to it.

The more clearly the criteria for assessment are stated, the less difficulty the teacher will be faced with in terms of reliability, sufficiency and validity. In this respect, some course specifications are more helpful than others, and some subject areas present the teacher with more decisions to be made in the process of planning for assessment than others. Where the specifications are set out by an external body, for example, the teacher has a great deal of guidance not only in exactly what to assess (evidence) but also as to what assessment method to use. The method is implicit in the criteria. If the learners' presentation skills are to be assessed, the learners must make a presentation.

Inclusiveness

Sometimes, however, the learning needs of an individual mean it is not quite so straightforward as that. In Chapter 3 we explored the issue of inclusiveness. It is important that we ensure equality in the design and application of assessment procedures. In Chapter 8 we read in Jim's journal that he had planned an alternative, but equally relevant, activity for a student called Gaz who might feel unable to join in the class auction. It may well be that Gaz would also find it difficult to carry out a presentation to the whole class or, if asked to do so under the same conditions as the other learners, he might be unable accurately to demonstrate his abilities. If this is the case, Jim will need to plan for Gaz an alternative method of assessment that is equally valid and that generates sufficient evidence of achievement.

Let's leave Jim and Gaz for now, though. They probably feel they've been in the limelight for long enough. Instead, we'll look at how another teacher endeavoured to build equality of opportunity into her assessment planning and how far, on reflection, she felt she had succeeded.

TASK TASK **TASK** TASK **TASK** TASK **TASK** TASK **TASK** TASK **TASK** TASK

Read the following extract from Dorothy's journal and consider the following questions:
- **What concerns does Dorothy express about the reliability, validity and sufficiency of the alternative assessment method?**
- **Are her fears well grounded on any of these issues?**
- **Can you suggest (and give a rationale for) an alternative strategy?**

---

15 Feb

Time for the Health and Social Care group's second round of presentations. They get very wound up about standing in front of the group, even though they're all fairly outgoing. One or two of them who think they made a bit of a mess of it last time got particularly anxious, and although I didn't want to arrive at a situation where they didn't show up, a couple of them did take time off 'sick' or something – so that now we'll have to keep arranging slots for them to do their presentations later. I'm not sure what would have been the best way to take the pressure off, without letting them think that the presentations don't matter. They're an integral part of the assignment, and the assignment's a part of their continuous assessment. And that's that.

For Claire and Shona, though, to apply the standard rules of presentation wouldn't be fair because of their impaired hearing. For example, they need longer at the end to take questions because these have to go through their signer. Shona experiences some difficulty in making herself understood, and so I needed to find some way around the criterion about speaking clearly. So what I decided to do was to adjust the allocation of time. The other learners had five minutes to present and three minutes to take questions. For Shona and Claire I reversed that, so that their presentations lasted only 3 minutes and they had more time to take questions. Shona chose to take and answer questions through her signer, who was able to help me assess how clearly she had communicated the answers. Claire took questions directly, but requested that whoever was asking the question should write it down for her as well as speaking it clearly. They both did excellent presentations and I felt my strategy had worked well. But I still have some worries about it which I'd like a chance to discuss with the external verifier. Was a 3-minute presentation enough when the other learners were required to do five? Does it matter that I've sort of adapted one of the criteria so that instead of assessing whether S. speaks clearly I've assessed whether she *signs* clearly? Was it OK for me to change the emphasis from presentation to taking questions when what I'm assessing, strictly speaking, is the learner's ability to make a presentation? Would it have been better to have secured exemption for Shona and Claire from the criterion on the grounds of their disability, or would this have been unfair and made them feel excluded? They both wanted to do the presentations and now I regret having tinkered with the timings because I think they'd have been all right without me doing that. I did discuss it with them beforehand, and it was what they both wanted. But I think for the third presentation I'll let them watch the video of this one again to remind them of how well they did, and encourage them to work within the same timings as the other learners.

Let's look first of all at the issues of reliability, sufficiency and validity. When Dorothy wonders in her journal whether she should have reduced Claire's and Shona's presentations to three minutes, she is focusing on the question of sufficiency. Is a learner's performance during three minutes of presentation sufficient upon which to base assessment decisions about his or her presentation skills? When she ponders on her decision to assess the clarity of Shona's communication through a mode other than speech, she is expressing concerns about both the reliability and the validity of the assessment. She worries the reliability is in question because another assessor in the same situation might have judged it necessary and right to apply the criteria rigidly and literally; and she fears the assessment may be considered invalid because she has used evidence of clear signing in order to make an assessment decision about whether the learner can 'speak clearly'. Moreover, the weight of the evidence is about the learner's ability to respond to questions rather than make a presentation.

CLOSE FOCUS CLOSE FOCUS CLOSE FOCUS CLOSE FOCUS CLOSE FOCUS

1. What would you say to Dorothy if she asked your opinion about any of this?

2. You may find it useful to discuss this case with an internal verifier at the institution where you work or carry out your teaching practice. Would he or she support Dorothy's assessment decisions? It is usually at this level, or at the level of external verifier, that such decisions need to be confirmed.

3. Do you think Dorothy should have secured exemption for these two learners? What might be the implications of this course of action?

4. Early in her journal extract, Dorothy mentions that some of the learners are getting into a flap about doing the presentations because their previous experience of doing these was not a very positive one. They don't turn up for the presentations and this avoidance tactic will cause planning problems for the future. In your opinion, was there anything Dorothy could reasonably have been expected to do to prevent this from happening? Could their nervousness be seen as grounds for making some special arrangement for them, such as was made for Shona and Claire?

Teachers talking about assessment

As we have seen, assessment in practice is never quite as easy as it looks in the textbooks. In this section we look at some of the practical issues to do with assessment which newly appointed teachers and student teachers have identified as causing them problems. In the section that follows, we'll focus closely on two of these issues in particular: assessing groupwork and giving feedback.

- **How do you assess learners on an ongoing basis throughout the lesson – particularly the ones who don't respond very much?**
- **How do we assess learners when they may be starting from different levels of ability?**
- **How do you translate assessment criteria from the course specifications into plain English the learners can understand?**
- **How do we differentiate between the achievement of individual learners when they've been working as a group?**
- **How can I give feedback to a learner in a constructive way when the work he or she has produced is very, very poor?**

Assessing groupwork

Earlier in this chapter we saw Jim struggling to assess individual learners' involvement in a group discussion, and we looked at some of the documentation he might use to monitor and record their achievement. The question we need to look at now is: how does the teacher go about assessing the achievement of individual learners involved in a group project which may involve both research and written work? The answer here, of course, is that you have to be able to identify exactly what each learner has contributed to the group effort. This kind of assessment needs careful forward planning if the teacher is to be saved unnecessary work and worry after the event because discovering exactly who did how much of what is very difficult in retrospect. Some strategies that can be put into place before work on the project begins are these:

- when setting out the briefing for the project, the first task required of the learners should always be to draw up an action plan for each member of the group, setting out clearly what that member's role and contribution to the project will be;
- the learners should be required to indicate clearly on all written work submitted as part of the project which group member was responsible for writing each section, and which group member was responsible, if appropriate, for carrying out the research;
- a final requirement for every learner involved in the project should be to evaluate how well the group succeeded in working together and to identify any problems that arose over the allocation or carrying out of tasks. This will not only help the teacher who is acting as assessor but it will also provide the learners with the opportunity to demonstrate some of the Key Skills involved in 'Working with others'.

With these strategies in place, the assessment of group work becomes much more straight-forward.

Giving feedback

It's always a pleasant task to tell learners they've done well. It's less pleasant when we have to tell them they've done badly – they've failed an assignment or been unsuccessful in an end-of-module test. And it's not only less pleasant but it can be more difficult, too, because the rule about giving assessment feedback is that it should always be constructive. Sometimes it can seem difficult to give bad news in a constructive way. Let's have a look at this teacher's efforts. He has the unenviable task of telling Scott, aged 14, his assignment is unsatisfactory and will have to be done again.

Teacher: *Now then, Scott, how would you say you did on this assignment?*
Scott: *All right.*
Teacher: *All right? No, Scott, not all right. You made a right pig's ear of it.*
You're going to have to do it again. I want it in to me by Friday. And I want it right this time. Is that understood?
Scott: *Yeah.*
Teacher: *Good. Now clear off.*

I suppose we could call this feedback of sorts, but it's not particularly helpful to Scott because he's none the wiser about what he has to change in order to do better next time. So let's try again.

Teacher: *Now then, Scott. How would you say you did on this assignment?*
Scott: *All right.*
Teacher: *Well, I have to tell you, I'm afraid, that there are some problems with it, and I need you to have another go at it, all right?*
Scott: *Yeah.*
Teacher: *You've not read the assignment brief properly, look. You've missed out most of task one. And the spelling's atrocious. Do it again and have it in to me by Friday. Right?*
Scott: *Right.*
Teacher: *Good. Off you go.*

This is a slight improvement, I suppose. At least Scott has some idea now of what he has to put right. But what this dialogue still has in common with the first is that Scott really doesn't get to say very much. He gets to listen, and then he gets dismissed. But what if there are questions he needs to ask – things he needs clarifying? Let's try again.

Teacher: *Now then, Scott. How would you say you did on this assignment?*
Scott: *All right.*
Teacher: *Well, I have to tell you, I'm afraid, that there are some problems with it, and I need you to have another go at it, all right?*
Scott: *Yeah.*

> Teacher: *Just have a look again at the brief for task one. Just take a minute now to read it through. OK? Finished? Now think about what you've written here, look. What do you think's wrong with that as a response to task one?*
>
> Scott: *I've only done the first bit. I haven't put the tables or graphs in.*
>
> Teacher: *OK. Well spotted. So do you not feel altogether clear about tables and graphs, or was it just …?*
>
> Scott: *No, I just forgot to do it.*
>
> Teacher: *Sure? OK. So I need that done and in to me by Friday. And I need you to look at the spelling as well. Read it through. Spot the mistakes. Run the spellcheck just to be sure. You should try and get into the habit of always doing that. Yeah?*
>
> Scott: *Yeah.*
>
> Teacher: *OK. So is there anything you want to ask about this?*
>
> Scott: *No. Thanks.*
>
> Teacher: *Well, look, what you need to remember from this is: always read the task carefully, right? Always read the task carefully and always use the spellcheck. Anything else you want to ask about?*
>
> Scott: *No.*
>
> Teacher: *OK, Scott. Off you go.*

This time the teacher's attempts at giving feedback are much improved. At last we are seeing three essential elements of constructive feedback emerging:

1. the learners should be told clearly what the weaknesses are in their work;

2. they should understand what to do to improve it;

3. and they should understand what action to take to improve their performance in future assessments.

CLOSE FOCUS CLOSE FOCUS CLOSE FOCUS CLOSE FOCUS CLOSE FOCUS

There is still an element missing – something that should always form a part of constructive feedback. Can you identify what it is?

Look again at that third conversation between the teacher and learner. Imagine you were that teacher and reflect for a moment on how you handled this situation. Is there anything you would want to change?

The missing element is this: the learner's attention should always be drawn to what he or she has done well, or what he or she has done best. Even if his or her work has not, as a whole, met the required criteria, it will be possible to identify relative strengths. It is important for learners' motivation that they should be made aware of their strengths and successes, even if these are only relative. These essential elements in the giving of feedback apply not only to spoken feedback given face to face but also to written feedback given to the learner after his or her assignment or performance has been assessed.

How might the teacher, on reflection, improve on that third feedback dialogue? There are two points you may have identified here. One is that Scott remains fairly taciturn. We still don't really know how confident he feels about being able to meet the assessment criteria on his second try. Does he say little because he genuinely doesn't have any questions, or might it be he just wants the conversation over with as quickly as possible? This brings us on to the second point. One approach the teacher might have used would have been to question Scott a little bit more, asking him, for example, how he would go about representing the information in the form of charts or graphs. This would help to reveal whether Scott needed further help on this topic and whether he had omitted that part of the task not through an oversight but because he had felt unable to complete it.

Reflecting on assessment information

How do you use the information gained from assessing achievement? There are three ways in which this information will be used. It will be:

1. fed back to the learners in order to help them with their learning – and we've already looked at some of the issues related to that;
2. passed on to appropriate stakeholders – who may include awarding bodies and/or employers;
3. used by the teacher to evaluate his or her teaching and to identify ways in which it might be improved as we saw in Chapter 9.

A SUMMARY OF **KEY POINTS**

In this chapter we have:
> **examined the purposes of assessment;**
> **looked at how to plan for assessment;**
> **considered ways in which you can plan learner activities which will make it possible for you to assess what learning has taken place;**
> **discussed ways to monitor learner achievement and record assessment decisions;**
> **explored the concepts of reliability, validity and sufficiency, and applied them to practical assessment situations;**
> **discussed the need for inclusiveness in assessment procedures;**
> **explored ways of assessing individual contributions to group-work;**
> **looked at strategies for giving positive, constructive feedback.**

Branching options

The following tasks are designed to allow you to apply or explore further some of the contents of this chapter. If you are using this book to support your CPD or your professional development leading to a teaching qualification, you may find it useful to choose a task according to the level at which you are currently working. These are indicated in brackets.

1. Reflection and self-evaluation (NQF level 5)

a) Look carefully through the following list of assessment methods and identify those that you use and are familiar with, and those which would be appropriate for the assessment of your specialist subject but which you have not yet any experience of using.

- Group tasks.
- Multiple choice tests.
- Projects.
- Observation of practical tasks.
- Question and answer.
- Written reports.
- Short answer tests.
- Presentations.
- Peer assessment.
- Student self-assessment.

b) Decide which new assessment method or methods you will implement with your current learners, and incorporate this into your professional action plan.
c) Against what criteria will you evaluate the effectiveness of the chosen method/s?

2. Evaluation: theory and practice (NQF level 6)

Read through the following list of assessment terminology. Using the internet, library, or discussion with your mentor or colleagues, discover the definition of any of these terms about which you are unclear.

- Continuous assessment.
- Criterion referenced assessment.
- Diagnostic assessment.
- Norm-referenced assessment.
- Profiling.
- Proficiency assessment.
- Phase assessment.

Now choose from the list one approach which you haven't used before and which you consider appropriate to the curriculum and assessment needs of your current learners, and describe in your professional action plan how you will implement it.

3. Engaging critically with the literature (NQF level 7: M level)

a) Using electronic or library resources, search the academic journals to find a paper on one of the following:
   - inclusiveness and assessment in the Lifelong Learning sector;
   - differentiated assessment in the Lifelong Learning sector;
   - equal opportunities for assessment in the Lifelong Learning sector.

You might find it useful to start your search with these journals:

Research in Post-Compulsory Education, Journal of Vocational Education and *Journal of Further and Higher Education*.

b) How would you summarise the argument of your chosen paper?
c) What critique would you offer of the paper's argument, based on your own experience and wider reading?

REFERENCES AND FURTHER READING REFERENCES AND FURTHER READING

Ecclestone, K. (1996) *How to Assess the Vocational Curriculum*. London: Kogan Page.

Gardner, J. (ed.) (2006) *Assessment and Learning*. London: Sage.

Tummons, J. (2010) *Assessing Learning in the Lifelong Learning Sector* (2nd edition). Exeter: Learning Matters.

14
Managing behaviour and motivating learners

The objectives of this chapter

In this chapter we shall look at how we can engage learners' interest, and at some of the barriers to motivation we have to overcome if we are to encourage their aspirations and keep their attention on their learning. It discusses how the selection and structuring of subject matter should be done with a view to facilitating and reinforcing learners' motivation. It links closely to the Professional Standards for QTLS, particularly in helping you to:

- **acknowledge the experiences and expectations that learners bring with them (AS1; AK1.1; AP1.1; BK2.5; BP2.5);**
- **help learners set own realistic goals (DS2; DK2.1; DK2.2; DP2.2);**
- **secure and maintain the involvement and motivation of learners (AP1.1; BS1);**
- **maintain a safe and supportive, and mutually respectful learning environment (BK1.1; BP1.1; BK1.2; BP1.2; BK1.3; BP1.3);**
- **structure and present learning in a way that that engages learners' interest (BK3.3; BP3.3).**

Introduction: removing barriers to learning

As a manager of the learning process, it is your responsibility not only to plan, facilitate, assess and evaluate, but also to try to ensure there are as few obstacles as possible in the way of your learners' learning. Sometimes referred to as barriers to learning, these obstacles can be as obvious and easy to solve as an over-heated classroom or as difficult to address as an individual's lack of self-confidence. We experience a barrier to learning when something else occupies our mind, preventing us from focusing the necessary attention on what is to be learnt. A growling stomach and a preoccupation with how long to go before lunchtime will get in the way of our learning, as will a fear the teacher is going to ask us something we don't know and make a fool of us. Now there's not a great deal you can do about the first (although I do know a teacher who carries biscuits around for just such an emergency), but it is certainly within your power to manage learners' learning in such a way as to avoid the second.

Maslow, as we saw in Chapter 7, argued there is a hierarchy of human needs, of which the more basic, such as the need for safety and comfort, must be met before we can give our attention to meeting our higher-order needs, such as developing our potential through learning. For now, let us keep this idea in mind: that a learner needs to feel comfortable – physically, emotionally and socially – if she or he is to achieve his or her full potential for learning.

TASK TASK **TASK** TASK **TASK** TASK **TASK** TASK **TASK** TASK **TASK** TASK

Read through the following report written by an experienced teacher on her observation of a trainee teacher's classroom practice.

- **What barriers to learning does she identify?**
- **What could the student teacher do to remove them?**
- **What additions could the student teacher make to his action plan in the light of this feedback?**

OBSERVATION REPORT

Name of trainee:..

Name of observer: ....

Subject: ....

Level: ....

Number of learners: ....

Date observed: ....

Planning

It would have been useful if you had let me have a copy of your lesson plan for this lesson. I think it would have been useful for the learners, too, if they had been made aware of the intended outcomes. You could have written these on the board at the beginning. It always helps if learners know the objectives of the lesson - they can put their own weight behind it then, and work with you. The sequencing was clear and logical; but you should consider the real advantages of taking as your starting point something the learners are already familiar with. Dropping them straight in the deep end as you did, no matter how carefully subsequent content is sequenced, is likely to cause them some panic. And it was this panic, I think, which lay behind their reluctance to venture any answers to your questions.

Communication

When you couldn't get anyone to volunteer an answer, I'm not sure it was a good idea to start picking on people. Especially when you're not yet familiar with their names. Jabbing your finger towards someone and saying 'You!' can seem a bit threatening, you know. And all the rest are wondering who it's going to be next. And just a tip: when a learner is obviously unable or unwilling to answer, you saying 'Come on! Come on!' loudly at them is probably not going to help things. If they don't know the answer, they can't give you it, however much you insist. And if they're unwilling to answer in case they get it wrong, putting them under pressure isn't going to help that either. Well done, though, for noticing afterwards that you'd made Emma cry, although I'm not sure that drawing everyone's attention to it was a good idea. This class is usually quite responsive and communicative. I'm sure they wouldn't take advantage if you adopted a more friendly approach.

Resources

I could have let you have a few more overhead transparencies if you'd asked me. Then you wouldn't have had to cram absolutely everything on to just one. How do you make your writing so tiny? It's almost too tiny for the human eye to see. And I was sitting at the front. Well done, though, for picking up the fact that no one could read it. It might have been a good idea, however, to have apologised to Scott when you realised that the 'strange face' he was pulling was only his effort to focus on the screen. Reading it to them was a sensible solution. But it would have been better to read it from the transparency itself rather than from the wall screen, because having your back to the class for so long meant you didn't see the wasp come in through the window. That was what all the murmuring and lack of attention was about. So it might have been better if you'd asked them what the matter was, rather than keep telling them to 'Settle down.' I'm sorry it was you who got stung, by the way; but I thought you handled that very well.

Observation report

How many of the following barriers to learning did you identify?

✗ The learners aren't clear about the objectives of the lesson.

✗ The learning does not start from a 'safe' point with which the learners are comfortable and familiar.

✗ Answers are being demanded of the learners which they don't yet feel confident or competent enough to give.

✗ The teacher's questioning is making the learners nervous, not only because they're not confident of the answers but also because they fear they are about to be picked on and exposed to embarrassment.

✗ The teacher's manner may be seen as aggressive or insensitive.

✗ The learners are unable to read the OHP projection.

✗ They are by now too nervous, apparently, to tell the teacher this straight away.

✗ Efforts to cooperate and make the best of it (squinting to see the screen) are met with rebuke.

✗ The teacher turns his back on the class to read from the screen, thus depriving the learners of eye contact.

✗ The danger presented by the wasp preoccupies the learners to the detriment of their learning.

I like the way the teacher-observer tries to draw some positive points out of all this. And certainly she provides guidance to the trainee teacher on how some of these barriers could have been avoided or removed. You will probably have added some points of your own. Taken all together, the advice we would want to give him would look something like this:

If the learners had been made aware of the planned learning outcomes and had not been left in the dark, they might have felt less nervous about this encounter with an unfamiliar teacher and an unfamiliar topic. When they failed to respond to your questions, it would have been better to take this as a sign they did not feel sufficiently confident about their knowledge and understanding and to have gone over the topic again more simply or from another angle, or to have invited them to question you. If you don't know a learner's name, you should make a point of learning it there and then, and using it. Quickly setting them a task and then having a quiet word with the tearful learner would have been better than drawing the attention of the whole class to her predicament. Never cram too much on to one OHT. It loses its impact and can appear daunting to the learners. If the writing on the OHT appeared too small, you could have tried moving the OHP further from the screen and then refocusing. And you could always have carried a whiteboard marker as your Plan B. You should have kept up eye contact with the class. This is an important element in human interaction. If eye contact is absent, for whatever reason, it is difficult to establish the rapport necessary for a good working relationship. And you should have been observing your learners anyway so you could effectively monitor how they were responding to your teaching. Signs of puzzlement or boredom are as important to spot as rogue wasps – and more potentially damaging in the long run.

This is a lot more directive than the tutor's evaluation. If the trainee teacher resolves to take this advice – and it's to be hoped he does – the additions to his action plan would ideally be to:

- set clear objectives and make sure the learners are aware of them;
- make a point of learning the learners' names, and use them;
- use with care and due consideration the direct questioning of individual learners;
- avoid a manner which could be interpreted as aggressive;
- avoid behaviours or interactions which make learners unduly anxious;
- make sure OHTs are legible and uncrowded;
- maintain eye contact with the learners whenever possible;
- be observant about what's going on in the classroom.

This last point is a key one for any teacher. You have a responsibility to manage the learning experience but you can't manage any situation unless you take accurate notice of what is happening. This inevitably demands that you are able to read the situation correctly – to use your powers of observation and your common sense – so you don't assume that learners who are straining to see the screen are simply pulling silly faces; or fail to see that all the flapping about isn't caused by an excess of energy but by fear of a wasp. Your ability to observe and interpret what is happening in the classroom or workshop accurately is your most useful asset in identifying potential barriers to learning. And this ability will improve as your experience and confidence increase.

But of course there is more to motivating learners than simply removing barriers to learning. Ensuring learners feel safe, comfortable and undistracted is an essential first step, but you can't stop there. You will still need to make sure you engage and retain their interest. The next two sections look at some of the ways in which this can be achieved.

Motivating learners

You – yes, you – know that learning can be an enjoyable and rewarding experience. You may always have known this or it may be something you discovered relatively late in life, after the age of compulsory schooling, for example. But you would not be here now, pursuing a career in teaching, unless you knew the experience of learning could be a positive one. However, this is not an attitude you can take for granted in your learners. For some of them, the experiences associated with learning may have been negative ones: failure, embarrassment, a sense of not belonging, low self-esteem. In the Lifelong Learning sector particularly, we often find learners, of whatever age, who have not thrived in mainstream compulsory schooling. Helping them to regain the confidence and motivation to learn is part of what makes teaching in the PCET sector such a challenging and rewarding profession.

One of the first steps in helping learners to feel confident and motivated is to remember they are all different. We looked at this in some detail in Chapter 12. They may be introduced to us initially as 'Health and Social Care 3' but we must never lose sight of the fact that the group is made up of individuals, each with his or her own aspirations, worries, abilities and experiences. Each one has his or her own story to tell about their journey through the education system. Some of these journeys will have been happier or more positive than others. But each learner will be carrying the effect of these experiences with them, and it will influence the way in which he or she responds to you, to the other learners and to the learning process. Now one way to begin to fathom this is to include in your planning those methods and strategies of teaching and learning that will enable you to get to know something about the group as individuals. This cannot be accomplished if, for example, you invariably use the formal lecture, which requires nothing of them but to be passive, silent learners.

Another way to gain some understanding of the individual and disparate needs of learners is to undertake a case study of one or two learners whose attitude or motivation you would like to understand more clearly. Such case studies are often built in as part of the coursework for programmes leading to a QTLS teaching qualification. Even if that is not so in your case, you will still find this a useful exercise.

TASK TASK **TASK** TASK **TASK** TASK TASK TASK TASK **TASK** TASK

The case study should be based upon a prepared interview with a selected learner. The interview should be designed to explore their learning needs and preferred learning styles, together with associated principles of teaching and learning. In writing up the case study, whether in your journal or more formally for assessment, you should be sure to maintain an ethical approach (for example, preserving the anonymity of the learner and others) as you describe and reflect upon the following:

- **the learner's attitudes to learning;**
- **what motivates them and what barriers exist to his or her learning;**
- **their previous route through education;**
- **their reasons for attending college and choosing his or her particular programme;**
- **their perceptions of the college and his or her programme;**
- **what you have learnt from this case study, and how you will use it to inform your future teaching.**

You might first like to read a part of what one trainee teacher wrote after carrying out such a case study.

I'll call the learner Barry, although that's not his real name. I first encountered him last term in the learning support group, where he was getting one-to-one help with his spelling and grammar. I found him a bit grumpy then. And this term he's suddenly appeared in my GCSE English class, and I've been quite worried about how he's going to cope with doing the whole thing in two terms. He's got a lot of coursework to catch up with before he even starts. And he's quite a lot older than the other learners, which probably makes it even more difficult for him. But I was worried about how I'd cope with him, as well, because he seems to look cross all the time – as though he might suddenly make trouble. But when I asked him if I could interview him for my case study he seemed really pleased. He was happy for me to tape-record the interview rather than take notes. I told him I'd give him the tape when I'd finished transcribing it but he said he was happy for me to use what he said in any way that was useful to other learners. Here's what he said.

He left school officially in 1987 when he was 16, but he hadn't been attending really since he was 14. He lived in [name of county], then, where they still had the 11-plus. Both his sisters passed it but he didn't, and he says he just gave up then because he felt he was a failure and so there was no point trying. He hated his secondary school because his writing was so poor he was always getting into trouble. In the end he gave up handing any work in at all. He said that, because he always got told off for his work anyway, he might as well be told off for not doing it and save himself the trouble. Because it was his writing and his spelling, it affected his achievement in every subject, so there was never anything really that he could get praised for. After he left school officially, with no qualifications, he went on a training scheme but he hated the college part of it because he ran into the same trouble over his written work. After that, he tried to join the army. They wouldn't have him. He didn't say why. Then there's a 10-year gap where he seems to have been in and out of casual employment, but never very happy with what he was doing. The turning point was last year when he met his partner. She told him that if he wanted to get a permanent job he could settle down and enjoy, he'd have to get himself GCSE English and maths as a minimum. So here he is. He strikes me as quite intelligent. He reads a lot and his spoken English is really good; and obviously he's motivated now to work hard and get some basic qualifications. But he's really not anything like as confident as you'd think he was from looking at him. His confidence is, I think, quite fragile.

In terms of what this tells me as his teacher, I realise I'll need to bolster his confidence and motivation because his previous experiences of learning have left him feeling very negative – about learning and about himself. He'll need a lot of positive reinforcement. And I think it'll be important to make sure he doesn't feel any embarrassment or awkwardness about being so much older than the others in the group. Because his oral English is so much better, still, than his written English, I can build up his confidence in that particular strength, and I'm going to have a word with my mentor to see whether we can take advantage of that strength, somehow, in his coursework. I feel that any minor setback could easily destroy his confidence and motivation and so I'm pleased I found all this out because I'm in a better position to help and support him now.

One of the most important things to notice here is that this trainee teacher is reflecting on what she has learnt about this individual in terms of its implications for her own practice. She is not just exhibiting the curiosity we all have about the lives of others; she is making a professional assessment about this learner's needs and about how she can help him to build upon the fragile confidence he has found. This is exactly the purpose of such a case study – that it should inform the teacher's future practice.

Another important point to note is that she has selected a learner whose attitudes and motives she is unsure of, rather than one with whom she feels entirely confident. She is intent on problem-solving here, rather than simply giving herself an easy time. It's interesting to read that she initially saw this learner as a potential trouble-maker. Until she had spoken to him, one-to-one, she would have had no idea that what she interpreted as an irritable expression was probably caused by anxiety. And so we have a clear illustration here of why it is important to sit down with learners and help them to plan their learning. I'm not suggesting we carry out a case-study investigation with each one – that would obviously be entirely impractical; but that we recognise the importance of one-to-one contact with our learners, even though time constraints may sometimes seem to advise against it. Such contact is essential if you are to be able to help the learners to:

- **identify their individual strengths and individual learning needs;**
- **develop their individual plan of learning and assessment;**
- **recognise what interests and motivates them;**
- **track their attainment of the Functional Skills;**
- **identify what aspects of study skills they need to develop so they can begin to take some responsibility for their own learning;**
- **evaluate their experiences of learning and express this constructively so you, as teacher, can respond to their needs as appropriate.**

Fostering enjoyment

There are a number of ways you can encourage learners to enjoy their learning and look forward to your lessons.

✓ Incorporate a range of appropriate learning and teaching methods so that learners don't become bored by the same old activities. Surprise them.

✓ Arrange the classroom or workshop in such a way that you are able to make eye contact with all the learners. A horseshoe of tables or a boardroom arrangement is better for this purpose than small clusters of tables where some learners may have their backs turned to you. To build up a relationship of trust, you all need to be able to see each other.

✓ Allow humour into your lessons. (Don't rehearse jokes, though – contrived humour can fall embarrassingly flat.)

✓ Use methods that are fun, such as games, debates, simulations.

✓ Give plenty of encouragement and praise. There are ways of encouraging a learner who volunteers an answer, even though you're having to tell him or her their answer is wrong.

✓ Be enthusiastic. Enthusiasm is infectious. Never say things like: 'We've got to do this. I know it's a bit boring, but . . . ' You can hardly expect effort or enthusiasm from learners after they've heard something like that.

✓ Show them you value the work they have done by assessing it thoroughly and accurately and giving full and constructive feedback – and by returning it to them promptly.

✓ Make your learning materials interesting. Develop and use a variety of materials that will engage learner interest and are appropriate for their level of ability.

✓ Reward success – by giving praise or by organising activities you know the learners will enjoy.

✓ Be fair and honest and expect the best of your learners, rather than fear the worst.

Fostering enjoyment

TASK TASK **TASK** TASK **TASK** **TASK** TASK **TASK** TASK **TASK** **TASK** TASK

Add three suggestions of your own to this list. If your experience of teaching is not yet very extensive, draw upon your experiences as a learner. What have your teachers done in the past to help you to develop an enjoyment of learning?

Take one of these suggestions – your own or one from the list – and incorporate it into your action plan for your next taught lesson.

Motivation: a wider view

It's not only what goes on in the classroom or workshop, however, which has an impact on learners' levels of motivation. There are social, political and economic factors too, as we saw in Chapter 4 of this book, which have an inevitable effect on current attitudes to learning, particularly among young people. For ease of reference, we can consider these factors under four main categories. Let's word them as the learners might express them to themselves:

'Is it really worth it?"
We used to be able to say to learners, 'Work hard, get your qualification, and you'll be able to get a good job.' For a number of reasons, this is no longer always the case. Widening participation means that more young people than ever before are coming into colleges and training organisations to undertake vocational qualifications. However much we might applaud this, an inevitable consequence of widening participation is that some of the learners being enrolled onto courses are arriving with fewer skills and needing more support than was traditionally the case. Many are being enrolled in level 1 and 2 programmes which will not lead directly to employment but will require progression through higher level training before the learner can realistically begin applying for a job. The question: *'Is it really worth it?'* inevitably arises when the learner can see no prospect of reward in the short or even in the medium term. What they're really asking themselves is why should they put any effort into learning if it's not going to get them anywhere?

'I'm rubbish at this, anyway.'
Many young people come into further education having had a negative experience of education. Many have not achieved well, have not found learning an enjoyable experience. For them it is a process which has undermined their self-esteem. They associate it with failure and feeling bad about themselves. They have labelled themselves as 'losers' as far as learning goes, and – unfortunately for us – tend to see 'the teacher' in the role of enemy, which means that any effort at reassurance on our part is often regarded with distrust.

'This is boring.'
There are three good reasons why learners might be bored. The work may be too easy for them, so they switch off. Or it may be too difficult for them, so they switch off. Or it may indeed be boring because the teacher isn't presenting it in an engaging way. So – you guessed it – they switch off.

'I'm too scared to engage with this.'
Young learners in particular are afraid of ridicule, and – from their point of view – there are two ways in which engaging with their learning might bring ridicule down on their heads. They might get it wrong and show themselves up as being stupid (which they may secretly believe they are); or they might attract the mockery of their mates for breaking ranks and turning into a swot or a boff or any one of those pejorative terms reserved for fellow learners who actually get down to some work.

So how is the teacher or trainer expected to respond to these wider motivational issues? Clearly it's not within our remit to address them at source. We aren't politicians, policy makers or psychiatrists – although you might aspire eventually to become any or all of these. Neither are we responsible for creating these problems. But there are ways in which we can begin to address them in our day-to-day dealings with learners. For example:

How to respond to: *'Is it really worth it?'*
- **Set short-term goals and rewards.**
- **Encourage learning for its own sake (in other words, make it enjoyable).**

(You can find examples of both of these strategies in the next chapter.)

How to respond to: *'I'm rubbish at this, anyway.'*
- **Persevere with being the nice guy. Act as though you're pleased to be there with them (even if sometimes you're not).**

- Give lots of positive reinforcement.
- Model the behaviour you expect to see. This involves treating the learners with respect.
- Don't take the negative attitude to 'the teacher' personally.
- Set achievable tasks and give lots of praise.

How to respond to: *'This is boring.'*
- Make sure it's not! Find interesting, lively ways to present the learning. (See Chapter 11 for some ideas.)
- Incorporate lots of learner activities into your lesson plans.
- Ensure you're taking the learners' needs into account when planning your lessons. (For example, don't present an activity that requires note-taking if learners don't have note-taking skills.)
- Employ differentiation (of task and of assessment) so that more able learners don't switch off.

How to respond to: *'I'm too scared to engage with this.'*
- Be approachable.
- Always handle answers sensitively, even if they're wrong. There's always something to praise, something to make the learner feel good about (*Good try! . . . Nearly! . . . A good answer, but not quite.*)
- Operate a zero tolerance of bullying or ridicule in your classes.
- Don't pick on people.
- Ask answerable questions and set achievable tasks.
- Draw on learners' own expertise wherever possible (for example, about computers, TV programmes, music) and draw on examples which will be familiar to them.

From the point of view of keeping yourself motivated, it's important always to keep in mind that learners' lack of motivation may well not be directly your *fault*. However, as their teacher, it is your *responsibility* to do what you can to address the symptoms, even though the cause may lie well outside your sphere of influence.

Motivation and behaviour

So how do we apply what we have learned here about motivation to the everyday practicalities of managing and improving learner behaviour? After all, the link is clear. We can see that in most cases it is a lack of motivation to learn which underlies behaviours that form a barrier to students' learning; or in some cases it may be inappropriate sources of motivation – such as the desire to impress peers, to 'fit in', or to avoid making the effort that learning demands – which get in the way. Understanding this helps us to observe disruptive behaviours more dispassionately, rather than panicking and taking such behaviours personally. It also enables us to draw on longer-term motivation strategies such as those we have discussed in this chapter so far.

But, of course, the opportunity to develop such longer-term strategies is sometimes not available to you, particularly if you are taking a class for the first time, or for only a short period, as part of your teaching practice for your QTLS programme. As a new teacher, a student-teacher, or as any teacher new to a class, it is useful to have a range of behaviour management or behaviour improvement strategies to draw on from the beginning. As well as making your task of teaching and supporting learning easier, such strategies help to prevent patterns of obstructive behaviour from becoming established within the class and affecting the motivation of those who *are* willing to learn.

Now, in the final part of this chapter, we are going to look at some strategies which other teachers have found useful for addressing the most common examples of non-compliant or disruptive behaviour.

Strategies for behaviour management and improvement

Learners using or playing with phones in class
- Begin the lesson by explaining that you operate a 'visible phones' policy, which requires that all phones should be switched off and placed in front of the learners where you can see them.
- Begin the lesson by explaining that you operate a 'phones away' policy, which requires that all phones should be switched off and put away.
- Avoid learners using the excuse that they have an 'emergency' at home or elsewhere by giving every learner the number of the college office on a card to leave at home so that they can be easily contacted in case of emergency.
- Make a deal with the class that they get extra break time but lose five minutes every time someone uses their phone or a call tone sounds.

Learners talking instead of listening
- Lower your voice and speak quietly.
- Say something unexpected or contentious, which will grab their attention – then use that opportunity to keep it.
- Move about the room and talk directly to the talkers from close up. Don't just stand in one place.

Learners are off-task and interacting with each other but not with you
- Again, do or say something to grab their attention (but remember: it has to be something that they *will find genuinely interesting*, and not just something you think they *ought to* find interesting!).
- Join their group and work with them.
- Manage the allocation of groups so that learners aren't with the people they usually sit with.
- Introduce some group work, rather than trying to engage them with teacher input. This means thinking on your feet and possibly deviating a little from your lesson plan, but that's OK if it gets them learning.

The learners seem hostile
- Remember, if this is the first time you have met them, it can't be personal.
- Before you can get them to like you, you have to make them believe that you like them, so smile, and act as though you do.
- Find something to praise them for. Almost anything will do, even if it's something they've done right by accident.
- Tell them you've been looking forward to working with them.

A learner is reluctant or refuses to join in with group work
- Invent for them a role that takes into account what you've seen of their behaviour. For example, if they find it difficult to sit still, appoint them as the go-between who moves and liaises between groups.
- Manage the composition of groups so that they're with people they want to work with or people who are likely to set an example that will encourage them to work.

Building behaviour management into your lesson planning

The strategies we've just seen are useful ones to try when thinking on your feet in a classroom situation. But there are ways in which you can make such behaviours less likely to arise by giving careful thought at the lesson planning stage. For example, your lesson plan should ensure that the learners are provided with:

Clear structure and direction

In comparison with the structured school environment from which they have come, the comparative anonymity and the more flexible regime of the college may tempt some younger learners to overstep the boundaries of acceptable behaviour. However, there are a number of ways we can provide a sense of structure and clear direction. For example:

- begin each lesson by explaining what they are going to do, and end it by recapping for them what they've done;
- give a clear time allowance for each task, a count-down as it proceeds (for example, *'You have five minutes left.'*), and a final clear and unambiguous indication when the time for the task is up;
- build in lesson time to make or negotiate your own classroom rules if appropriate;
- establish a pattern to your lessons. This should include always starting on time and beginning with a recap once they've settled down; always having breaks at the same time; always having a question time at the same point in the lesson; and so on.

Frequent changes of learner activity into your lesson plan

Younger learners particularly have a lot of physical energy and can get restless. You should try to accommodate this in your planning. Here are some ways.

- Keep teacher exposition (verbal inputs) as brief as possible. Avoid lengthy lectures. It's better to have several short periods of exposition interspersed with periods of learner activity, than to require that younger learners listen to you attentively for any length of time.
- Select methods which involve active learning and which require learners to be doing rather than listening and watching.
- In classroom-based lessons, plan activities that allow for some physical movement. For example, learners working in small groups could choose a member of their group to move on to the next at a pre-arranged signal in order to share ideas and information. Or you could build in to your plan one-minute 'breaks' every twenty minutes where everyone stands up, rolls their shoulders or stretches, and sits down again.

Clear links to the context of the workplace

Learners need to know – and be frequently reminded – that what they are doing is relevant to their vocational aspirations and interests. This helps them to recognise the *purpose* of this aspect of their learning. Here are some strategies to incorporate into your planning.

- Begin by introducing, discussing and agreeing rules of behaviour *based on what would be acceptable in the workplace*.
- Remind them frequently of the purpose of their learning by building in opportunities to say things such as: *'When you're doing this at work what you'll need to do is...'* and: *'When you're at work you'll be doing this every day and you'll find you just keep getting better and better at it.'*
- Plan time to explain health and safety rules in terms of the workplace, asking them questions such

as: *'If we were at work, what might happen if we left these tools about?'* Or, *'If we ran about in the salon what could happen?'*

- Plan to use resources that relate to their vocational area of interest. For example, if you're teaching Functional Literacy Skills to students of transport and engineering, you could use an extract from a glossy motoring magazine for comprehension questions; and if you're teaching Functional Numeracy to learners in beauty therapy, take your examples from timings for nail extensions or lengths of appointments.

Reminders about the rules of the college or the institution

Make college rules clear. Plan time to discuss them. And, of course, make sure you uphold them consistently.

When to refer it on

Very occasionally you may encounter learner behaviour which it is wiser to refer on to some one with more specialist knowledge or seniority. Although this is rare, you need to be able to recognise when a situation with a learner has reached a point where this becomes necessary both for the learner's sake and for your own. This may include cases where:

- their lack of motivation endangers the health and safety of themselves or others;
- you suspect the underlying problem may be drugs or alcohol related;
- you suspect they may need specialist psychological help;
- you have reason to suspect problems at home, such as abuse, neglect, bereavement.

A SUMMARY OF **KEY POINTS**

In this chapter we have:

> identified factors in the planning and delivery of lessons which may present barriers to learning, and considered how they might be overcome;

> discussed motivation in relation to learners' individual needs;

> looked at ways to foster enjoyment of learning;

> provided examples of ways in which independent learning can be used to improve learner motivation;

> discussed some of the wider factors which have an impact on learner motivation, and considered the extent to which the individual teacher can be expected to address these;

> examined what we can learn from this about managing and improving learner behaviour.

Branching options

The following tasks are designed to allow you to apply or explore further some of the contents of this chapter. If you are using this book to support your CPD or as part of your professional development leading to a teaching qualification, you may find it useful to choose a task according to the level at which you are currently working. These are indicated in brackets.

1. Reflection and self-evaluation (NQF level 5)

a) Look again at the four main causes of de-motivation listed in the previous section. How well do these match your own experience of teaching and supporting learning? Are there ways in which you would want to expand on this list? For example, under *'It's boring!'* you may wish to add something about some young learners' short attention span. What argument would you present for including this?

b) Choose a strategy for combating one of the four de-motivators listed in the last section – one which you haven't tried before – and incorporate it into your Action Plan. You should also set out the criteria and timescale you will apply to judge whether the strategy has been successful.

2. Evaluation: theory and practice (NQF level 6)

Drawing on the theories of learning we discussed in Chapter 8, and on your wider reading, what theoretical rationales would you offer to support each of the suggested strategies for addressing de-motivation set out on pages 188–9? For example, the strategy of setting short-term achievable goals and rewards to combat the attitude of *'Is it really worth it?'* clearly draws upon Neo-behaviourist theories of motivation in that it provides a reward for the desired behaviour (in this case, engaging with learning).

3. Engaging critically with the literature (NQF level 7: M level)

For a detailed analysis of the socio-economic factors underlying low levels of motivation among young learners in the Lifelong Learning sector, you will find it useful to read:

- **Ball, S.J., Maguire, M. and Macrae, S. (2000)** *Choice, Pathways and Transitions Post-16: New Youth, New Economies in the Global City.* **London: RoutledgeFalmer.**
- **Wallace, S. (2002) No Good Surprises: intending lecturers' preconceptions and initial experiences of further education.** *British Educational Research Journal, Vol 28 No. 1,* **pp 79–93.**

Use your library resources to access one of these and make a critical analysis of its argument about the causes of poor motivation amongst young learners. How does the argument compare with (a) the one set out in this chapter, and (b) your own experience and reflection?

REFERENCES AND FURTHER READING

Ball, S.J., Maguire, M. and Macrae, S. (2000) *Choice, Pathways and Transitions Post-16: New Youth, New Economies in the Global City.* London: RoutledgeFalmer.

Dearing, R. *et al.* (1996) *Review of Qualifications for 16–19 year-olds.* London: SCAA.

DfES (2006) *FE Reform: Raising Skills, Improving Life Chances.* Norwich: TSO.

Foster, A. *et al.* (2005) *Realising the Potential: A Review of the Future Role of Further Education Colleges.* Annesley: DfES.

Wallace, S. (2002) No Good Surprises: intending lecturers' preconceptions and initial experiences of further education. *British Educational Research Journal, Vol 28 No. 1,* pp 79–93.

Wallace, S. (2007) *Managing Behaviour in the Lifelong Learning Sector.* Exeter: Learning Matters.

Wallace, S. (2007) *Getting the Buggers Motivated in FE.* London: Continuum.

15
Learning and teaching 14–16

The objectives of this chapter

This chapter expands on some of the ideas set out in the previous one, and is designed to help you identify and address some of the issues specific to working with 14–16 year-old learners. It draws on areas of essential knowledge, skills and values covered in other chapters, and relates them here directly to this age group. In particular, it will help you to:

- **motivate learners and respond to their aspirations (AK1.1; AP1.1);**
- **create a safe and supportive learning environment (AS6; AP6.2; BK1.1; BP1.1);**
- **maintain engagement and active participation of learners through use of appropriate learning techniques (DP1.1; DP1.2: DP1.3; BK2.2; BP2.2);**
- **establish ground rules and encourage respect (BK1.2; BP1.2);**
- **structure and present information clearly, in a way appropriate to the learners' needs (BK3.3; BP3.3);**
- **identify and remove barriers to effective communication (BS3; BK3.1; BP3.1; BK3.2; BP3.2).**

Introduction

One of the biggest – and certainly one of the most talked-about – changes to the teacher's professional responsibilities in post-compulsory education and training in the last few years has been the advent of 14–16 year-olds as learners in PCET 1. Yet why should the arrival of this particular group of learners have created such a stir? Aside from the issue of parity with school teachers (and that's certainly an important one), perhaps it was because there was little current experience within the sector of supporting the learning of this age group. Perhaps, too, it was immediately recognised that younger learners can have different needs when it comes to planning learning activities for them, engaging their interest, and keeping them motivated. In this chapter we shall be looking at some of these needs and discussing how we can effectively address them. So this is, above all, a very practical chapter. The strategies we'll look at are based on advice from teachers in PCET 1 who have substantial and successful experience of teaching this energetic and sometimes challenging group of learners.

But first, let's remind ourselves why it is that some 14-16 year-olds are now recommended for participation in PCET 1. The official, short answer is that they are here to be motivated. In the White Paper, *14–19 Education and Skills* (DfES 2005) we are told that young learners who have not been sufficiently engaged by the National Curriculum are considered more likely to be motivated by a more practical, vocational curriculum. Some colleagues who have taught this age group may beg to question some of the broad assumptions implicit in this policy. Certainly, as educational professionals, we know very well that we cannot rely on an alternative curriculum alone to motivate disengaged learners. A great deal will also depend on the activities we plan for them, and how we relate to and communicate with them.

The learning needs of 14–16 year-olds

So what makes these younger learners any different from the slightly older learners we teach every day? Is it useful or even fair to treat them as a distinct group on the basis of their age? Most teachers who work with them would say that yes, there are characteristics and needs displayed by 14–16 year-olds which it is important for us to take into account if we are to effectively support their learning. Some characteristics we can expect as a consequence of the 'selection' process which determines which learners should be directed towards a vocational curriculum. Often (although certainly not always) these are learners who are not achieving well in the National Curriculum. And so these characteristics might include:

- **having low self-esteem and a lack of confidence in themselves as learners;**
- **having a history of negative relationships with teachers;**
- **expecting to have the same sort of negative relationship with you;**
- **expecting you not to like them;**
- **having low expectations of the learning experience – their past experience of school has convinced them they won't enjoy it.**

In addition, they may present behaviours and characteristics which are attributable to their age. A 14-year-old has not, after all, been 'grown up' very long. As a consequence, you may find that younger learners:

- **have a shorter attention span than older learners;**
- **find the comparative freedoms presented by FE frightening, or tempting, or both;**
- **feel intimidated by being a small fish in a big pond – where all the other learners are older, possibly bigger, and sometimes meaner;**
- **lack the experience or skill to take responsibility for their learning;**
- **have boundless energy and need to let off steam.**

Put these two lists of characteristics together and it's not surprising that some teachers find this age group a bit of a challenge. It is, of course, unwise to generalise too much about our learners, and it would be unprofessional to take any group and 'lump' them together as having identical learning needs. The 14–16 year-olds you teach will include some who cope very well with the transition to FE, who are self-motivated, hard-working, and who have made a conscious choice to pursue a vocational curriculum in order to achieve their career aspirations. And among those who cope less well, each will have her or his own individual learning needs. But the characteristics we've identified above will help us to start thinking about ways we can respond as teachers, in order to enhance the quality of the learning process, both for the learners and for ourselves.

Strategies we can use

If we're looking for broad strategies, the following list is a good starting point.

- **Appear approachable and enthusiastic.**
- **Create structure.**
- **Communicate clearly.**
- **Remove barriers, such as fear and boredom.**
- **Use reward.**
- **Engage and motivate.**

Although all these tactics can be useful for supporting the learning of any age group, 14–16 year-olds respond particularly well to this combination of *structure* and *positive reinforcement*. And there's a useful mnemonic for remembering this list: put it into practice, and there's every chance that success will ACCRUE.

Now let's look at each of these strategies in more detail, and explore what they involve in practical terms.

1. Appear approachable and enthusiastic

There's nothing less likely to inspire learners' interest than a teacher who themselves demonstrates no real interest in the subject or topic being taught. Even less inspiring is the teacher who says, *'I know this is boring, but we've got to do it'.* How could anyone expect learners – particularly young learners – to want to engage after an introduction like that? So we need to look enthusiastic, talk enthusiastically and with animation, and trust that our enthusiasm will prove to be catching. Even if we're having to fake enthusiasm for a topic we don't personally feel much interest in, our teaching will have more sparkle than if we made no effort at all, and so we – just as much as our learners – are likely to enjoy it more.

As well as appearing enthusiastic, you also need to appear approachable. Approachability will help to allay the fears of younger learners who feel intimidated by their first experience of a large college environment; and it will challenge the preconceptions of those learners who have negative expectations of all teachers. Building a positive relationship with your learners will be the single most effective way of helping them to engage with their learning. Being scary can have short-term benefits; but in the long run, if learners like and trust you they'll be more inclined to seek your approval and work hard 'for you' (although, of course, the person who'll be benefiting is themselves).

But let's be very clear here about what 'being approachable' means. It doesn't mean being a walkover, or being the learners' best friend. It doesn't mean abdicating or compromising your professional role. It just means responding to learners in a way that encourages trust and respect, showing them respect in return, and making sure they feel comfortable about coming to you with questions and problems related to their learning.

2. Create structure

Structure helps to create a sense of security and purpose. For some young learners, the transition between the 'safe' and comparatively regimented environment of school and the more adult, anonymous culture of the college with its fewer rules and restraints will prove difficult to handle. If we build clear structures into the planning of our lesson, and provide explicit direction in terms of learning goals and expected behaviour, we create the reassurance of certainty and routine, which can be particularly important to 14–16 year-olds. Here are some of the ways we can do this.

- **Always start on time.**
- **Make the aims of the course or programme clear, and go over them every session if necessary.**
- **Give your lessons a predictable shape. For example, the timing and length of the break (if you have one); where question time comes in the lesson; how and when you take in homework or assignments; and so on.**
- **At the start of every lesson tell learners what you are all going to do in the course of the lesson; and at the end recap by summarising what's taken place.**

- Create a safe and supportive learning environment by maintaining a routine in the way you begin and end lessons.
- For example, it can be useful to always begin the lesson with a 'settling' activity. Settling activities are widely used in schools, and help not only to establish a sense of order and routine from the outset of the lesson, but also keeps the noise down during that crucial time so that you can more easily be heard as you explain the lesson objectives and tasks. Settling activities can include things such as a game of hangman using essential subject-specific terms; a puzzle or question displayed on the board; a brief video clip with a 'quiz' to complete afterwards; a short gapped handout in the form of a quiz to check how much they remember of the previous lesson; and so on. When designing a settling activity, remember that it will serve not only to provide routine and an orderly start, but also to signal to the learners that the lesson has started and not a minute must be wasted.
- As you progress on to other learning activities, state the learning objectives of each activity clearly before the activity and reiterate them after the activity, saying something like: *'Here's what you're going to learn to do.'* And, *'Now you've done that, you're able to...'*
- Signal clearly how much time is allowed for each task, and provide reminders as the task proceeds; for example, *'Ten minutes left. You should be on the final question now.'* You should also state clearly and firmly when that time is up.
- Don't allow too long for group tasks. Keep up the pace. A lack of apparent urgency will make learners more likely to stray off-task.
- Be absolutely clear about organisational or college rules, and be consistent and fair in applying or upholding them. State or negotiate any additional rules of your own (for example, about language or behaviour), and be consistent and fair in the application of those, too. And make sure your own behaviour always abides by the rules. This all helps learners to feel secure and to understand what parameters they must set to their own behaviour.
- Always make the recap at the end of the lesson a positive one, involving praise (and possibly other rewards) for those who've earned it. Routines make learners feel safe. And an orderly ending, with an emphasis on what's been achieved, means that learners are taking away with them a positive impression of the lesson and of themselves. This will make them more likely to feel positive about coming to the next one.

One of the barriers to creating a sense of order is a messy beginning to the lesson. This is almost inevitable if there is a problem with learners' punctuality. This will make it difficult for us to establish a settling activity. However, it's usually best to resist the temptation to delay the start of the lesson to wait for habitual latecomers, because this can simply result in learners delaying their arrival even longer as they learn that we don't mind waiting for them. (Remember Chapter 7?) If you design settling activities that are interesting and enjoyable (learning activities disguised as games, as in the suggested list above), you may well find that this works to get learners to the lesson on time, because they don't want to miss out.

CLOSE FOCUS CLOSE FOCUS **CLOSE FOCUS** CLOSE FOCUS **CLOSE FOCUS**

So what other strategies can you think of to encourage punctuality? You might want to develop some of the ideas from Chapter 15, if you've not done so already.

3. Communicate clearly
- Always break tasks down into a number of smaller steps. It's a good idea to do this for all tasks, not just the very complex ones.
- When briefing learners for a task, make sure the instructions you give are clear, and delivered one step at a time. One of the things this allows you to do is to ensure that no learner is rushed on to

the next step in the task until they have thoroughly grasped the one before. In this way it helps provide a secure learning environment in which learners are not set up to fail.

- Make sure any instructions you give are *heard*. This is not always easy in a noisy classroom or workshop. It may sometimes be necessary to raise our voice above the sound of equipment or machinery; but we should try to avoid raising our voice in competition with noisy learners, other than briefly, to gain their attention. It's much more effective to create a relative quiet in which to give instructions. Surprisingly, lowering the voice, rather than raising it, can be an effective way to achieve this.

- It's often, however, a good idea to display instructions – on the board, screen, flipchart – as well as going through them verbally, to make sure they are communicated to everyone and there is no ambiguity. This is a good way of overcoming the problem of background noise, whether that's machinery working or learners *not* working. (This will not, of course apply, in cases where learners' literacy skills are not yet sufficiently developed to enable them to read instructions accurately.)

- Be prepared to repeat instructions as many times as necessary. This isn't about trying to compete with learners' inattention; it's about making sure everyone has a secure understanding. This can be particularly important for younger learners who may not yet have developed note-taking skills. Ask and answer questions until you're sure everyone has fully understood what they should be doing.

- If learners are having difficulty understanding you, think of different ways of explaining the same thing. Try to relate it to their world. Use something they'll be familiar with, such as a sporting analogy, something on a current TV show or in the music charts.

- Move around the room checking individuals' understanding, and providing an opportunity for them to ask for clarification that they may have shied away from seeking in front of the whole class.

- Always explain to learners WHY they are doing something. Wherever you can, relate this to the vocational area they are interested in, or to the world of work generally. Don't take it for granted that they'll see the point in what you're asking them to do. Always spell it out for them.

- Wherever possible, provide worksheets or gapped handouts. 14–16 year-olds often haven't developed note-taking skills and need some help in recording important lesson content. Gapped handouts can provide a sort of scaffolding which helps them to identify the key points and key words, and get them down in a logical order for future reference.

- If you do use gapped handouts, always be sure to check them before learners file them away, in order to ensure that the information they've recorded on them is correct.

- When designing worksheets and gapped handouts, make sure they aren't overcrowded with text. (Remember the guidelines in Chapter 9?) Stick to main points and essential diagrams, and use bullet points wherever possible. Leave plenty of spacing and a legible sized font (at least 12 point).

- Think carefully about the language you employ in handouts. Use a vocabulary the learners will be familiar with – at least as your starting point. When introducing technical or specialist language, define it clearly, providing a glossary if necessary. Handouts that are too demanding in terms of their language will simply not be read.

- Don't overdo the handouts. The more you give out in one lesson, the less chance they'll be read. Better one handout that you go through carefully all together, than half a dozen that end up crumpled in the bottom of sports bags.

- Don't distribute handouts until the point at which you want the learners to read it. You don't want them reading when they need to be listening to what you're saying. This creates confusion, not structure.

- If you make sure the handouts are hole-punched, there's more chance that learners will put them safely in their files for future reference.

- If you refer back to previous handouts occasionally in subsequent lessons, the learners will begin to realise that these are important and are required reading. This establishes continuity and a pattern to their learning.

4. Remove barriers, such as fear and boredom

When we looked at the characteristics of 14–16 year-olds we considered some reasons why they might feel threatened or uneasy in the college environment. These reasons are not just to do with unfamiliarity, but may also be to do with a lack of confidence in their own ability to succeed in what is demanded of them. In Chapter 14 we discussed how this fear can act as a barrier to learning for learners of any age; but some 14–16 year-olds selected for a PCET 1 route may have particular reason to doubt their ability to cope. Two very good strategies for removing fear, as we've seen before, are to build up the learner's confidence and create a safe and supportive learning environment. Clear structure and clear communication can go a long way towards achieving this. So what else can we do?

We can build learners' self-esteem by:

- planning activities into your lessons which give you opportunity and time to talk to individual learners so that you can get to know something about their aspirations and their worries. Show them that you're interested in them;
- always appearing pleased to be teaching them (even if you're not!);
- finding things to praise them for – both as individuals and as a group. There's always something, even if it's only something small and nothing directly to do with the curriculum – moving a bag out of the way to let someone pass, for example;
- giving them tasks that won't defeat them. Build into your lesson plans opportunities for them – all of them – to get a sense of achievement. This may involve planning carefully for differentiation;
- providing positive reinforcement whenever you can. *Good... Well done... Well tried... Not quite, but nearly, so well done.* And so on. Even if they get something wrong, show them you're pleased with them for trying. This will make them more likely to try again next time.

CLOSE FOCUS CLOSE FOCUS **CLOSE FOCUS** CLOSE FOCUS **CLOSE FOCUS**

Go back and look again at the theories of learning in Chapter 7. In what ways do those theories underpin each of the points in the list we've just looked at?

A low boredom threshold can be the other main barrier for this age group. The claim, *'It's boring!'* can sometimes seem to us to be an automatic defence put up against having to engage with the work. But it can genuinely be very difficult for younger learners to sit still for long periods of time, or to listen or give their attention to one task in other than short bursts. Some academics blame our channel-flipping culture; but common sense tells us that a lot of this is also to do with youth, energy and hormones. There are plenty of ways to combat boredom. They include:

- incorporating plenty of learner activities into your lesson plan;
- making sure you have frequent changes of learner activity;
- keeping any periods of exposition as brief as possible, and avoiding lengthy 'lectures'. Plan several short periods of exposition and alternate them with periods of learner activity, rather than planning a lesson which requires 14–16 year-old learners to listen to you attentively for any length of time;
- selecting teaching and learning methods (see Chapter 10), which involve active rather than passive learning. Make sure the learners are going to be spending more time 'doing' than they are listening and watching;
- planning for some activities that allow learners to move around if you can, and if it's safe to do so, even if this is simply to form or reform small working groups;
- planning to have a one minute 'break' in activity every 20 minutes or so, for learners to stand up,

stretch, and sit down again;
- incorporating two smaller breaks rather than one long break (but bear in mind that younger learners must not wander unsupervised, so these may have to be restricted to the classroom or workshop);

5. Use Reward

We're going to look at three kinds of reward here. We can refer to them as:

- prizes;
- praise;
- promises.

Prizes: It may seem a little patronising to suggest rewarding learners with little prizes such as sweets or raisins. But many teachers have found that this tactic works well – and not only for younger learners. It injects an element of fun, which, in addition to the initial idea of reward, also disarms those learners whose personal baggage includes the idea that learning can never be enjoyable; and gives attention-seeking learners a more useful focus – answering questions, for example, rather than disrupting learning. You can use prizes in the following ways:

- for punctuality;
- for correct answers;
- for best group effort;
- for the learner or group nominated by the rest as 'best performance';
- at the end of the lesson for those who've stayed on task.

You'll no doubt be able to think of ways to add to this list. The important thing to remember is that we are using 'prizes' to help learners understand that learning can be a positive experience. If we can't get them engaged with learning in the first place, we'll never achieve that. So 'prizes' are an intermediate step. Our end goal is that they'll learn to find it rewarding in itself.

Praise: We saw earlier how we can use praise to raise learners' self-esteem. We can also, of course, use it to reward them, as we explored in some detail, and in relation to all groups of learners, in Chapters 7 and 14. Two key points to bear in mind when rewarding younger learners with praise are:

- don't restrict your praise to their achievements in skills, knowledge and understanding. Find opportunities for praising their behaviour and attitude, too; for example: punctuality, behaving within the rules, using appropriate language;
- create opportunities to give praise, if necessary. For example, ask them to get into groups and then praise them for doing as you asked. Perhaps you can praise them for doing it quietly or quickly; but if neither of these would ring true, just praise them for doing it. Similarly for individuals, if you ask someone to pass some handouts to the rest of their group, and they do it, make a point of thanking them. Just a *'Thank you. Well done'* will do. It may be the only opportunity you get to praise them for anything, so make it count!

In this chapter we've looked at two uses of praise: to build self-esteem and to give reward. How do these two functions relate to the theories of learning we looked at in Chapter 7? Which theory or theories in particular would you use to justify each of these uses of praise?

Promises: Promises are about deferred gratification. They enable us to say, as teachers, 'If you do this, then this will be the reward.' However, learners have to be confident that you're going to deliver, and so this strategy is effective only if you use it fairly and consistently. Empty promises are no good. This applies to withholding a reward as well as to giving it. For example, if you've promised them an early break if they get a task completed, but they don't complete it – then they don't get the early break. But if they do complete it, they do. If they can't be sure of this, promises won't work.

The sort of promises you can make include:

- an activity at the end of the lesson that has the appearance of a game; for example, a quiz, using vocationally-relevant terms. Learners may see this as finishing early, but you know differently;
- an additional use of this activity is to deduct time from it to compensate for time lost during the lesson through learners being off-task. So you might say, for example, 'Please remember there'll be a minute knocked off the team event at the end for every minute you spend fiddling with that phone instead of getting on with the task';
- promising a brief 'Check your Texts' time twice during an hour's lesson as a reward for keeping phones turned off and put away during the rest of the time. (Of course, you can't use this tactic if there's a no-phones rule operating.);
- alternatively, promising a couple of one-minute 'stretch your legs' or 'talk about TV' breaks each lesson on condition that learners remain on task and don't wander about during the rest of the lesson.

6. Engage and motivate
We looked at motivation in detail in Chapter 14, and everything covered there applies equally to younger learners. But in addition, you might like to consider the following strategies, which many teachers report as being particularly effective in engaging and motivating this age group.

- Relate everything you possibly can to the work situation. The reason why they're in PCET 1 and not at school is because they have 'chosen' to follow a vocational curriculum. You can use this to kick-start their enthusiasm, and to sustain it. So when you demonstrate a task, for example, you make a point of stressing that that's how it's done at work. This also applies to health and safety issues, and to appropriate ways of interacting (see Chapter 2).
- Extend this to behaviour as well as to learning objectives. Make a start by agreeing with them a set of rules about behaviour, stressing that these must be based on what would be acceptable in the workplace.
- Choose resources and texts applicable to their vocational area. This is another way of encouraging learners to take pride in themselves as skilled workers-in-waiting. Always make their learning as near as possible to the real thing, whether it's hairdressing, electronics or trowel trades.
- Showcase your own vocational skills. Encourage the learners to think of you not only as a teacher but also as an accomplished and experienced professional in the line of work to which the learners themselves aspire.
- Encourage them to think of themselves as people who will be successful in the workplace if they

learn to...whatever it is they need to do. But remember, don't make false promises; and this includes not encouraging unrealistic expectations. If the initial award they're working towards won't be sufficient to gain them employment, find some way to encourage a longer view.

Reflecting on theory

We've had a look, from a very practical point of view, at strategies for engaging and encouraging younger learners. We've talked about communication, structure, reward and motivation. Now let's go back to the argument for the entry of 14–16 year-olds into PCET 1, some of which is set out in *14–19 Education and Skills* (DfES 2005); and look at it carefully, while keeping in mind the issues encountered in practice by teachers in the classroom or workshop.

TASK TASK **TASK** TASK **TASK** TASK TASK **TASK** TASK **TASK** TASK TASK

Read carefully through the two passages below, and then answer the questions which follow. You may wish to make some notes so that you can discuss your answers with others.

Passage 1
Economic and social change mean that the need for education and high-level skills is greater than ever before.

2.5. In this interdependent world, currents of economic change in other parts of the world can quickly affect this country and technology increasingly means that even service industries serving one country can be sited in another. Changes in the traditional industrial base have already profoundly changed the nature of many of our communities. The availability of low-skill, manual jobs has declined over a long period and for most, physical strength alone is no longer a sufficient basis for employment.

2.6. The changes to our expectations of working life, too, have been profound. The modern world in the labour market and beyond makes greater demands on a young person's capacity to communicate, present themselves, work in teams and understand diversity. No longer is there an assumption that the sector in which a young person starts work is the one in which they will end their career. For most, movement between jobs is the norm; for many, movement between entirely different sectors of the economy a realistic prospect. Young people may also want to further their careers in other countries. We must expect that the ability to move successfully between jobs in this way will be a growing necessity for the young people of today over the course of their working lives.

2.7. In this context, the need to offer every young person the opportunity to become educated and skilled is not only an economic imperative, but a moral one. Young people who do not have a good grounding in the basics and the right skills and knowledge for employment will not have much prospect of making the most of themselves in life and at work. If young people leave full-time education without well-respected and recognised qualifications, then they are unlikely to be able to gain employment and then cope with the changing context of work through their lives. And the ongoing social and technological change that affects our world demands that more young people are prepared not only with transferable skills but also to adapt and learn throughout their lifetime. In simple financial terms, as Figure 2.2 shows, those who achieve higher levels of qualification will earn more.[1]

Figure 2.2: Education increases the productivity of the workforce, reflected in higher wages. Analysis of gross weekly earnings from the labour force survey shows that earnings increase with qualification levels.

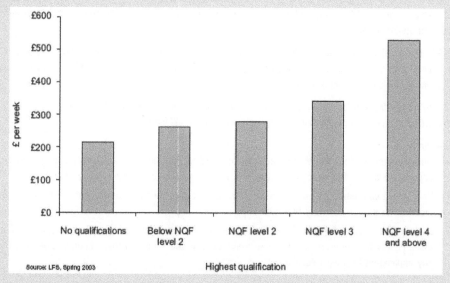

Source: LFS, Spring 2003

2.8. The wider economic need is significant too and the cost for all of us if we do not succeed, great. If we are to continue to attract many of the high value-added industries to this country, and to compete effectively on the global stage, then we will need far more of our population to have high levels of education. A critical mass of highly-skilled people will continue to attract those employers to this country.

Figure 2.3: Correlation between offending behaviour and truancy.

	Males		Females	
	12–16	17–30	12–16	17–30
	% offender	% offender	% offender	% offender
Truant at least once a month	47	21	30	9
Occasional truant	13	16	18	3
No truant	10	8	4	2

Source: YLS 1998/9 HO RS 209 – note 12–16 year olds were asked about truanting in the last year. Those aged 17+ were asked about truanting in their last year of school.

We also need to ensure that our population is not making choices based on stereotypes, but on the basis of clear advice and guidance. The benefits of more engaging work, higher living standards and prosperity will flow to all of us.

[1] Levels refer to National Qualifications Framework (NQF) levels. Level 2 is intermediate level (equivalent to 5 or more A*-C grade GCSEs); level 3 is advanced level (equivalent to 2 or more A levels); level 4 is equivalent to first degree level.

2.9. Wider society's need for young people to achieve educational success goes beyond the needs of the economy, however. There is a strong and well-documented association between poor attendance and behaviour at school and later anti-social behaviour and criminality, as Figure 2.3 shows.

2.10. Tackling disengagement, truancy and poor behaviour at school are essential; providing motivating routes to success a necessity. It is in all our interests that we avoid the costs of failure to the individual and to wider society. And if we are to have a healthy society of responsible, active citizens, well-prepared to take a role in our democracy and the international community, then our education system provides us with the means of achieving that.

2.11. For all of these reasons, the need for an education system which offers high-quality routes to success for all young people has never been greater. For all the progress of recent years, there remain significant challenges to be overcome.

(Taken from: DfES (2005) 14–19 Education and Skills, London: HMSO. Available at: www.education.gov.uk/publications/eOrderingDownload/CM%206476.pdf

Questions

1. What arguments does the White Paper put forward for 'the need to offer every young person the opportunity to become educated and skilled' (2.7)? You should be able identify at least three.

2. How would you, personally and as a professional, prioritise these? In other words, which reason of those given do you consider the most important?

3. Look carefully again at Figure 2.3. What argument are these figures being used to support? Could these figures be interpreted in any other way? What is the source of these figures? Does this have any implication for their reliability?

Passage 2

2.16. Of course, there are concerns about even the well-established academic route. There are concerns about lack of breadth post-16 in the A level programmes even of those who do get 5 A*-C grade GCSEs.

Figure 2.5: Attainment at 16 and post-16 participation.

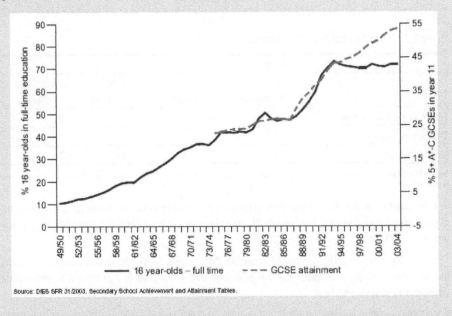

Source: DIES SFR 31/2003. Secondary School Achievement and Attainment Tables.

There are concerns about the extent to which the most able are really stretched with some young people acquiring large numbers of GCSEs, which individually do not challenge them. And, as achievement rises, some of our most prestigious universities report increasing difficulty in differentiating between very strong candidates for the most popular courses, since their educational records appear very similar.

2.17. Perhaps more seriously, there has been little choice of high-quality curriculum and qualifications pathways. The GCSE and A level route has been by far the most well-recognised and understood route to success. But for those who prefer to learn in a different way, who would benefit from greater variety of learning styles or who are more interested by learning in ways with direct practical applicability, there has not been real choice. These young people (although many might do well in GCSEs and A levels) have to wait to develop their talents until later in the education and training system.

2.18. For some pupils in this category, achieving well in GCSEs and A levels enables them to flourish at university, on an academic or vocational course, and then to go on to success in employment. For others, though, the existing curriculum on offer switches them off. They may take GCSEs without success. As Figure 2.6 shows, very few of those who do not get 5 or more A*-C GCSEs at 16 go on to study at level 3. Since the success rate for those retaking GCSEs is not high (only around 20% of those retaking get a higher grade than they did first time around), young people may easily get stuck in a qualifications blind alley. Furthermore, there is currently little scope to take a little more time over GCSEs in order to reach a higher standard.

2.19. The post-16 alternatives to GCSEs and A levels in schools and colleges need to be more widely available and to be credible with employers. Too many young people experience qualifications 'dead ends', where despite pursuing a further qualification, there are no clear onward routes to employment or progression to a higher level of learning.

Figure 2.6: Post-16 courses pursued by young people, by attainment at 16. Main study aim at 17 by year 11 attainment: % of those studying.

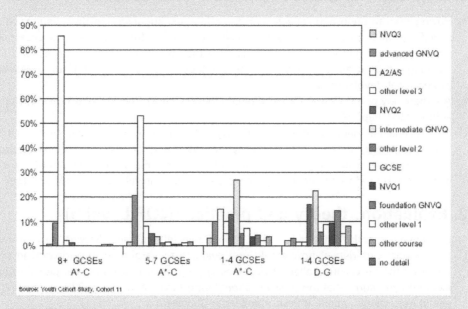

Source: Youth Cohort Study, Cohort 11

(Taken from: DfES (2005) *14–19: Education and Skills*, London: HMSO. Available at: www.education. gov.uk/publications/eOrderingDownload/CM%206476.pdf

Questions
1. What concerns are identified about the existing academic route? You should be able to identify at least four.
2. What are the arguments expressed here for providing alternative routes for young learners?
3. To what extent does 14–16 provision within your own organisation reflect this ideal of an alternative route? How does it fit with the organisation's overall vision and purpose?

Branching options

The following tasks are designed to allow you to apply or explore further some of the contents of this chapter. If you are using this book to support your professional development leading to a teaching qualification, or other formal CPD accreditation, you may find it useful to choose a task according to the level at which you are currently working. These are indicated in brackets. Alternatively, you choose to work through them all.

1. Reflection and self-evaluation (NQF level 5)

a) Having read through and reflected on the strategies suggested in this chapter, what specific professional skills do you consider are called for in order to successfully support the learning of 14–16 year-olds? Are they the same skills as are needed for teaching other groups of learners, or do they suggest the need for additional professional development?

b) Are there any points you would wish to add to your own professional action plan in the light of this chapter?

c) Looking again at that first extract from the White Paper we used in the final task, what, in your view, is the difference between being 'educated' and 'skilled'? The context in which both words are used suggest the writers of the White Paper are assuming there's a distinction. How do you see your purpose as a teacher in relation to each of these?

2. Evaluation: theory and practice (NQF Level 6)

a) Looking again at the extracts from the White Paper (above), and drawing on your own professional experience, how would you evaluate the argument put forward in that paper for the provision of alternative routes of progression for young people? To what extent do you agree that this policy is about 'opportunity' and 'choice'? (You may find it useful here to look again at your notes from Chapter 3.)

b) Taking this White Paper together with the Foster Report (2005) and the subsequent White Paper, *Further Education: Raising Skills, Improving Life Chances* (2006), what patterns and progressions in policy can you identify? (Foster Report: www.natecla.org.uk/uploads/documents/doc_2797.pdf; *Further Education: Raising Skills, Improving Life Chances*: www.eauc.org.uk/sorted/files/fe_white_paper_1.pdf)

3. Engaging critically with the literature (NQF level 7: M level)

a) Look again at the extracts from the White Paper set out above, and conduct a discourse analysis, looking particularly at the choice of language used to describe the disengagement of young learners.

b) What factors identify this as polemic?

c) Go to the DfE website and look at the next section of this White Paper: paragraphs 2.20-2.23 (**www.education.gov.uk/publications/eOrderingDownload/CM%206476.pdf**). Analyse the reasons being put forward here to explain why vocational education has been 'a cause for concern'. What would be the argument for viewing this as only a partial explanation?

d) Paragraph 2.2 refers to policy initiatives which have 'failed to resolve the issue'. Which initiatives do you think are being referred to here, and why?

REFERENCES AND FURTHER READING

DfES (2005) 14–19 Education and Skills. London: HMSO.

DfES (2006) *FE Reform: Raising Skills, Improving Life Chances.* Norwich: TSO.

Donovan, G. (2005) *Teaching 14–19: Everything You Need to Know About Teaching Across the Phases.* London: David Fulton.

Foster, A. *et al.* (2005) *Realising the Potential: A Review of the Future Role of Further Education Colleges.* Annesley: DfES.

Lumby, J. and Poskett, N. (2005) *14–19 Education: Policy, Leadership and Learning.* London: Sage.

16
Professionalism and scholarship 3: reading critically and reflectively

The objectives of this chapter

This chapter encourages you to explore and reflect upon extracts from texts written by key figures in educational theory and research, and to relate these to your own experience as a teacher and learner, and to the context in which you work. Working through these questions at the appropriate level will help you to:

- **recognise the importance of reflecting on your own professional practice and values (AS4);**
- **find opportunities for continuing your professional development (AS4; AS7);**
- **explore principles, frameworks and theories which underpin good practice (AK4.1; AP4.1);**
- **draw on research to enhance your own professional development and practice (AK4.3; AP4.3).**

Introduction

One of the key purposes of this chapter is to support the skills in thinking, reflecting and academic writing which you will need to successfully complete the written assessments (coursework assignments) that are a major component of your QTLS programme. To do this we shall explore some landmark texts in order to reflect upon and critically analyse some of the theories, arguments and conceptual frameworks underpinning policy and practice in post-compulsory education and training. The first two will focus on professionalism and the teacher, and the third and fourth on vocational education, status and work. Each extract we look at will be followed by three sets of questions designed to help you analyse and interrogate further what you have read. The questions are aimed at three levels:

- reflection;
- analysis;
- critical analysis.

This will allow you to engage with the text at the level you consider appropriate to your own professional development needs. For some or all of the texts you may like to work through all three levels in order to build up your understanding of all the ways in which what is being said there can illuminate aspects of your own professional practice or the contexts in which you teach.

TASK TASK **TASK** TASK **TASK** **TASK** TASK **TASK** TASK **TASK** **TASK** TASK

1. Professionalism and the teacher

The following passage explores what we mean by 'professionalism', and particularly the professionalism of the teacher. Read it through carefully, making notes if necessary, and then chose one (or more) of the sets of questions which follow.

Most discussions about teaching as a profession focus on the extent to which teaching conforms to the criteria normally employed in distinguishing professional from non-professional occupations. Briefly, these are, first, that the methods and procedures employed by members of a profession are based on a body of theoretical knowledge and research. Part of the reason why medicine, law and engineering are regarded as professional occupations is because they involve techniques and skills supported by a body of systematically produced knowledge. A second distinguishing feature of professions is that the over-riding commitment of their members is to the well-being of their clients. Both the medical and legal professions are governed by ethical codes which serve to ensure that the interest of clients is always the predominant concern. Thirdly, to ensure that they can always act in the interest of their clients, members of a profession reserve the right to make autonomous judgments free from external non-professional controls and constraints. This professional autonomy usually operates at both the individual and the collective levels. Individually, professionals make independent decisions about which particular course of action to adopt in any particular situation. Collectively, professionals have the right to determine the sort of policies, organization and procedures that should govern their profession as a whole. The medical and legal professions, for example, select their own membership and determine their own disciplinary and accountability procedures.

Even this very brief description of the characteristics of a profession is sufficient to convey some idea of the limited extent to which teaching, as we know it today, can legitimately be regarded as a professional activity. It is clear, for example, that theory and research play a much less significant part in teaching than they do in other professions. Indeed, what little evidence there is suggests that most teachers regard research as an esoteric activity having little to do with their everyday practical concerns. Likewise, the relationship of teachers to their clients is much less straightforward than in other professions. To doctors and lawyers, the client is either 'a patient' or 'a case' and professional concern is limited to effecting a cure or winning a case. A teacher's professional concern for his pupils, however, cannot be limited in this sort of way. In the case of the doctor or lawyer, a specific condition, such as an illness or a real or alleged grievance, exists before the professional is called in. This is not so for the teacher. A lack of education is a diffuse and open condition, too general to be regarded as specific 'ignorance', except in some special cases of a very basic kind (total illiteracy, for example). The business of educating is diffuse and prolonged, and teaching requires a much more diverse range of skills than those required by either doctors or lawyers. A further complication arises because it is not at all self-evident that the pupils are the teachers' only clients. Parents, the local community, government and employers all make claims to be considered as legitimate clients and their interests may not coincide with what teachers believe to be in the educational interest of their pupils.

It is, however, in the area of autonomy that the professionalism of teachers is most seriously limited. For although teachers can, and do, make autonomous judgments about their everyday classroom practices, the broad organizational context within which these practices occur is something over which they have little control. Teachers operate within hierarchically arranged institutions and the part they play in making decisions about such things as overall educational policy, the selection and training of new members, accountability procedures, and the general structures of the organizations in which they work is negligible. In short, teachers, unlike other professionals, have little professional autonomy at the collective level.

What all this suggests is that if teaching is to become a more genuinely professional activity, three sorts of development will be necessary. First, the attitudes and practices of teachers must become more firmly grounded in educational theory and research. Secondly, the professional autonomy of teachers must be extended to include the opportunity to participate in the decisions that are made about the broader educational context within which they operate; that is, professional autonomy must be regarded as a collective, as well as an individual matter. Thirdly, the professional responsibilities of the teacher must be extended so as to include a professional obligation to interested parties in the community at large.

Now these three requirements are closely related. For example, any extension of the professional autonomy of teachers will have important implications both for the kind of knowledge required from research and the kind of relationship that exists between researchers and teachers. Thus, the sort of knowledge required from research would not be limited to that which affects classroom practices and teaching skills. Rather, it would include the sort of knowledge that would facilitate collaborative discussion within the teaching profession as a whole about the broad social, political and cultural context within which it operates. Moreover, if professional autonomy was extended in this way, research findings could not be regarded as something that teachers accepted from researchers and slavishly implemented. Instead, researchers would be required to devise ways of helping the teaching profession to organize its beliefs and ideas (both individually and collectively) so as to facilitate the making of informed judgments about professional activities and to fulfil its responsibility to defend these judgments to other interested parties.

From: Carr, W. and Kemmis, S. (1986) *Becoming Critical: Education, Knowledge and Action Research.* Lewes: Falmer Press, pages 7–10.

Questions

Set 1: reflection

a) Which three key features do the authors identify as distinguishing what we mean by a 'profession'? Are there any features which you would want to add to this list?

b) How far do you agree with the writers that, given their analysis, teaching can 'only to a limited extent' be regarded as a profession?

c) Do you think the writers are correct in claiming that most teachers don't see research as having much to do with their everyday working practices? In what ways have you used research to support your professional practice?

d) Which three requirements do the writers consider necessary if we are to make teaching a more genuinely professional occupation? To what extent do you agree with their analysis?

Set 2: analysis

a) Summarise the writers' argument, identifying those steps where you might wish to contest what they are saying, or question them further.

b) The writers draw attention to the complicated nature of the relationship between teachers and their 'clients'. In what ways is this further complicated in the case of teachers in the post-compulsory sector? Who are our 'clients' and is this the appropriate term to use?

c) Analyse the relationship the writers draw between research and the professional development of teachers. To what extent do you agree with them?

Set 3: critical analysis

a) How far does the writers' ideal of the autonomous teacher (both collectively and individually) fit with the discourses which construct the role of teacher within the post-compulsory sector?

b) The writers refer to differences in 'the kind of knowledge' required from research. What do you understand them to mean? How would you extend their argument here in the context of post-compulsory education and training (PCET)?

TASK TASK **TASK** TASK **TASK** TASK TASK **TASK** TASK **TASK** TASK TASK

2: The 'competent' teacher?

It is interesting to compare the next passage to the one we've just read. It addresses the same question, but from a slightly different angle, exploring the question of whether competence-based professional development for teachers would in fact serve to limit their claims to professionalism. It is taken from a book which looks in detail at post-modernism and education, and therefore employs, in places, a specialised vocabulary which you may find unfamiliar at first. Read the passage through, more than once if necessary. Make notes if you find it useful to do so. Then chose one (or more) of the sets of questions which follow.

Discourses of competence attempt to repress certain conceptions of knowledge and understanding in order to sustain an agenda where competence-based qualifications appear to be the appropriate response. A regime of truth is established which derides certain forms of knowledge as 'theory' irrelevant to 'getting the job done well'. This is most noticeable in neo-conservative governments' approaches to the training of teachers in which 'theory' is constructed as the reason for the failure of progressive tendencies in education since the 1960s and which can only be countered with a greater emphasis on the practice of classroom management. Here the competent teacher is constructed not as one who knows that something is the case or knows how to teach but who can actually teach competently according to pre-determined criteria of competence. The veiling of certain terms of knowledge as 'theory' to be removed from the curriculum of teacher training is something which also finds support among many trainee teachers who thereby deny themselves the forms of autonomy and the right to be critical which were previously the defining characteristics of the teaching profession.

This emphasis on performance is also part of the 'no nonsense' management style of discourse that has become so powerful since the 1980s. The greater emphasis being put on the notion of 'practice' in the training of teachers to which 'theory' is subordinated and instrumental is reflected in institutional arrangements and forms of assessment to which trainees are subject. More emphasis is placed on teachers training within the schools rather than 'out of touch' education departments in higher education institutions and portfolio-based assessment is given greater importance than the more traditional essay. Trainee teachers therefore become increasingly subject to the on-going self-monitoring of their own experience and practice within which the possibilities for alternative and resistant formulations and discourses are severely limited. Dissatisfactions will still be articulated but the framework is more likely to be 'moaning in the staff-room' than any more considered response. In this sense.

...privileging practice without due consideration of the complex interactions that mark the totality of theory/practice and language/meaning relationships is not simply reductionist; it is a form of theoretical tyranny. Theory... becomes a form of practice that ignores the political value of theoretical discourse within a specific historical conjuncture.

(Aronowitz and Giroux, 1991, p92)

Paradoxically, therefore, in becoming more occupationally competent, teachers may relinquish a capacity for contextualising and reflexively understanding their practices. The management of the classroom, the learning programme, the curriculum, displaces wider practices from educational agendas. The provision of education is reconstituted on the twin bases of central state control –

of curriculum, of testing and of teachers – and free-market, parental choice. These modes of regulation are intended both to provide social and political stability and to isolate and neutralize, as far as possible, the influence of reformist public educators . . .

(Ball ,1990c, p58)

The co-implication of notions of occupational competence with a greater emphasis on the 'effective' and 'efficient' management of organizations and people is effected not simply in the rapid development of management competences, but is further demonstrated in the very structure of NVQ awards. NVQs actually inscribe a division of labour into the qualifications structure, so that the higher levels of award within each occupational sector are for management competences. In every sphere of occupationally related learning, therefore, it is managers who are attributed higher levels of competence than those in supervisory or non-supervisory positions. The competent shop manager is therefore more highly qualified than the competent shop assistant. The desire for mastery of particular occupational competences is compounded by desire for mastery within the division of labour.

References

Aronowitz, W. and Giroux, H. (1991) *Postmodern Education: Politics, Culture and Social Criticism.* Minneapolis: University of Minnesota Press.

Ball, S. (1990) *Politics and Policy Making in Education: Explorations in Policy Sociology.* London: Routledge.

From Usher, R. and Edwards, R. (1994) *Postmodernism and Education.* London: Routledge, pages 115–116.

Questions

Set 1: reflection
a) How far do you agree that competence-based learning can lead to an undervaluing of theory? How would you construct a counter-argument to this?
b) The writers suggest that trainee teachers 'become increasingly subject to the ongoing self-monitoring of their own experience and practice.' What examples can you give of self-monitoring? For example, are you required to keep a professional development journal or log? Are you asked to evaluate your own teaching performance? Why do you think the authors see this as problematic?
c) What do the writers identify as a major drawback of competence-based professional development for teachers? (The answer can be found in the final paragraph.)

Set 2: analysis
a) How would you summarise the argument contained in this extract?
b) At the end of the first paragraph, the writers use the term 'autonomy'. How does their use of this term compare with that of the authors of the previous extract?
c) How far do you agree that 'discourses of competence attempt to repress certain conceptions of knowledge and understanding'? What 'conceptions of knowledge and understanding' do you think the writers are referring to here?

Set 3: critical analysis
a) How far do you agree with the writers' attribution of the decline of 'theory' as a component of teacher training?
b) Although on the surface they are making a similar point, in terms of discourse, this extract is very different from the previous one. How do these two extracts compare in

terms of their philosophical stance and conceptual framework?

c) The argument about 'self-monitoring' reflects Foucault's work on *'surveillance'* (Foucault, 1979). What is the point that's being made here, and might it equally well apply to learners' self-monitoring through the use of self-assessment and self-evaluations?

TASK TASK **TASK** TASK **TASK** TASK **TASK** TASK **TASK** TASK **TASK** TASK

3: *Vocational Education: the status of work in contemporary society*

For our third extract we look at an analysis of the status of work in today's society, as it is perceived by young people. Teaching within the newly redefined Skills Sector, it is more than ever important for us to understand young learners' attitudes towards the world of work. When you've read this passage through carefully, making notes if necessary, choose one (or more) of the sets of questions which follow it below.

Occupation, status and identity are inextricably interwoven – we are what we do – and not to work is in many ways to become excluded, a 'non-person'. However, here we want to register two caveats. First, occupational status and work may not be that important in the lives of 'the young'. Indeed, evidence is suggesting that many post-adolescents are trying to 'postpone' or keep their work identities 'on hold' (Clarke, 1999; Du Bois-Reymond, 1998). Other sources of identity and identification deriving from music, fashion and leisure may be more central to how they think about themselves. Second, the fact of occupation may be more important in terms of economic security to specific constituencies; the status of occupation and its interpenetration with identity may well be primarily a middle-class phenomenon. So while the primary concern of youth researchers (e.g. Banks, 1992; Brice Heath and McLaughlin, 1993; Bynner et al., 1997; Ferri and Smith, 1997), 'remains the economic transition from school into the labour market and the unequal occupational opportunities that befall young people as they progress towards adulthood' (MacDonald, 1997, p. 20), they may be misreading the primary concerns of young people themselves. Nonetheless, in our society where work is central to inclusion, access to work and concomitantly education and training provide the major 'contexts of opportunity' through which to tackle what Mandelson (1997) has called 'the scourge and waste of social exclusion'.

The relationships between work and identity play around and upon young people in another more general sense. That is, through the 'rhetoric and reification' of a continuing demand for an upskilled, technologically literate and flexible workforce which will contribute towards national economic competitiveness. This rhetoric is embedded in policy condensates like 'life-long learning' and the 'learning society'. In respect of this, the current Labour administration display some distinct continuities with policies developed by the previous Conservative governments (Cockett, 1996). On the one hand, 'The philosophy underlying the proposed reforms is perhaps not as focused on market solutions or as ideologically driven as that of the previous administration' (Bartlett et al., 1998, p. 1). On the other, there is perhaps an even closer connection and a blurring of distinctions between education and the needs of the labour market – the point of the first being to service the requirements of the second (Ball, 1999). White's (1998) discussion of the Third Way represents this as 'employment-centred social policy' – 'a prime example of the dual commitment to the values of opportunity and personal responsibility' (p. 6). (Again there are links back to our previous discussion of 'individualization' and 'responsibilitization'.) In effect, social and educational policies are collapsed into economic and industrial policy. As David Blunkett explained in his 1998 Labour Party Conference Speech:

We recognise the very real challenge facing manufacturing industry in this country and the way in which we need to support and work with them for skilling and re-skilling for what Tony Blair has described as the best economic policy we have – 'education' (p. 5)

Within all this 'learning' and the 'learning society' is a new and powerful normativity, a moral economy – the government Reports and Papers which address post-16 education and training seek to establish a 'new culture of learning' (DfEE 1999, p. 1). Learners are encouraged to see themselves as a constantly renewable skill resource, the acquisition of skills ensuring 'national competitiveness and personal prosperity' (DfEE 1999, p. I); 'people are to be treated first and foremost in relation to their potential contribution to the economy', as Coffield (1999, p. 9) puts it

[...] In a sense you are your skills. This is strongly represented, in one respect, in the commonly held view, right across our study sample, that qualifications are the key to obtaining and progressing in work. However, many of those outside of education and training post-16, the 'others' to the 'learning society', carry with them 'learner identities' (Rees et al., 1997) often severely damaged by their experiences in compulsory education. More learning is the last thing they are interested in.

References

Banks, M. H. (1992) Youth employment and training, in J. C. Coleman and C. Warren-Adamson (eds) *Youth Policy in the 90s: the Way Forward*. London: Routledge.

Bartlett, W., Roberts, J.A. and LeGrand, J. (1998) The development of quasi-markets in the 1990s, in J. C. Coleman and C. Warren-Adamson (eds) *Quasi-market Reforms in the 1990s: A Revolution in Social Policy* (pp 1–16). Bristol: Policy Press.

Brice Heath, S. and McLaughlin, M. W. (eds) (1993) *Identity and Inner City Youth: Beyond Ethnicity and Gender*. New York and London: Teachers College Press, Columbia University.

Bynner, J., Ferri E. and Shepherd, P. (eds) (1997) *Twenty-something in the 1990s: Getting On, Getting By: Getting Nowhere*. Aldershot: Ashgate.

Clarke, D. (1999) Work hard, play hard: consumption, lifestyle and the city. *Research Counts* (Vol. UpDates (dave@geog.leeds.ac.uk), Swindon: ESRC.

Cockett, R. (1996) Thatcher's final victory: a labour win. *New Statesman*, pp. 56–7, 20 December.

Coffield, F. (1999) *Breaking the Consensus: Lifelong Learning as Social Control*. Newcastle: Department of Education, University of Newcastle.

DfEE (1999) *Learning to Succeed: a New Framework for Post-16 Learning*. London: DfEE.

Du Bois-Reymond, M. (1998) 'I don't want to commit myself yet': young people's life concepts. *Journal of Youth Studies*, 1 (1), 63–79.

Ferri, E. and Smith, K. (1979) Where you live and who you live with, in J Bynner, E. Ferri and P. Shepherd (eds) *Twenty-something in the 1990s: Getting On, Getting By, Getting Nowhere*. Aldershot: Ashgate.

MacDonald, R. E. (1997) *Youth, the 'underclass' and social exclusion*. London and New York: Routledge.

Mandelson, P. (1997) *Tackling Social Exclusion*. London: The Fabian Society.

Rees, G., Fevre, R., Furlong, J. and Gorard, S. (1997) History, place and learning society: towards a sociology of lifetime learning. *Journal of Education Policy*, 12 (6), 485–498.

White, S. (1998) *Interpreting the 'Third Way': a Tentative Overview*. Cambridge, MA: Dept of Political Science, MIT.

From: Ball, S. Maguire, M. and Macrae, S. (2000) *Choice, Pathways and Transitions Post-16: New Youth, New Economies in the Global City*. London: RoutledgeFalmer, pages 7–8.

Questions

Set 1: reflection

a) What is the main point being argued in the first paragraph?

b) How far does this reflect your own experience and knowledge of young learners?

c) How would you go about designing a piece of research to put this argument to the test?

d) The authors say, 'In a sense you are your skills'. What do they mean by this? Do you agree with them?

Set 2: analysis

a) One of the authors of this extract (Ball) was cited in the previous passage. In what ways do the ideas expressed in that passage relate to those set out in this one?

b) What do you understand the authors to mean when they write, 'This rhetoric is embedded in policy condensates like 'life-long learning' and the 'learning society'?

c) What argument do the writers put forward to support their claim that 'social and educational policies are collapsed into economic and industrial policy'? How convincing do you find this argument, and why?

Set 3: critical analysis

a) The writers suggest a possible link between occupational status, identity and social class. What are the implications here for the Lifelong Learning sector?

b) Explain the writers' critique of the 'life-long learning' discourse.

c) The extract points to 'a blurring of distinctions between education and the needs of the labour market'. Taking one recent White Paper on post-compulsory education, test this claim by carrying out a discourse analysis to highlight any direct links made between education and employment or the economy. (White Papers can be accessed at: www.education.gov.uk)

TASK TASK **TASK** TASK **TASK** **TASK** TASK **TASK** TASK **TASK** **TASK** TASK

4: *What is the distinction between education and training?*

For our final extract we turn to a passage which sets out some of the arguments that have been used to distinguish between vocational and general or liberal education. Read the passage through, making notes if you find it useful to do so. Then choose one (or more) of the sets of questions which follow. The passage begins by referring to:

> ... the origins of the vocational/academic divide in the nineteenth-century gentleman ideal based on a classical education. Wiener (1981) has suggested that this 'gentry ideal' ensured that, alongside the Industrial Revolution in England, there emerged a suspicion of technology and a distaste for and evasion of the realities of manufacturing and commerce. It was this ideal which was associated until quite recently with exclusively academic and professional pursuits in the classical tradition, with technology, business and even science struggling for admission to privileged status. There is some justification for the comment by Silver and Brennan (1988) that it was the persistence of such 'gentrified' notions which fuelled prejudice and 'public ignorance' (p. 23) about the nature of industry at the root of current dualisms (in contrast to the rather different historical developments and traditions in France and Germany).
>
> The prejudices associated with the gentry ideal of classical studies can be traced back to ancient Greek notions, particularly Plato's ideas about the nature of knowledge and the purpose of education. The original meaning of 'liberal' education as the 'freeing of the mind from error' can be traced to Plato's distinction between 'genuine' knowledge (knowledge acquired through rational reflection' and mere 'opinion' (knowledge acquired through practical activity for specific purposes; Schofield, 1972, p. 151). The former concept of knowledge, disinterested knowledge, came to be thought of as

intrinsically valuable (knowledge for its own sake), whereas the latter, instrumental knowledge, came to be associated with more practical and less valued vocational pursuits (see Lewis, 1991).

However, this differential value basis for vocational and academic studies has nothing more than historical association to support it. Beyond the contingent fact that the classical gentry ideal came to be associated with the most powerful political and economic groups in Britain, there are no intrinsic or logical reasons for the liberal/vocational dichotomy in education. Certainly, there are epistemological and moral criteria to be satisfied before a process can be legitimately called 'educational' in Peters' 'normative' sense which is associated with a 'liberal education' (Peters, 1966, pp. 144ff.). However, Peters' justification of education in terms of involvement in 'worthwhile activities' can apply as equally to so-called vocational as it can to academic activities.

Hirst's (1974) concept of liberal education based on the evolved and historically developed 'forms of knowledge', for instance, is concerned broadly with 'the comprehensive development of mind in acquiring knowledge... aimed at achieving an understanding of experience in many different ways' (p. 47). Certainly, the development of knowledge and understanding at the heart of this conception of education will be subject to certain formal criteria (concerned with breadth, means of transmission, and so on), but there is nothing here which necessarily legislates for hard and fast distinctions between vocational and other legitimately educational endeavours.

The distinction between 'instrumental' and 'non-instrumental' (or between 'practical' and 'theoretical') activities tends to break down when applied to concrete cases, since, as Peters (1978) observes, both theoretical and practical activities can be pursued 'for their own sakes' (p. 9). It is often the context of learning and the ends to which it is directed which are decisive. As Dearden (1990) notes in discussing the vexed questions surrounding the differences and relations between education and training, there are no *a priori* reasons why they should not in some circumstances be compatible; a 'process of training could be liberally conceived in such a way as to explore relevant aspects of understanding, and in a way which satisfies the internal standards of truth and adequacy' (p. 93). A similar point is made by Peters (1966), who, in citing 'cognitive perspective' as one key feature of educational activity, would 'not deny value to activities which have a limited cognitive content'. Thus, although 'cooking... is obviously an activity which is necessary for the maintenance of a way of life', it can be 'done just as a tiresome chore, or it can be delighted in for the opportunities for skill and ingenuity which it affords' and can 'become an extremely absorbing and worthwhile pursuit' (pp. 176–7).

All this is not to deny that there are, of course, real distinctions to be made between 'liberal' and 'illiberal' processes and between intrinsic and instrumental value. The point is that it would be a mistake to think that these sets of terms can be applied in a way which rigidly demarcates liberal and vocational education. Moreover, when we come to consider the ultimate ends of educational activity, the notions of intrinsic and instrumental value tend to merge for, as Bailey (1984) reminds us, 'it is precisely its *general and fundamental utility* that provides part of the justification of a liberal general education' (p. 28, author's italics).

In addition to the general utility of liberal education – 'its capacity to liberate a person from the restrictions of the present and the particular' – Bailey provides a range of supplementary reasons for the provision of education which is 'fundamental and general' (p. 29). There are, for instance, cogent moral duties incumbent on any legislation for compulsory education. If we are to impose any education system on others, this, at the very least, ought to be shown to be in their best interests and to promote rather than restrict their capacity for autonomous personal development. Being autonomous and making choices depends both on knowledge about all the options on offer and also on possessing the wherewithal to reflect on these options and to make rational choices. And, since 'autonomy' is here being used in a sense which is rather broader than the sense it has in some of the NCVQ literature (where it often means the freedom to achieve competence outcomes!), it requires a good general educational grounding for its realization. As White (1973) argues in looking at arguments used to justify the compulsory curriculum in terms of helping students to make choices, if choices are to be genuine and rational, then a person 'must know of all the possible things he [*sic*] may want to choose for their own sake, and he must be ready to consider what to choose from the point of view not only of the present moment but of his life as a whole' (p. 22).

What all this implies is that a good general education is a prerequisite, no matter what choices are made or forms of life chosen. In practice, of course, the realities of life, particularly working life, mean that none of us has absolutely open and free choices, but the point is that our choices would be even less free and open without access to the knowledge and skills provided by general education. This also serves to remind us that vocational education – 'initiation into work as part of a worthwhile form of life' (Corson, 1991, p. 178) – needs to be integrated with and not separated from the general objectives of education. Dearden (1990) expresses this point well when he observes that

> Work is an extremely important part of the lives of those who have work to do. It not only provides material rewards; it also structures time, choice and activity. It modifies the worker in all sorts of ways; in his [*sic*] skills and sensitivities, in his knowledge and attitudes, and in his self-concept. It confers status. A general education which failed to find any place to consider something of such importance would be importantly defective. (p. 93)

References

Bailey, C. (1984) *Beyond the Present and the Particular*. London: Routledge and Kegan Paul.

Corson, D. (ed) (1991) *Education for Work*. Clevedon: Multilingual Matters Ltd.

Dearden, R. F. (1990) Education and training, in G. Esland (ed) *Education, Training and Employment*. Wokingham: Addison-Wesley Publishing Co./Open University Press.

Hirst, P. H. (1974) *Knowledge and the Curriculum*. London: Routledge and Kegan Paul.

Lewis, T. (1991) Difficulties attending to new vocationalism in the USA. *Journal of Philosophy of Education*, 25 (1), 95–108.

Peters, R. S. (1996) *Ethics and Education*. London: Allen and Unwin.

Peters, R. S. (1978) Ambiguities in liberal education and the problem of its content, in K. A. Strike and K. Egan (eds) *Ethics and Educational Policy*. London: Routledge and Kegan Paul.

Schofield, H. (1972) *The Philosophy of Education: an Introduction*. London: Allen and Unwin.

Silver, H. and Brennan, J. (1988) *A Liberal Vocationalism*. London: Methuen.

Weiner, M. (1981) *English Culture and the Decline of the Industrial Spirit (1850–1980)*. Cambridge: Cambridge University Press.

White, J. P. (1973) *Towards a Compulsory Curriculum*. London: Routledge and Kegan Paul.

From: Hyland, T. (1994) *Competence, Education and NVQs*. London: Cassell, pages 116–118.

Questions

Set 1: reflection

a) This passage begins by offering two theories to explain why vocational education is accorded a lower status than general or liberal education. What are they, and which one does the author appear to favour?

b) What does this passage have to say about 'the differences and relations between education and training'?

c) What definition/s of vocational education can you find in this passage? To what extent is this consistent with your own?

Set 2: analysis

a) What arguments does the writer put forward for not making too rigid a demarcation between intrinsic and instrumental education?

b) This passage again uses the word 'autonomy'. How does the sense in which it is used here differ from, or relate to, its use in passages 1 and 2?

c) An argument about 'choice' is quoted in this passage. How does the definition of *choice* as it's used here compare with its usage in current and recent White Papers on post-compulsory education? (www.education.gov.uk)

Set 3: critical analysis

a) Critically analyse the argument the writer is putting forward here for the importance of general education.

b) The writer argues that 'there are epistemological and moral criteria to be satisfied before a process can be legitimately called 'educational'.' What would you understand these criteria to be?

c) In this extract it is suggested that distinctions between the 'practical' and the 'theoretical' cannot easily be made. What are the implications here for the argument set out in the second extract we considered in this chapter (The competent teacher)?

A SUMMARY OF KEY POINTS

This chapter has provided an opportunity for you to:

> reflect upon, analyse, and/or critically analyse passages from key texts in the field of post-compulsory education;

> explore the concept of professionalism in relation to the role of teacher in the post-compulsory sector;

> consider the advantages and disadvantages of a competence-based view of professional development for teachers;

> examine the ways in which young people's perception of work impacts upon their motivation to engage with vocational education;

> explore the distinction between vocational, general and liberal education, and consider what implications these have for your own professional practice.

REFERENCES AND FURTHER READING

Ball, S., Maguire, M. and Macrae, S. (2000) *Choice, Pathways and Transitions Post-16: New Youth, New Economies in the Global City.* London: RoutledgeFalmer.

Carr, W. and Kemmis, S. (1986) *Becoming Critical: Education, Knowledge and Action Research.* Lewes: Falmer Press.

DfES (2006) *FE Reform: Raising Skills, Improving Life Chances.* Norwich: TSO.

Foster, A. *et al.* (2005) *Realising the Potential: A Review of the Future Role of Further Education Colleges.* Annesley: DfES.

Foucault, M. (1979) *Discipline and Punish: The Birth of the Prison.* Harmondsworth: Penguin Books.

Hillier, Y. and Thompson, A. (eds) (2005) *Readings in Post-compulsory Education.* London: Continuum.

Hyland, T. (1994) *Competence, Education and NVQs.* London: Cassell.

Unwin, R. and Usher, R. (1994) *Postmodernism and Education.* London: Routledge.

Wallace, S. (Ed.) (2010) *The Lifelong Learning Sector: Reflective Reader.* Exeter: Learning Matters.

17
Achieving your teaching qualification in the Lifelong Learning sector

The objectives of this chapter

This chapter is designed to draw together everything we have considered in the previous chapters and to show how you can use it all – the theory, the advice, the practical strategies – to successfully achieve your teaching qualification in the Lifelong Learning sector. Although the chapter as a whole is clearly designed for the trainee teacher, the section on preparing for, and carrying out, observed teaching will also be helpful to qualified teachers who aim to achieve the best possible grade when observed for college self-assessment or for inspections by external agencies such as Ofsted. Because of its focus, this chapter is relevant to the whole range of knowledge, skills and values encompassed by the professional standards.

Introduction

As you will be well aware by now, gaining QTLS depends on much more than simply being able to get up in front of a class and teach. It involves you in producing a range of important evidence in order to demonstrate the care and reflection that have gone into the planning and evaluation of your lessons, as well as requiring you to complete other, more formal assignments for assessment. In addition, it demands evidence of your interpersonal and communication skills; your organisational skills and ability to manage your time effectively; and your scrupulously professional conduct. In this chapter we shall take each of these elements of the qualification and discuss ways in which you can ensure that you meet the criteria and perform at your very best.

Preparing for being observed

For most QTLS programmes you will be required to produce a set of documentation for each observed session. This will usually include a lesson plan; a justification or rationale for that lesson plan; a scheme of work showing where the lesson plan fits into the scheme; and an indication of which aspect of your own professional action plan you are focusing on for this observed session. Below are some tick lists designed to remind you of key points to address in this documentation.

Lesson plan
1. List the learning outcomes or objectives clearly.
2. Cross-reference them to the scheme of work.
3. Devise an appropriate range of learner activities.
4. Ensure the activities will allow you to assess whether the outcomes have been achieved.
5. Show clearly how each activity is assessed, and reference each to the learning outcomes you have listed. (If you number the learning outcomes, or use the numbering/designation employed in the scheme of work this will make cross-

referencing easier.)

6. Show on your plan the opportunities for developing functional skills.
7. Indicate how you have planned for inclusive learning and opportunities for differentiation.
8. Have a plan B or extension activity in case learners complete the lesson you've planned earlier than you expected.

Rationale/justification

1. Describe how your knowledge of the learners' characteristics have informed your planning.
2. Are there any individual learners whose needs you have had to take particular note of in your planning?
3. Explain the sequencing of this lesson within the scheme of work. What has proceeded it and what will follow?
4. In what ways will your planning help you to achieve elements of your own professional action plan?
5. What advice (if any) have your mentor or other colleagues given you about this group of learners?
6. What point have these learners reached in terms of their assessment, and how will this lesson fit into their overall assessment?

Scheme of work

1. It is highly unlikely that you will be required to write the scheme of work yourself, so you will have to ensure that you are able to obtain a copy of it well ahead of the observed session. If you have difficulty obtaining a copy, ask your QTLS tutor for advice or intervention.
2. Highlight on the scheme the section or content that your lesson will be covering. If the learning outcomes/objectives are numbered or lettered in the scheme, use this same enumeration in your lesson plan and rationale so that the cross-referencing is clear.

Action plan

1. Identify clearly on your professional action plan the action points that you will be addressing in the observed lesson.
2. If these action points have arisen out of previous observations of your teaching by your tutor or mentor, indicate that this is the case.
3. If they have arisen out of your own reflections on your teaching experience so far, make this clear.

Teaching an observed lesson

The anticipation of being observed can cause quite a build up of anxiety, even in experienced teachers. But this can be taken as a good sign. The fact that you feel nervous means that you *care* whether you do well or not, and that you feel a commitment to succeed. Good! But what you don't want to do is to *look* anxious, and it's this – the fear of looking anxious – that can make you feel even more nervous. So we're going to start this section with a reminder about the importance of body language, because – no matter how nervous you feel – wise use of body language can prevent it from showing. So:

- **Act as though you feel confident. Anxiety is catching. If you look nervous, the learners will pick it up and react to it in ways that may have a negative impact on your own attempt at confidence.**

You will project confidence if you get out from behind the desk. Sit on the edge of it if your legs feel wobbly. Drop your shoulders and unclench your hands. Don't refer to notes which are on sheets of paper that will tremble and give you away. Use cards, or refer to a flip chart or screen. Make firm eye-contact. Smile as much as you can. Remember: it is a proven fact that the more confident you appear, the more confident you'll start to feel.

- *Demonstrate your enthusiasm*. It's important to generate energy and enthusiasm in any lesson, and particularly in one where you want your observer/s to see you at your best. You can't expect the learners to be enthusiastic if you yourself are not. Any lack of enthusiasm on your part will be immediately evident in your voice and body language. So it's important to adopt the appropriate stance, gestures and tone. Stand up, move about, smile, nod, lean towards learners when they speak to you. All these are ways of conveying to the learners that you like them and enjoy their company; and this is important, because an observation is a crucial time to have the class on your side. Use your voice and gestures to be expressive. Look happy to be there.
- *Don't remain static*. It is important to move about the classroom or workshop. By occupying the space, you demonstrate that you're in control. It also allows you to join in with different groups or engage with individuals one-to-one, and this demonstrates to the observer a fuller range of your competence. It can also work well to keep learners on task if you move over in their direction in a purposeful manner. Moving around can be another way to demonstrate enthusiasm for the learners and the subject. But you should avoid simply pacing up and down for the sake of it, as that may make you appear agitated and would almost certainly distract learners from their learning.

An important aspect of your observed session is that it provides an opportunity for you to demonstrate your ability to form a positive and productive working relationship with your learners. Some of the many ways you can do this are summarised in the following list.

- Interact with learners as individuals, as well as a group.
- Make sure you learn their names and use them. If this is the first time you've met the group, you can pick up a few names as you go along.
- Make sure that you make opportunities to listen to the learners as well as requiring them to listen to you.
- Model at all times the positive interpersonal skills you expect the learners to display.

Receiving feedback from the observer

A good observer will always give you an opportunity to say how you felt the lesson went. Try to be as objective as you can. If you think it went well, say so. If you were disappointed by some aspects of it, explain why. The two most useful criteria for forming this initial evaluation will be:

- whether the planned outcomes were achieved;
- the quality of learning, as indicated by the general levels of learners' enthusiasm and engagement.

You will normally be encouraged to elaborate and reflect on your views in a formal written evaluation of the lesson and/or in some other format such as a reflective professional journal.

Having – hopefully – had your own say, you will need to listen attentively to the observer's feedback. The feedback is designed to help you. In that sense it should be considered as formative rather than summative assessment. You will need to reflect upon it and draw points for development from it to incorporate into your on-going professional action plan. Always seek clarification of any feedback you don't understand.

Post-observation documentation: reflecting and planning

Following the observation and any verbal feedback and evaluation, you will normally be expected to produce your own formal written evaluation of the observed lesson. Again, you will need to comment on whether outcomes were achieved and on the quality of the learning experience you provided for the learners. In addition you should demonstrate that you have reflected on:

- the range and appropriateness of methods and how well you implemented them;
- the quality and appropriateness of resources and your ability to utilise them;
- the opportunities for assessment, taken or missed;
- the appropriateness of the accommodation in terms of classroom or workshop layout, and whether there were any changes you could or should have made;
- the success or otherwise of your strategies for inclusion and differentiation;
- opportunities for developing functional skills, taken or missed;
- any significant incidents or issues;
- the extent to which you achieved your selected action point/s.

If you have disagreed with any aspect of the observer's feedback you should, after discussing it with the observer, take the opportunity to argue your case or set out your point of view in this written evaluation.

Completing written assessments: organisational skills and time management

We have concentrated so far on the practical teaching aspect of your QTLS and the associated documentation; but, of course, there is also the formal coursework to complete in the form of assignments. The detail and format of these assessments vary from provider to provider, but what they all demand in common is that to complete them successfully you will need to be able to get yourself organised and manage your time as effectively as possible.

Getting organised

The major part of getting organised is not so much about doing as about clear thinking. For example, here are some useful ways to help your thinking about organising your workload:

- Think of the tasks you have to do in terms of looking after a house. There will be *maintenance* tasks – the things that have to be done regularly to keep everything running smoothly (lesson planning, answering e-mails, marking/assessing learners' work, etc.) and *building* tasks, which are those that create something new and constitute substantial steps towards your ultimate goal of gaining your QTLS (writing assignments, preparing and teaching observed sessions, etc.). Separate these in your mind and it will help to make your workload feel more manageable.
- Read your QTLS programme handbook or other documentation very carefully and actively seek clarification for any points which you don't fully understand. This will enable you to feel confident that you know exactly what is required of you, and when. If you remain in a 'fog' about this it will make getting organised very difficult.

Time management

The QTLS programme places huge demands on your time. To avoid feeling overwhelmed you need clear strategies for time management if you are to complete your assessments successfully and on time. Again, thinking things through clearly is half the battle. Here are some examples.

- Faced with a multitude of tasks, try categorising them into those that are *urgent* and those that are *important*. The *important* tasks – in this case those that contribute substantially towards gaining your QTLS, such as key assignments – will need to have more time spent on them. Urgent tasks, obviously, are those which need to be done quickly, but they may or may not be important. Categorising tasks like this should help you to prioritise and also to achieve a sense of proportion about your workload.
- Set milestones or 'achieve by' dates. Make these realistic, and then stick to them.
- Never waste time doing a job twice. For example, deal with e-mails on the spot wherever possible. Don't close them, intending to answer them later. This just builds up pressure on top of your already heavy workload.
- Don't waste time worrying. If something needs doing and can be done – just do it.

Professionalism and identity

In embarking on a QTLS programme you are taking on a number of different roles, some of which may appear to be conflicting. When you are in the classroom you are a teacher with lessons to plan and marking to do; and yet, as a trainee, you are also a learner, with assignments to complete and criteria to meet. During your practical teaching experience you are, in relation to your learners, an expert in your subject; but in relation to your subject specialist mentor you are still a learner. You may also be holding down a job in order to help you to pay your fees, and at the same time you are also carrying out the common roles of life, as friend, parent, lover, carer, child. All this can be exhausting, and to survive with your energy and enthusiasm intact you will need to effectively address the issues of identity, organisation and time management.

If you are finding it difficult to adapt the role of 'learner' – whether in relation to your tutors or your mentor or other teachers you encounter on your placement, it may help if you try not to think in terms of either/or. For example, the sort of thinking that it is easy to fall into when you are feeling tired or disaffected goes something like this: *"Either you have subject expertise or you don't; either you are a teacher and deserve to be treated with appropriate respect by other teachers, or you are not and therefore should not be expected to cope with difficult classes alone or undertake onerous planning and marking...."* And so on. But thinking like this only makes you feel worse. And so it's important to remind yourself, whenever you fall into this sort of polarised thinking, that these apparently conflicting roles are entirely compatible within the context of your QTLS programme. You are both a teacher *and* a learner; you are both an expert *and* have much about your subject still to learn. And if we want to be good at our job this will remain true – for all of us – however well qualified.

Keeping yourself motivated

All this is hard work, and keeping on top of it all requires you to keep up your own levels of motivation. In the course of this book we have discussed at length the *what* and the *how* and the *who* of teaching in the Lifelong Learning sector. In terms of the *what,* we've explored the issues of subject specialism; of modelling appropriate behaviour; and of the vocational qualification framework and curriculum. We've discussed the *how* by looking at our range of methods; our lesson planning; our assessment strategies; our interactions with learners; our application of learning theory; our values in relation to equality and diversity; and our role as members of a professional team. And we've talked about the *who* in our exploration of learners' entry behaviour; their learning needs; their motivation; their age-specific characteristics and so on. But we haven't really said much about the *why.* What is it that motivates us and keeps us going, particularly through the QTLS programme. *Why* do we do it? Why do we choose to teach in this sector that's been called variously the 'Cinderella' and the neglected 'Middle Child' of the education system?

If I were to answer this one myself, based on my own experience of teaching in and with FE, I'd have to say there were two main reasons. One is about achievement and the other is about values. My guess is, as I explain these two a little further, that most colleagues working in the sector will recognise what I'm talking about here, however recent or lengthy their teaching experience.

Job satisfaction and a sense of achievement

As we've seen, this sector has traditionally been known as the sector of the second chance. People who've been alienated by their experience of school, who regard themselves as failures, as 'not clever', as no-hopers, can discover in FE and training a sense of achievement and direction, and an appetite for learning. Granted, it doesn't always happen. But when it does – when you find that your teaching and support have helped someone to develop their confidence, raise their aspirations and regain their self-esteem – at that moment your job feels like the most satisfying profession in the world. And, of course, there are all those learners who come into post-compulsory education and training already enthusiastic and motivated – because we mustn't forget that there are plenty of those in the sector, too – and teaching them brings its own rewards.

In a book like this one there is necessarily an emphasis on problem solving. But it would be a great mistake to conclude from this that teaching in the Lifelong Learning sector is simply a series of problems to be overcome. And where problem solving does become necessary, it would be unfortunate to view this as necessarily a negative factor. A problem to be solved is a challenge, and everyone recognises the sense of achievement in a challenge successfully overcome. So, whether you find your teaching challenging because you have constantly to overcome the disengagement of your learners; or whether you find it challenging because the learners' determination and life experience are driving you to constantly update and improve your subject specialist skills, one thing you can be sure of: the greater the challenge, the greater the satisfaction in having met and overcome it.

Job satisfaction and our sense of values

The other source of job satisfaction I cited was to do with values. Perhaps more than in any other sector, Lifelong Learning requires its teachers to confront and address issues of equality and diversity. Our learners represent the widest possible range of ability and age. They come to us from all walks of life and from disparate cultural, racial and religious backgrounds. And within this microcosm of a multi-ethnic, differently abled, and variously aged society, we, as teachers, have the opportunity to model good practice in promoting

Key

equality and valuing diversity. By setting an example of integrity ourselves, we have the possibility to encourage positive values, such as tolerance, in our learners. In terms of its value to society as a whole, there is little that can be more rewarding than that.

A SUMMARY OF KEY POINTS

In this chapter we have:

> considered a checklist of key points to cover when preparing for your teaching to be observed;
> considered a checklist of key points to cover when teaching an observed lesson;
> looked at key aspects of post-observation documentation;
> discussed the organisational and time management skills which are necessary for timely and successful completion of assessments;
> looked at issues of identity and role conflict.

REFERENCES AND FURTHER READING

To help you to plan your observed lessons

Tummons, J. (2011) *Assessing Learning in the Lifelong Learning Sector* (3rd edition). Exeter: Learning Matters.

Wallace, I. and Kirkham, L. (2007) *Pimp your Lesson! Prepare, Innovate, Motivate and Perfect.* London: Continuum.

To help you to carry out your observed lessons successfully

Appleyard, N. and Appleyard K. (2010) *Communicating with Learners in the Lifelong Learning Sector.* Exeter: Learning Matters.

Duckworth, V.; Wood, J.; Bostock, J. and Dickinson, J. (2010) *Successful Teaching Practice in the Lifelong Learning Sector*, Exeter: Learning Matters.

Roffey-Barentsen, J. and Malthouse, R. (2009) *Reflective Practice in the Lifelong Learning Sector*. Exeter: Learning Matters.

To help you succeed in your written assignments

Gravells, A. (Ed) and Williams, J. (2010) *Study Skills for PTLLS*. Exeter: Learning Matters.

Gravells, A. (2010) *Passing PTLLS Assessments*. Exeter: Learning Matters.

Gravells, A. and Simpson, S. (2011) *Passing CTLLS Assessments.* Exeter: Learning Matters.

Wallace, S. (Ed) (2010) *The Lifelong Learning Sector: Reflective Reader*. Exeter: Learning Matters.

Appendix 1

Glossary of abbreviations

This glossary is to help you decode some of the many acronyms and abbreviations related to the Lifelong Learning sector. You can use any search engine to discover more about the terminology and organisations referred to here. Entering the object of your search in full (rather than in its abbreviated form) will save you time and avoid ambiguity.

You will no doubt discover further acronyms to add to this list. Some of these will be local or 'in-house' abbreviations applied within your own institution.

A4e	Action for employment
ACCAC	Qualifications Curriculum and Assessment Authority for Wales (currently under review)
ABS	Adult Basic Skills
AE	Adult Education
ALI	Adult Learning Inspectorate (now incorporated into the new Ofsted structure)
ALBSU	Adult Learning and Basic Skills Unit
ALP	Association of Learning Providers
AoC	Association of Colleges
APEL	Accreditation of prior experience and learning
APL	Accreditation of prior learning
AQA	Assessment and Qualifications Alliance
AV	Audio-visual
AVA	Audio-visual aid
BECTa	British Educational Communication and Technology agency
BERA	British Educational Research Association
BTEC	Business and Technology Education Council
CACHE	Council for Awards in Children's Care and Education
CAL	Computer assisted learning
CEP	Career entry profile
CAT	Credit accumulation and transfer
CCW	Curriculum Council for Wales
CEL	Centre for Excellence in Leadership
CETT	Centre for Excellence in Teacher Training
CERI	Centre for Educational Research and Innovation
CoVE	Centre of Vocational Excellence
Cert Ed	Certificate of Education
CGLI	City and Guilds London Institute
CTC	City Technology College
CVA	Contextualised value added
CPD	Continuing professional development
DfE	Department for Education (formerly DFES and DCSF)
DENI	Department of Education Northern Ireland
e2e	Entry to Employment

EAZ	Educational Action Zone
ELW	Education and Learning Wales
EMA	Education maintenance allowance
ERA	Education Reform Act (1988)
EIS	Educational Institute of Scotland
EFL	English as a foreign language
ETP	Employer Training Pilots
EAL	English as an additional language
ESL	English as a second language
ESOL	English for speakers of other languages
ESF	European Social Fund
EV	External verifier
ECM	Every Child Matters
FE	Further Education
FENTO	Further Education National Training Organisation (now replaced by LLUK and SVUK)
FERL	Further Education resources for learning
FTE	Full-time equivalent
GNVQ	General National Vocational Qualification
HE	Higher Education
HEFC	Higher Education Funding Council
HMI	Her Majesty's Inspectorate
HNC	Higher National Certificate
HND	Higher National Diploma
ICT	Information and Communication Technology
IfL	Institute for Learning
ILT (1)	Information Learning Technology
ILT (2)	Institute of Learning and Teaching
ILP	Individual learning plan
IEP	Industry Education Partnership
IT	Information technology
ITT	Initial Teacher Training
IV	Internal verifier
JISC	Joint Information Systems committee
JCNVQ	Joint Council of National Vocational Qualifications
LLUK	Lifelong Learning UK
LSC	Learning and Skills Council
LSDA	Learning and Skills Development Agency
LSN	Learning and Skills Network
LTS	Learning and Teaching Scotland
MLE	Managed learning environment
NCC	National Consortium of Colleges
NEET	Not in education or employment
NGfL	National Grid for Learning
NGfLS	National Grid for Learning Scotland
NIACE	National Institute of Adult Continuing Education
NLT	National Learning Target
NLS	National Literacy Strategy
NNS	National Numeracy Strategy

NOF	New Opportunities Fund (to become the Qualifications and Credit Framework (QCF))
NPQ	National Professional Qualification
NQF	National Qualifications Framework
NQT	Newly qualified teacher
NSA	National Skills Academies
NTO	National Training Organisation
NVQ	National Vocational Qualification
OCR	Oxford, Cambridge and Royal Society of Arts
OFSTED	Office for Standards in Education
OLAS	Offender Learning and Skills Services
PAYP	Positive activities for young people
PCET	Post-compulsory Education and Training
PGCE	Postgraduate Certificate of Education
PPP	Public Private Partnership
QAA	Quality Assurance Agency
QCDA	Qualifications and Curriculum Development Agency (formerly QCA)
QIA	Quality Improvement Agency
QTLS	Qualified Teacher Learning and Skills
QTS	Qualified Teacher Status
RAE	Research Assessment Exercise
SAR	Self-assessment Report
SAT	Standard Assessment Task
SEED	Scottish Executive Education Department
SEN	Special Educational Needs
SENCO	Special Educational Needs Coordinator
SFEU	Scottish Further Education Unit
SMT	Senior Management Team
SQA	Scottish Qualifications Authority
SSR	Staff-student ratio
StAR	Strategic Area Review
SUfI	Scottish University for Industry
SVUK	Standards and Verification UK
TAFE	Technical and Further Education (Australia)
TQ(FE)	Teaching Qualification for Further Education (Scotland)
UCAS	Universities and Colleges Admissions Service
UCU	University and College Union
UfI	University for Industry
U3A	University of the Third Age
VET	Vocational Education and Training
VLE	Virtual Learning Environment
VLP	Virtual Learning Portal
VQR	Vocational Qualifications Reform
WBL	Work-based learning
WEA	Workers' Education Association

Appendix 2

Standards for teachers in the Lifelong Learning sector outside England, Wales and Northern Ireland

The LLUK Professional Standards for teachers in the Lifelong Learning sector are not unique. If you are a teacher or trainer in countries with a comparable vocational education framework, such as Scotland or Australia for example, you will know that similar Standards are in place there. While not worded identically, these various sets of Professional Standards nevertheless cover the same areas of skills, knowledge and values we have explored in this book, as can be seen from the table below.

A comparison of domains/units/areas included in Professional Standards

LLUK	Scotland (QT(FE))	Australia (TAFE)
Professional values and practice	Professional practice and development	Values
Learning and teaching	Teaching/facilitating learning	Tasks
Specialist learning and teaching	Quality and standards	Activities *(e.g. updating)* and Knowledge
Planning for learning	Planning and preparing the learning experience	Tasks *(e.g. planning)*
Assessment for learning	Assessment	Tasks *(e.g. carrying out assessment)*
Access and progression	Guidance and support	Activities *(e.g. identifying developmental needs of learners)*

You can find current and updated details of these Standards on a number of websites.

For the Professional Standards for Lecturers in Scotland's Colleges (both for initial teacher training (ITT) and for continuing professional development (CPD)), go to:

www.scotland.gov.uk/Publications/2006/06/13164029/4

For the skills, knowledge and values required of Vocational Education Teachers in Australia , in the sector known as TAFE (Technical and Further Education), go to:

http://www.jobsearch.gov.au/joboutlook/
default.aspx?PageId=AscoDesc&ASCOCode=2422 and click on *'explore this job'.*

Index